BURDENED VIRTUES

STUDIES IN FEMINIST PHILOSOPHY
Cheshire Calhoun, *Series Editor*

Published in the Series
Gender in the Mirror: Confounding Imagery
Diana Tietjens Meyers

Autonomy, Gender, Politics
Marilyn Friedman

Setting the Moral Compass: Essays by Women Philosophers
Edited by Cheshire Calhoun

Woman and Citizenship
Edited by Marilyn Friedman

Burdened Virtues: Virtue Ethics for Liberatory Struggles
Lisa Tessman

Burdened Virtues

Virtue Ethics for Liberatory Struggles

LISA TESSMAN

2005

OXFORD
UNIVERSITY PRESS

Oxford University Press, Inc., publishes works that further
Oxford University's objective of excellence
in research, scholarship, and education.

Oxford New York
Auckland Cape Town Dar es Salaam Hong Kong Karachi
Kuala Lumpur Madrid Melbourne Mexico City Nairobi
New Delhi Shanghai Taipei Toronto

With offices in
Argentina Austria Brazil Chile Czech Republic France Greece
Guatemala Hungary Italy Japan Poland Portugal Singapore
South Korea Switzerland Thailand Turkey Ukraine Vietnam

Published by Oxford University Press, Inc.
198 Madison Avenue, New York, New York 10016

www.oup.com

Library of Congress Cataloging-in-Publication Data
Tessman, Lisa, 1966–
Burdened virtues : virtue ethics for liberatory struggles / Lisa Tessman
p. cm.—(Studies in feminist philosophy)
Includes bibliographical references and index.
ISBN-13 978-0-19-517914-9; 978-0-19-517915-6 (pbk.)
ISBN 0-19-517914-5; 0-19-517915-3 (pbk.)
1. Virtues. 2. Ethics. 3. Women—Conduct of life. 4. Feminist ethics.
5. Oppression (Psychology) I. Title. II. Series.
BJ1531.T27 2005
179'.9—dc22 2004059975

9 8 7 6 5 4 3 2 1

Printed in the United States of America
on acid-free paper

For Ami and Yuval

Acknowledgments

Research that I did for several chapters of this book was made possible by a Dean's Research Semester Award that I received in the fall of 2002 from Binghamton University.

Most parts of the book have been presented in draft form and have been shaped by the responses I received to these presentations. An early version of chapter 1 was presented in 1998 at the University of Göteborg, Sweden, by invitation from the Department of Philosophy and the Department of Feminist Studies, and at the spring 1998 meeting of the Eastern Division of the Society for Women in Philosophy. Portions of chapter 2 were presented at the 1998 Radical Philosophy Association conference and at the 1999 Feminist Ethics Revisited conference. The beginning of chapter 3 was presented at the 2001 meeting of the Association for Feminist Ethics and Social Theory and at the 2001 National Women's Studies Association conference; later pieces of this chapter were presented by invitation at the Feminist Moral Philosophy conference at the University of Western Ontario in 2002. Chapter 4 began as a paper for the International Association of Women Philosophers conference in 2002 in Barcelona, Spain, and was also presented at the Colloquium on Ethics in the History of Philosophy, sponsored by the Program in Social, Political, Ethical and Legal Philosophy at Binghamton University in 2003. Parts of chapter 5 were presented at the 2002 conference of the Radical Philosophy Association and other parts at the 2003 Feminist Ethics and Social Theory conference. Chapter 6 emerged from a paper that I wrote in 1997 and presented at that time to the Philosophy Departments at Temple University, Michigan State University, and DePaul University. The conclusion grew from a presentation at the 2004 meeting of the International Association of Women Philosophers in Göteborg, Sweden. I wish to thank the audiences at all of these presentations for their comments and questions, which spurred my revisions.

Members of the Binghamton University Philosophy Department's junior faculty discussion group—Charles Goodman, Christopher Knapp, Steve Scalet, and Melissa Zinkin—closely read, commented on, and discussed most of the manuscript while it was in progress. I have benefited enormously from their work, especially because the insights they offered came out of such widely diverging sorts of philosophical training, areas, and moral commitments. This group of my colleagues has also supported and encouraged me at every step of the process of completing this book. Members of the Socialist and Feminist Philosophers' Association (SOFPHIA) read a large portion of the penultimate draft of the manuscript and discussed this draft in the spring of 2004. I am grateful to all of them for undertaking this and for their thought-provoking comments. Richard Schmitt, in particular, read the entire penultimate draft and presented it for discussion at this SOFPHIA meeting, in addition to offering me substantive comments of his own. I thank him for this. I also would like to thank each of the students in my spring 2004 graduate seminar on virtue ethics; I taught this course while doing the final revisions on the manuscript, and the students gave interpretations of the course material that pushed my thinking in important ways. Margaret Walker, Hilde Nelson, and Sara Ruddick provided me with extensive comments on the manuscript; I am grateful for the suggestions that they made—many of which I followed—and I thank them for their careful consideration of my work. Cheshire Calhoun, editor of the Studies in Feminist Philosophy series, and Peter Ohlin, Lara Zoble, and Stacey Hamilton at Oxford University Press have been wonderful to work with, and the reviewers, one of whom was Alison Jaggar and the other of whom remained anonymous, wrote valuable and encouraging comments.

I owe intellectual debts to all of my teachers, but there are three who stand out: María Lugones, who lured me into the field of philosophy (and introduced me both to Aristotle and to feminist philosophy) twenty years ago when I was her undergraduate student at Carleton College; Robert Paul Wolff, who made my graduate education difficult but from whom I learned a good deal about how to do philosophy; and Ann Ferguson, who directed my dissertation at the University of Massachusetts and who has been a friend, intellectual and otherwise, ever since.

In addition to the individuals named above, I would also like to thank Barbara Andrew, Sandra Bartky, Samantha Brennan, John Brentlinger, Joan Callahan, Claudia Card, Chris Cuomo, Peggy DesAutels, Chris Frakes, Bob Gooding-Williams, Lisa Heldke, Ulla Holm, Kimberly Leighton, Amie Macdonald, Margaret McLaren, Desirée Melton, Andrea Nicki, Peg O'Connor, Max Pensky, Lisa Schwartzman, Tom Wartenberg, and Joanne Waugh. And my parents and sister, and each of their families.

My deepest thanks go to Bat-Ami Bar On. As my life partner and lover, she has sustained me in every possible way throughout my work on this book. As a philosopher, she has also been my most consistent interlocutor, and our philosophical disagreements have enriched my thinking. Ami endured countless discussions with me about the ideas in this book; she also read numerous drafts of every chapter, generously offering comments on the large and small problems that needed working out. If a fraction of the depth with which Ami ponders and theorizes is present in this book, I shall be glad. And to our daughter, Yuval, thank you just for being.

Parts of this book have been previously published. Chapter 1 is a revision of "Moral Luck in the Politics of Personal Transformation," which appeared in 2000 in *Social Theory and Practice* 26 (3): 375–395. Chapter 2 is based on an article that was called "Critical Virtue Ethics: Understanding Oppression as Morally Damaging," which was published in 2001 in *Feminists Doing Ethics*, edited by Peggy DesAutels and Joanne Waugh (Lanham, MD: Rowman and Littlefield): 79–99. A very short excerpt from a previous version of chapter 3 was published in *American Philosophical Association Newsletters: Newsletter on Feminism and Philosophy* 1 (2) (Spring 2002): 59–63, under the title "Do the Wicked Flourish? Virtue Ethics and Unjust Social Privilege." Other sections of an earlier version of chapter 3 were also published, appearing in 2002 as "On (Not) Living the Good Life: Reflections on Oppression, Virtue and Flourishing" in the *Canadian Journal of Philosophy* Supplementary Volume 28 on Feminist Moral Philosophy. A portion of chapter 5 is being published in 2005 as "The Burdened Virtues of Political Resistance" in *Feminist Interventions in Ethics and Politics*, edited by Barbara S. Andrew, Jean Clare Keller, and Lisa H. Schwartzman (Lanham, MD: Rowman and Littlefield). Chapter 6 is a revised version of "Dangerous Loyalties and Liberatory Politics," which was published in 1998 in *Hypatia: A Journal of Feminist Philosophy* 13 (4): 18–39. All are reprinted with permission.

Contents

Introduction: Moral Trouble 3

1. Regretting the Self One Is 11

2. The Damage of Moral Damage 33

3. The Ordinary Vices of Domination 53

4. Between Indifference and Anguish 81

5. The Burden of Political Resistance 107

6. Dangerous Loyalties 133

Conclusion: Eudaimonistic Virtue Ethics under Adversity 159

Works Cited 169

Index 179

BURDENED VIRTUES

Introduction

Moral Trouble

In situations of moral conflict, acting for the best does not always yield a morally clean result. Oftentimes a residue persists from the moral demand that was overpowered or opted against. Moral conflicts are ineliminable and can be encountered anywhere—and thus these disturbing moral remainders may be scattered widely—but my interest is in a context that is primed for moral trouble: the context of oppression and of the liberatory struggles that take place against oppression. My concern is with the *selves* who endure and resist oppression and, in particular, with the way in which the devastating conditions confronted by these selves both limit and burden their moral goodness.

Because I want to examine the moral state of selves—rather than, say, analyze the moral flaws in social practices and institutions, or develop a normative account detailing what is to be done to counter specific injustices—I turn to a tradition of ethical theory that is agent-centered and that foregrounds questions of character: virtue ethics. I spend some time early in the book pointing out the advantages of a virtue ethics framework for thinking about oppression. Throughout the book I depend upon this framework, sometimes situating my thinking in it rather loosely simply by emphasizing issues of character and, at other times, drawing more specifically and directly on Aristotelian and neo-Aristotelian virtue ethics, a project that requires doing a good bit of critique since such theory is in its unfiltered state not suited for feminist or other liberatory purposes.

Part of what attracts me to the Aristotelian virtue ethics tradition is that it is eudaimonistic: it assumes that the pursuit of flourishing—qualified in certain ways and especially by the requirement that one develop and maintain the virtues—is morally praiseworthy. Eudaimonism provides an interesting way of thinking about liberatory political struggles, for one might portray oppression as a set of barriers to flourishing and think about political resistance as a way of eradicating these barriers and enabling flourishing. I believe that there is some notion of flourishing implicit in the projects of political resistance, for without some idea of what is a better and what is a worse life, there is no explanation of nor motivation for the commitment to change systems of oppression. This book explores the possibility—or lack thereof—of flourishing in the context of oppression and resistance.

Something grim emerges when one tries to work with a eudaimonistic moral theory while examining oppression, for one centers the importance of flourishing and then confronts the terrible fact of its distortions or absence under conditions of oppression. Thus I will follow Sandra Bartky in warning, as she does in the introduction to *Femininity and Domination*, that what follows has "a rather pessimistic cast" (Bartky 1990, 7). Despite this pessimism—and perhaps because I think that something extremely grim must indeed be revealed—I hold onto this virtue ethics framework since it does allow one to investigate the relationship between oppression and flourishing in complex ways. I noted that oppression could be thought of as creating barriers to flourishing. Activists focused on transforming systems of oppression tend to fight against the external barriers that put a good life out of reach for many people in the obvious ways; for instance, members of targeted groups may be subject to violence or abuse; refused recognition and respect as full persons; forced to survive with inadequate housing, food, health care, child care, transportation or other goods; denied access to education or to their own cultural traditions; exploited and alienated in dead-end jobs; unjustly imprisoned; exposed to environmental hazards; and so on. On top of all these troubles faced by subordinated people, I expose one more: moral trouble. Like the other sorts of trouble, moral trouble spawned by oppressive conditions can stand in the way of a good life.

This moral trouble appears in two forms. The first, which has already received some attention by both feminists and critical race theorists, is that the self under oppression can be morally damaged, prevented from developing or exercising some of the virtues. Viewing the phenomenon of moral damage through a virtue ethics lens reveals new depths of this damage. Moral damage occurs when there is a certain sort of a self that one ought to be, but the unconducive conditions of oppression bar one from cultivating this self. In an Aristotelian schema, such moral damage in turn disqualifies one from flourishing, for virtue is necessary for flourishing. Moreover, if the virtues that are interfered with include those that could enable people to resist their own subordination, moral damage will actually help to sustain structures of oppression.

The second form of moral trouble that appears under oppression persists even for those who do manage to locate and embody moral virtues. I ran up against this second form—which has not yet received the theoretical attention that it deserves—as I tried to think through the question of which character traits could be recommended as virtues within the context of liberatory political movements. The fruitlessness of the search for traits that could unambivalently be morally praised led me to see instead a set of virtues that, while practically necessitated for surviving oppression or morally necessitated for opposing it, carry with them a cost to their bearer. To explain this set of traits, I introduce what I call *burdened virtues*, virtues that have the unusual feature of being disjoined from their bearer's own flourishing. A virtue ethics such as Aristotle's that denies that virtue is sufficient for flourishing leaves room for there to be virtues that do not, at least in certain circumstances, contribute to their bearer's well-being. However,

Aristotle did not anticipate that such virtues would be pervasive, because he did not theorize about how the bad luck that produces adverse conditions (for basically good people) could be systemic and unrelenting. This unlinking of virtue from a good life can take place under conditions of moral conflict, where the competing demands produced by great injustice force even the most virtuous agent to leave some "ought" unfulfilled and to subsequently be regretful or sorrowful or ill at ease with her/himself; and a similar unlinking can follow from maintaining character traits that are praiseworthy due to their efficacy for a politics of resistance, but that forfeit their bearer's well-being because they are self-sacrificial or corrosive or crowd out other valuable traits.

The idea, offered by Bernard Williams, of a moral residue or remainder has helped illuminate for me the phenomenon of the burdening of the virtues; such burdening takes place under conditions—such as those regularly faced by oppressed and politically resisting selves—where doing what is best falls far short of what one would have chosen given better conditions. Williams suggests that in situations of moral conflict, correctly answering the question of what is to be done or what, given the circumstances, is for the best does not by itself release a moral agent from concern about competing moral obligations that thereby are left unmet. This unreleased agent stays in a morally uncomfortable position, saddled with a moral remainder that is often expressed in the form of regret or even stronger emotions such as anguish (Williams 1973). Similarly with the moral agent who, due to moral luck and thus beyond the limits of her/his own control, takes part in a blameworthy action; this agent, too, is left in the disquieting position of being responsible for something that she/he would not have chosen and may feel what Williams dubs "agent-regret" (Williams 1981b). These forms of moral trouble are common under oppression, arising as they do when adverse conditions make even the very best possibility a morally problematic one or when bad luck leads one to engage in morally problematic ways or even to develop a morally problematic character.

This book, then, dwells on what may be missed by much feminist and other liberatory prescriptive moral theory. For while such theory can help determine what is the best way to live or to act under or in opposition to oppression, it does not typically pause to lament the fact that the best—in the circumstances—is really not very good at all. By lamenting this, I hope to increase the breadth of the complaint about systems of oppression, to name moral limitations and burdens as belonging on a list of harms that oppression causes, and to express both anger and grief over these harms.

The first three chapters of the book focus on the first form of moral trouble by drawing out different implications of the phenomenon of moral damage, especially considering the insight supplied by a virtue ethics framework that a morally "healthy" self is crucial for flourishing. In chapter 1, "Regretting the Self One Is," I argue that liberatory struggles not only must strive to change oppressive structures but also must work on transforming the selves who have been shaped by dominant values. I examine one oppositional practice that has attempted to respond in critical and practical ways to the fact that selves have been morally damaged under oppression. This practice, known by feminists as the *politics of personal transformation*, recognizes that participants in social justice movements must remake their own desires or inclinations so that they better reflect the commitments of the movement. While feminists such as Claudia Card (1996) have used the concept of moral luck to characterize oppression and its resulting moral damage as a matter of systemically patterned bad luck, I point out that luck also impacts heavily on the possibilities of transforming one's own character in the context of political resistance. Because the constitution of one's own self is subject to luck and thus not entirely in one's own control, one may actually be *unable* to develop or sustain inclinations that are in line with one's own liberatory principles, unable to embody what from a liberatory perspective would count as virtues. This fact is interesting because it explains an impediment to flourishing. But it also suggests a basis for Williams's agent-regret, an attitude that one can have toward what one would not have chosen but came to enact anyway precisely because of one's own lack of control. I argue that experiencing this discomforting agent-regret about one's own character—as well as experiencing anger at the systemic forces that ingrained objectionable values into one's self—is appropriate, and yet the very need for a self-reflective attitude that is so disturbing should be considered a harm.

Having relied on the concept of moral damage in chapter 1, in chapter 2, "The Damage of Moral Damage," I begin to worry about the use of the concept in reference to subordinated people. I name two reasons for believing that characterizing the oppressed as lacking in virtues—that is, as morally damaged—can be problematic. First, it seems that it is primarily the beneficiaries rather than the victims of oppression who should be understood as morally damaged (a point to which I return in the third chapter). A second, quite serious, problem is that highlighting what are actually wounds due to oppressive conditions can unintentionally lend credibility to a victim-blaming stance that attributes a group's subordination to an inherent or self-perpetuating inferiority. Indeed, this is exactly the fate met by African Americans, who have been persistently portrayed as damaged and as exhibiting character traits such as "criminality" and "dependency." Even if one exposes the systemic sources of moral damage and points to this moral damage in the oppressed as evidence of injustices against them, such an argument may not be heard against a background in which the supposed character flaws of members of subordinated groups have been used to condemn these groups as the source of their own problems. And yet, simply denying that there is anything wrong with the self obscures from the view of liberatory thinkers the need to theorize what sort of a self one ought to try to be to survive and resist oppression and steers activists away from projects—difficult as they may be—of transforming the self. Thus, despite the strategic dangers of exposing moral damage in the oppressed, I argue for its value. Acknowledging the moral shortcomings of the self under oppression sets up the task of the last three chapters of the book (after a detour in chapter 3 to consider those selves who are in dominant positions): to critically search for character traits that one could recommend to those who devote themselves to both undoing the damage of oppression and engaging in political resistance. As it turns out, such traits are rather elusive because those that seem praiseworthy under oppression or for purposes of resistance leave a trail of moral remainders.

Chapter 3, "The Ordinary Vices of Domination," differs from the others in that it focuses on members of privileged groups. Virtue ethics seems to present a puzzle about the privileged: if moral virtue is necessary for flourishing (which is a core assumption of virtue ethics), then members of privileged groups can only flourish if they are morally good. However, it is more plausible to conceive of the privileged as morally deficient than as morally good, since their privileges result from *unjust* social positions. Thus it appears that they are barred from flourishing, which is odd since one would expect conditions of oppression to prevent the victims rather than the beneficiaries of these conditions from living the good life. The puzzle begins to dissolve when one distinguishes between the contemporary understanding of happiness and the ancient Greek conception of flourishing, for it turns out that privileged people can be said to be happy without granting that they flourish. The distinction helps to uncover a key assumption of interdependence behind the belief that even the so-called other-regarding virtues are necessary for one's own flourishing; if people are interdependent in such a way that the flourishing of one is tied to the flourishing of all, then for the privileged to flourish, they would have to worry a lot more about the well-being of the disadvantaged. However, since in contemporary hierarchical societies members of dominant groups may ignore the sufferings of their subordinates without sacrificing their own subjectively felt happiness, that interdependence is clearly limited. As it turns out, it was limited for Aristotle, too, for he never intended the *polis* to be an inclusive one. This suggests a critical revision to his eudaimonistic theory, by the addition of the claim that a trait that contributes to one's own well-being cannot count as morally praiseworthy if it detracts from the flourishing of an inclusive social collectivity. A form of eudaimonism like Aristotle's—without this restriction—does not ensure that morality will require attention to subordinated people.

Eudaimonistic theories must be modified in other ways as well to be useful for describing (and prescribing responses to) conditions of oppression: the contingency of the relationship between virtue and flourishing must be not just acknowledged (as it is by Aristotle), but emphasized, for this relationship is constantly disrupted under oppression. It is not simply that the virtues must be accompanied by adequate external conditions in order to be sufficient for flourishing, though this fact is certainly central for directing the efforts of activists toward changing those inadequate conditions that are unjust. Adverse conditions can also affect what will actually qualify as a virtue, and the traits that are assessed as virtues for facing great adversity will likely not be those that meanwhile (or thereby) are good for their bearer. Vast suffering, the urgency of stopping injustices and thus the demands of oppositional struggle, and the complicated allegiances that resistance movements have called for, all potentially give rise to "mixed" traits that deserve praise only in the qualified sense of being the best that is possible under awful conditions. Virtues warranting this sort of praise tend to burden their bearer. Chapters 4 through 6 locate and examine these burdened virtues that are symptomatic of the second form of moral trouble.

In chapter 4, "Between Indifference and Anguish," I present the idea of a burdened virtue as I search for a praiseworthy trait in the realm of sensitivity and attention to others' suffering, a trait that ought to lie somewhere between the poles of indifference and anguish. What I encounter in the search is a field of moral dilemmas, where the enormity of unjust suffering in the world produces constantly conflicting, dire needs to which one must attend even as one is supposed to balance this focus on others with some direct self-care. Every point in this sphere is at once too indifferent (for one always turns one's back on so many) and too anguished (by the pain of those to whom one does attend). Even if one can determine a "best" disposition to have and make the right decisions regarding which actions to take in the face of all this suffering, one still leaves strong moral demands unsatisfied. Here there is a stark example of a moral remainder, where the weight of regret and guilt at what one cannot do burdens the moral agent. Additionally, what one *can* successfully do in the way of being attuned to others' suffering is burdensome too, for such sensitivity, even in moderation, is intrinsically painful. There is one further issue regarding painful sensitivity to others' suffering: I argue that, like Aristotelian pity, such sensitivity proves unreliable for motivating action aimed at alleviating suffering or for eradicating the injustices that cause suffering. Nevertheless, its absence is morally horrifying.

Chapter 5, "The Burden of Political Resistance," looks at the fact that liberatory movements—and I focus on both feminist movements and black liberation movements—offer praise for their fiercest, bravest, and most dedicated fighters, holding them up as models of the character traits that best enable political resistance. But this praise appears strange given a eudaimonistic ethics in which character traits that are morally praiseworthy are usually conducive to or constitutive of flourishing, for the character traits recommended for resistance often *disable* resisters themselves from flourishing. Relying on Aristotle's discussion of "mixed actions," I describe the political resister as displaying mixed traits that are routinely unlinked from flourishing and thereby burdened. Resisters experience a special vulnerability, not only due to their encountering dirty hands dilemmas regularly in political struggle, but also due to the pressure to develop certain character traits needed for fighting injustice. While in the first chapter I worried about a self's failure to heal from moral damage and to transform into an effective resister, in this chapter I am concerned with the dangers for those selves who succeed in transforming themselves. The problematic traits of the politically resistant self include those, such as anger, that contribute to maintaining a hard resolve against the oppressors; those, such as courage, that help resisters to take risks and to accept loss and sacrifice; and those that resisters must display in their relationships with one another, such as loyalty coupled with an openness to criticism and self-criticism. In an extended analysis of one of these questionable virtues—anger—I juxtapose Aristotelian warnings about how anger can go wrong with compelling arguments that feminists have made in favor of exactly the kind of anger that would normally be quite wrong but that under the extraordinary conditions of oppression are actually morally recommended. But while the feminist arguments may correctly identify what sort of anger is best under the circumstances, they do not reconcile this with its corrosive effects. I thus reframe the old question about consistency between means and ends, asking whether one employs acceptable means to liberatory political goals if the character of the resister is corrupted badly as it is fashioned for struggle.

Loyalty, which I consider briefly in chapter 5 as one of the traits that is praised within oppositional movements, becomes the focus of chapter 6, "Dangerous Loyalties," where I suggest that not only might a loyal disposition be detrimental for the one who is loyal, but it may actually turn out not to truly support liberatory ends. In order for group loyalty to even be available as a virtue, there must be a worthy object of loyalty. Feminist communities and communities that ground liberatory racial movements are potential objects of group loyalty. However, loyalty requires a certain restraint in—though not an absence of—dissent and criticism; specifically, loyalty forbids doing anything aimed at undermining the existence of the object of loyalty. Because liberatory principles sometimes do indeed call for dissolving the identities to which one might have allegiances, there may be no morally acceptable opportunities for group loyalty for a political resister. This is a loss, and it is one that results from the need for constant critique, including critique that threatens the continued existence of the very groups that form to oppose oppression. Political resisters who do sustain loyalty to a community by accepting the challenge of being a loyal critic may become burdened in several ways: they may find themselves tied to a community whose practices reflect internal dynamics of dominance and subordination, or they may belong to the community only uncomfortably, for their critical activities will tend to alienate them from other community members. Maintaining a critical stance either leaves one burdened by ties to a problematic object of loyalty or makes group loyalty as a virtue entirely unavailable.

The book's conclusion, "Eudaimonistic Virtue Ethics under Adversity," addresses a question that emerges given all of the critical revisions to a eudaimonistic virtue ethics that I suggest in the course of the book and especially given my proposed addition of this rather odd category of virtues—burdened virtues—which lack the usual feature of virtues because they are exercised in contexts in which flourishing tends to be diminished or unattainable. I ask how one could identify the virtues under conditions in which the link between virtue and flourishing is so unreliable. Given that the burdened virtues tend to fail to enable their bearers to flourish, one cannot find these virtues simply by beginning with a conception of flourishing and then working backward from there to see which traits are conducive to or constitutive of such flourishing. I propose instead a variety of ways in which a trait, despite being costly or detrimental, could be otherwise identifiably praiseworthy.

In choosing to focus on moral life under and in resistance to persistent oppression—rather than on strategies for achieving victory over oppression—and in emphasizing the limitations and burdens that characterize this moral life, I draw attention to some of the hardships of oppression rather than spark hope for liberation. It is for this reason that I cautioned of this book's pessimism. However, the pessimism must not be understood as indicating resignation nor as suggesting the pointlessness of struggle. Quite the opposite: revealing how destructive oppression is of the possibilities for flourishing underscores its evil and points to the necessity of oppositional politics. Derrick Bell has described being "pessimistic in a *victory* sense" (1992, x) as consistent with the assumption that resistance is necessary, for even the resister who is expecting defeat must continue to protest so as not to imply that the terms of the defeat are acceptable. I would like to temper my pessimism in one other way as well by noting that even while drawing out the problems of moral life under and in resistance to oppression, I believe that no self—and no moral life—can be described exhaustively by reference only to oppression and resistance. The moral troubles that I describe are not necessarily consuming. Something about life itself—something that is not captured by oppression and not captured by resistance either—asserts itself under even the worst of conditions.

1

Regretting the Self One Is

I

I find a virtue ethics approach to be useful in theorizing about oppression and resistance in part because it directs one to focus on the self. Other sorts of normative theories are crucial for identifying structural causes of injustice and for recommending strategies for bringing about structural change. But in prescribing actions, such theories may overlook the limitations of the selves who are to act: the victims of and the resisters to oppression. I believe that feminist and other liberatory theory and practice can be enriched by focusing on these selves, not just by inquiring, as virtue theories traditionally will, how they can be good or virtuous, but also by examining how their moral limitations may reveal some of the less-obvious harms of oppression.[1] If moral goodness is necessary—though importantly, not sufficient—for flourishing, as virtue theories in an Aristotelian tradition assume that it is, then moral damage to one's self interferes with one's living the "good life."

1. Thus I disagree with Sarah Conly, who argues that feminists should oppose feminist virtue ethics. Her argument is based on the claim that "the cultivation of virtue is a moral task from which there is no respite" (2001, 13) and that this task will be detrimental because (1) continual self-evaluation "may be alienating" and thus may threaten agency, and (2) these self-evaluations are likely to "find us wanting" (2001, 13). Her argument depends on the assumption that all that a virtue ethics may do is to prescribe a route to perfect virtue and to condemn those who fail. This is not what I intend to do in making use of a virtue ethics framework. Susan Moller Okin (1996) also cautions against a feminist virtue ethics, though it turns out that her concern is not about virtue theory per se, but rather the particular flaws of an unrevised Aristotelian theory (and also Alasdair MacIntyre's virtue theory). Several feminist theorists have recently been exploring the contribution that virtue ethics may make to feminism. Those who explicitly draw on an Aristotelian tradition of virtue theory (while modifying, departing from, or adding onto Aristotelianism to various degrees) include Halwani 2003; Homiak 1999; McLaren 2001; Potter 2001, 2002; Snow 2002; Tessman 1998, 2000, 2001, 2002a, 2002b; and Woolfrey 2002.

The idea of "constitutive moral luck" can be used in the context of virtue ethics to understand the formation of the oppressed self as a morally damaged being. As Claudia Card (1996) has argued, while the constitution of any self is partly a result of luck, that is, beyond the control of that self, those who are oppressed are likely to meet with particular conditions that negatively affect the developing self. That is, being subjected to oppression influences the chances of developing a good or virtuous character. Following Card's insight, but working more explicitly within a virtue ethics framework and therefore connecting the virtues to human flourishing, I will be analyzing the moral implications of the damage that is done to character by institutionally embedded social forces, namely, the damage done as a result of one kind of constitutive bad luck. In particular, in this chapter, I will be considering the possibilities for those selves who, in an oppositional response to their own subordination, attempt a self-transformation that aims to both undo the aspects of their own characters that cause them to suffer and cultivate character traits that best enable resistance.

Through the *politics of personal transformation*—politics in which transformation of one's self or character is meant to go hand in hand with working to bring about other sorts of liberatory changes—many feminists have tried to work critically on questions of self and character. I will point out that the concept of moral luck complicates the issue: if not only the way in which one's character is formed but also how much it can be changed is subject to moral luck, particularly the bad luck of being affected by systems of oppression that can damage one's self by creating conflicts between one's dispositions and one's own liberatory principles, then one cannot just *will* one's dispositions to change. Thus, it is not clear that a politics of personal transformation can really succeed, for its success would depend upon participants being able to bring their dispositions into line with their principles. Feminists may be in a position where they recognize and accept that they ought to engage in personal transformation (and ought to carry out actions that this transformation would enable) but find that they *cannot* because one does not entirely control one's character.

I will suggest that in the absence of reliable practices for transforming one's character, one might still make use of a virtue ethics framework to raise questions about the self who—due to luck—is in a position she/he would not have chosen. One might ask, for instance, what the morally recommended disposition is when feminist or liberatory prescriptions fall on those who cannot enact them; what is the virtue for reflecting on (and carrying on within) one's own moral limitations, when those limitations result from bad moral luck? Bernard Williams has suggested that one might appropriately feel regret over a wrong action that luck has brought one to be implicated in; he calls this regret *agent-regret* to emphasize that the regret is felt by one who takes at least partial responsibility despite lack of complete control (Williams 1981b, 27). I extend this suggestion by applying it not just to incident luck—luck that bears on an event—but also to constitutive luck; that is, I claim that one might appropriately regret the self that one has come to be and that one finds oneself unable to change. However, in the case that one's bad constitutive luck is not accidental but rather a result of systemic oppression, agent-regret cannot be the only recommended emotion; anger, coupled with agent-regret, maintains a critical recognition of and oppositional stance toward the forces that inflicted one's moral damage.

II

Moral luck—an oxymoron in Kantian ethics, where the will must be unconditioned—is that which is not within an agent's own control and yet affects the agent in a morally relevant way by, for instance, influencing character, decisions, or actions. The concept of moral luck implies, as Margaret Urban Walker puts it, that "*responsibilities outrun control*" (1993, 241); that is, one can be morally responsible, though in complex ways, for more than just that over which one has complete control. Moral luck may be good luck or bad luck; I take it to be bad luck when it interferes with living well or flourishing.[2] While moral luck is always outside of the agent's own control, its sources can vary: it could result from a natural event, such as a disease striking oneself or a loved one or a hurricane destroying one's home; it could be caused by another person's actions (whether intended or unintended), such as a friend's moving away or—to use Williams's example—such as the case where a child dashes into the street in front of one's car; additionally, it could be due to what Claudia Card calls the "unnatural lottery," namely, circumstances that are systematically arranged and that tend to affect people as members of social groups. I will call the luck that is doled out by the unnatural lottery *systemic luck* to indicate its source in social systems—particularly systems of oppression; it is in this way distinguished from luck that is natural, accidental, or idiosyncratic. For example, it can be due to systemic luck (in this case, bad luck) that a person suffers from the deprivation of poverty; there is nothing about this luck that is natural, accidental, or idiosyncratic, in that one can point to its systemic source in, for instance, capitalism.

Because social positioning is complicated and very few people can be described as fully occupying a position of dominance or alternatively as being subordinated in every possible way, analysis of how systemic luck affects any given person will be complex; it will have to attend to the ways in which an individual is disadvantaged and the ways in which she/he is privileged by social systems and thus to numerous ways in which the unnatural lottery would be likely to lead that person to encounter systemic barriers as well as open opportunities for developing certain virtues and for flourishing. One might wonder, given the ways that systems of oppression intersect or interlock, how to understand luck—or anything else—as systemic. Groups of people will be composed of individuals who differ from each other in socially significant ways, and generalizations about the group's luck will be like any other generalizations

2. I will put off discussing the question of how to define *flourishing* or a *good life*. I take up the problem—though I do not try to answer the question—in the chapters to come.

about a social group, namely, they will probably fail to accurately apply to many group members. For instance, the claim above that being subject to certain deprivations is a form of bad luck that accompanies poverty fails to take note of how the poverty of whites and of blacks entail different deprivations (and similarly for gender difference, and so on). However, that there is complexity to a society structured by multiple oppressions does not suggest that there is any randomness or lack of pattern to people's experiences in the society. Thus without necessarily being able to name the features of the patterns except through overgeneralizing, one can still assume the presence of patterns or systemic sources for experiences that have formative effects on the characters of people whose social positions are hard to capture by broad labels such as "working class," "Asian-American," "gay," "able-bodied," and so on, or by an even broader term, such as "member of a subordinated group." Throughout the book I will have occasion to use some of these broad terms, and I use them without the implication that people fall neatly under them but rather simply to make points such as the present one, that there is a difference between luck that is systemic and luck that is not.

The distinction between systemic and nonsystemic luck is not recognized by Bernard Williams (1981b) and Thomas Nagel (1979), who initiated the contemporary discussion of moral luck with their symposium on the topic;[3] however, they do draw other sorts of distinctions between kinds of moral luck, distinctions that I also find useful. Williams, on whom I will focus here, draws a distinction between what he calls constitutive luck and incident luck, where *constitutive luck* is that which affects the formation of character and is considered by Williams to be general, with sources that are not readily or precisely identifiable, and where *incident luck* is that which is directly relevant to whatever project, decision, or action is under moral evaluation. Given Williams's description of constitutive luck, he clearly did not have in mind systemic forces that affect character in patterned ways. He sets constitutive luck to the side, presumably because he considers it to be too broad to raise any specific questions of moral responsibility, since it "affects everything" (1981b, 25). Incident luck he further divides into what he calls *intrinsic* and *extrinsic luck.* Luck whose source is intrinsic to a project that is a result of a decision that is to be morally evaluated is, for him, the most important, since bad intrinsic luck makes the decision retrospectively morally unjustified. Williams's primary example of this is in a fictionalized account of Gauguin, who abandons his wife and children to live the sort of life that he deems necessary for actualizing what he hopes is his potential to be a gifted artist. If it turns out—and one can know this only in retrospect—that he had no such potential after all, then what is revealed is a failure of something intrinsic to the project. He fails as an artist as a result of something not within his control and therefore due to moral luck, but the something is intrinsic to his project of becoming a great artist; his decision to abandon his wife and children becomes retrospectively unjustifiable due to this

3. Originally published in Williams and Nagel 1976.

luck. Were he to have had good intrinsic luck—namely, were he to indeed have had the potential for great art—but bad extrinsic luck (and here Williams asks us to suppose Gauguin were to be injured on his way to Tahiti), his project would still fail, but he would not necessarily be morally unjustified in having made the decision to abandon his family.

While feminists can and have complained about Williams's assumption that if the project of becoming a great artist succeeds for Gauguin then he is morally justified in sacrificing his personal relationships and responsibilities,[4] there are good reasons for revising not just Williams's examples but also his distinctions among varieties of moral luck. It is useful, for purposes of theorizing about oppression, to think of the most important distinction within moral luck as that between what I am calling systemic luck and that which is nonsystemic, being natural, accidental, or idiosyncratic. Within what is systemic, one can then draw a further distinction by thinking, on the one hand, about the impact of systemic forces on the development of character and, on the other hand, about the effect systemic forces have on making good and bad incident luck more or less likely. For instance, being an African-American male makes it more probable that one will face police harassment or brutality; encountering such treatment while carrying out a specific project can be described as bad incident luck, while the long-term effect that accumulated experiences of this sort may have, such as regarding oneself with double-consciousness, is an effect on character and thus is constitutive luck.

I will be focusing, following Card, on systemic, constitutive moral luck. It is the sort of luck that interests me the most because thinking about it facilitates an analysis of the self under oppression. Additionally, using Williams's distinction between intrinsic and extrinsic luck, I will focus even more specifically than Card does: I will examine those cases in which systemic, constitutive moral luck is *intrinsic* to one's project, for it is in the cases in which luck is intrinsic to a project that luck bears most heavily on one's taking moral responsibility with respect to the project.[5] For a simple example of this, consider the case of "pride" movements such as Black pride or gay pride, the success of which depends upon the possibilities of changing internalized forms of racism or homophobia, which are socially formed character traits; that is, the project is *about* changing character or disposition. If one's constitutive luck has been such that one's disposition proves impervious to change in the relevant respect, the project will fail and will fail due to something intrinsic to the project itself. This is an example of a case of systemic, constitutive, intrinsic moral luck.

More generally, any ethicopolitical project that fits under what feminists have come to call the politics of personal transformation will provide cases in which to examine systemic, constitutive, intrinsic moral luck. I take it that a project counts as enacting a feminist politics of personal transformation only if it centrally involves changing disposition or character in accordance with a

4. See, for instance, Marilyn Friedman's "Liberating Care" in Friedman 1993.
5. Notice that Williams only considers intrinsic luck within incident, not constitutive, luck.

feminist transvaluation of traditional virtues and vices.[6] Thus these are cases where failures and successes with respect to character are intrinsic to the project. In most such cases of a politics of personal transformation, a changed character is linked with liberation. For example, traditional "feminine virtues" like self-sacrifice reflect dominant (in this case, patriarchal) values. Rejecting these values entails seeing such feminine virtues as interfering with a woman's capacity for valuing her own aspirations along with those of others; character traits such as these are thus critiqued and targeted to be changed through a politics of personal transformation. A change in character both enables and is enabled by changed social arrangements. For instance, freed from a self-sacrificing disposition, many women may choose not to become a wife and/or mother under existing conditions and may insist on changed conditions; those changed conditions, in turn, may discourage the development of a self-sacrificing disposition.

Conceiving of the politics of personal transformation as presenting cases of systemic, constitutive, intrinsic moral luck suggests the value of borrowing from virtue ethics a focus on character, the central factor in constitutive luck. The politics of personal transformation also implicitly endorses the assumption at the core of virtue ethics that having a praiseworthy character (in this case praiseworthy from the perspective of liberatory rather than dominant values) is necessary for flourishing, for those who are trying to transform themselves do so because they recognize that changing their own characters is a necessary part of their work toward making the good life accessible to all (including themselves). Traditional accounts of virtue ethics will, of course, not offer all of the conceptual apparatus needed here for thinking about the self under oppression. Such accounts will fail to ensure that attention be paid to systemic forces such as those of oppression when examining the constitution of the self and will define the virtues in ways that may support rather than undermine dominant

6. Ann Ferguson comments about this sort of transformation that "to reconstitute ourselves as anti-racist, antisexist, and so forth requires work, struggle, new habits, new virtues, and new social practices as well as reconstructed social identities" (1995, 370) and that in order to carry out the reconstruction of values "we need to form intentional or chosen communities of resistance, or what I call 'oppositional communities.' Such communities are attempts to partially realize some of our ideals in the present as we struggle to change the world in the future" (1995, 372). She elaborates on her understanding of an oppositional community—the location of the anticipated transformation—as

> not just people who live together or in the same neighborhood, such as in a communal household or progressive barrio or neighborhood, but a network of actual and imagined others to whom one voluntarily commits oneself in order to empower oneself and those bonded with others by challenging a social order perceived to be unjust, usually by working on a shared project for social change. Connecting to an oppositional community is at some level an act of rebellion or resistance. The choice to do so involves a resolve to reconstitute one's personal identity and, in so doing, to reassess the values to which one is committed and the responsibilities one has for others. (1995, 372)

In this book I use the term *oppositional community* interchangeably with *community of liberatory politics*, *community of resistance*, and similar variations.

values and will neglect or badly distort what will count as the flourishing of those who are subordinated.

Bringing moral luck into the discussion of the politics of personal transformation (once such a project is viewed through a lens of virtue ethics) raises questions about how possible it really is to take responsibility for changing one's character, the very thing that such a politics prescribes. If systemic, constitutive, intrinsic, bad moral luck interferes seriously with being able to retrain one's character in accordance with one's liberatory principles, then a politics of personal transformation will not succeed as a feminist ethicopolitical project. I will thus turn next to Claudia Card's investigation of the possibilities for taking responsibility in the face of systemic, constitutive moral luck, especially when it is bad luck and luck that is intrinsic to feminist ethicopolitical projects.

III

Card suggests that for feminists aiming to create moral or political change, what will be particularly relevant about moral luck is the questions it raises about moral responsibility—not in the backward-looking sense of assigning praise or blame for choices already made (which is the sense of responsibility central to Williams and Nagel's discussions of moral luck)—but rather in the forward-looking sense of "taking responsibility" for future possibilities, including one's own future character. For her, moral agency is exercised through taking responsibility, and one who cannot take responsibility cannot fully be a moral agent. Since she focuses on the cases of those whose systemic, constitutive moral luck has disadvantaged them—that is, has given them an unequal opportunity for developing the virtues—her questions about taking responsibility presuppose that this is to be done given damage already sustained and given continuing conditions that create barriers against successfully repairing this damage. These background conditions complicate the taking of responsibility, but they do not, for Card, eliminate its possibility.

According to Card, taking responsibility in any forward-looking way requires that one ask and answer the question of what is to be done, that is, what is worth doing, and the additional, important question of whether one is capable of doing it, given one's virtues and vices at the "starting position" from which one takes a forward-looking perspective (1996, 27). Card notes that "luck is involved both in the motivation to take responsibility and in our ability to carry through. Where that seems unfair, we may be able to take the unfairness into account, morally, in some of our evaluations" (1996, 27). Taking unfairness—particularly the unfairness resulting from the unnatural lottery—into account does not mean excusing anyone from responsibility, since, as Card points out, "that our motivations and carryings through are embedded in factors beyond our control does not imply that there is no control after all" (1996, 27); rather, taking responsibility while recognizing unfair luck means that "we locate ourselves as morally relevant centers of agency" (1996, 28) while understanding that, as Williams puts it, "one's history as an agent is a web in which anything that is the product of the will is surrounded and held up and partly formed by things that are not" (Williams 1981b, 29).

It is because one cannot cleanly separate what is a product of the will from what is not that Card rejects a requirement for autonomy in the exercise of moral agency. Other people with whom one has relationships affect how one's character is constituted and are thus a part of one's moral luck; significant relationships "affect our basic values, our sense of who we are, our commitments, even our abilities to live up to those commitments" (Card 1996, 30). While conceiving of an agent as autonomous would require an assumption of immunity from some forms of moral luck, conceiving of an agent as—at least potentially—having integrity does not depend upon this assumption. It is thus integrity, which "involves considerations of consistency, coherence, and commitment" (1996, 32), that Card considers to be important to the exercise of moral agency in the taking of responsibility.[7] However, integrity is not a simple achievement for those who have suffered moral damage as a result of oppression. Card claims that "to develop and maintain integrity, we need to discover, assess, and sometimes make changes in our values, traits, and capacities," a process that is affected by luck to such an extent that "to determine whether it makes sense to hold an agent responsible, we need to know whether that agent's luck made the development or maintenance of integrity impossible or impossibly difficult" (1996, 33).

Part of what makes moral integrity difficult, when it is possible at all, is understanding and possibly changing aspects of character that are acquired early in life, if one later comes to see these as problematic, and reconciling the resulting changes in moral commitments (Card 1996, 33). Integrity—and thus responsible moral agency—may be unattainable for those who cannot fully ferret out the sources of their dispositions, change these when appropriate, or manage to carry out old commitments without violating more recently gained convictions. Card claims that the sort of fragmentation that threatens integrity can be characteristic of those who are formed under conditions of oppression. In the case of those who develop multiple personalities—for instance, as a way of surviving childhood abuse—such fragmentation is quite literal, but even in other cases, Card notes that the oppressed "are likely to be sites of seriously warring inclinations, moods, likes, and dislikes elicited by the double-binds of oppressive institutions" (1996, 42).

Card understands integrity in terms of the integration of these opposing dispositions (1996, 46). The task of acquiring integrity is necessary for resisting oppression and taking responsibility for—or being able to "stand behind" (Card 1996, 28)—whom one becomes, but it is a task that in turn requires discovering which of one's character traits are constitutive of moral damage and should be forgone in favor of a disposition that consistently supports one's own—and others'—flourishing. While there are both virtues and vices associated with

7. For other feminist considerations of the problems and possibilities of integrity under oppression, see Davion 1991, Calhoun 1995, and Walker 1998, chap. 5.

social disadvantage (and likewise with social privilege), the special problem of figuring out how to resist oppression creates the question of how to change the vices in the oppressed that may contribute to their own suffering and that may prevent them from (successfully) pursuing liberation.[8]

It will be helpful, then, to know concretely what damaging effect oppression may have on one's character. Here I only explore how victims of oppression are morally damaged; in chapter 3 I take up the question of how beneficiaries of oppression may also—though differently—be damaged. Of course, since actual people cannot be separated into distinct groups—of advantaged and disadvantaged—analyzing moral damage in any particular case will require attention to the peculiarities of an individual's social positioning. However, one might still usefully describe the results of the experience of some kind of subordination, noting that one will have to take care in seeing who tends to have experiences of this sort and who does not. Oppositional political groups, for instance, could undertake projects using techniques of consciousness-raising to better understand the experiences of their members and could move from there to the practical task of changing traits that stand in the way of their well-being or of their ability to resist oppression.

Card suggests some traits that seem to result from the damage of being subordinated, and traits such as these could serve as a starting point for groups' investigations of the particular forms of moral damage their members may have sustained:

> Misplaced gratitude is one kind of moral damage women have suffered. There are others. . . . The oppressed are liable to low self-esteem, ingratiation, affiliation with abusers (for example so-called female masochism), as well as to a tendency to dissemble, fear of being conspicuous, and chameleonism—taking on the colors of our environment as protection against assault. (1996, 53)

Damaged character traits typically develop as survival mechanisms under oppressive circumstances. For instance, Card speculates that because of women's "political inability to end bad relationships, we have not learned to discriminate well between good ones and bad ones," which contributes to women's having a tendency to focus on maintaining relationships—no matter what—rather than a tendency to value separation and autonomy (1996, 64). Someone who has these damaged character traits and who meanwhile is committed to liberatory principles through which she can identify these traits as bad (for her)

8. I will complicate the connection between virtue and flourishing in later chapters, for while the virtues are necessary for flourishing, they are—especially under conditions of oppression—not sufficient. One cannot simply identify virtues, or praiseworthy dispositions, by determining which traits contribute to or are constitutive of flourishing. However, until I introduce these complications, I will assume that the liberatory principles and goals of an oppositional movement or community can serve to point in the direction of desirable character traits: those traits that are consistent with bringing about and living lives free from oppression and domination.

will experience an internal conflict that Card would describe as a lack of integration.

Taking responsibility for oneself in a forward-looking sense will require being able to make of oneself a person one is willing to be accountable for, a person whose values, practices, and disposition one can support. Being a self whose desires are seriously at odds with one's principles will complicate taking responsibility since one may not want to fully stand behind such a self. Learning how to undo the damage would enable one to unproblematically stand behind one's self, but this may not be easy or even possible to learn. As Card asks, "[H]ow is it possible for us as damaged agents to liberate ourselves from the damage?" (1996, 41) and thus to become a self whose inclinations are not at war with deeply held convictions, a self one could thereby stand behind and more easily take full responsibility for becoming?

IV

Card's question about liberation from moral damage needs to be taken seriously by feminists or others engaged in liberatory struggles, whether in an attempt to answer it or in an attempt to proceed beyond it by exploring how to engage ethically in a context in which one cannot liberate oneself from some moral damage. My sense is that an action-centered approach to ethics tends to deflect attention away from Card's question, since the question is primarily about the *character* of the agent who may potentially resist oppression. I would like to suggest that rather than (or in addition to) using the idea of right action as a starting point for feminist or liberatory ethics, and then, if at all, asking what sort of virtues are required for the actions, one might do well to ask questions focused on character and framed by a recognition of the moral damage done to character through systemic bad luck. If systemic bad luck impacts heavily on one's being able to take responsibility for whom one becomes, as Card suggests, then feminist (or liberatory) ethical theory can only address this problem by focusing on character.

Once focused on character, one might begin by identifying and trying to determine how to acquire the virtues that will be needed to not only consistently and dependably carry out the actions that liberatory principles suggest are good ones, but to do so as a self with integrity; however, I assume that this first line of inquiry will meet with difficulties or failures due in part to bad luck, so there will need to be a second set of questions, about how one takes responsibility for a self whose constitution is not fully in one's control and which one cannot necessarily "repair." The assumption behind this second path of inquiry is that since, as mentioned before, "*responsibilities outrun control*" (Walker 1993, 241), one may be led to "stand behind" a self that one would not have chosen to be.

To have a sense of the limitations of an action-centered feminist ethics for pursuing these issues, consider as an example Alison Jaggar's account of what she calls the "minimum conditions of adequacy for any approach to ethics that purports to be feminist" (Jaggar 1989a, 91).[9] Jaggar's first condition, which is the only one on which I will focus here, is: "Within the present social context, in which women remain systematically subordinated, a feminist approach to ethics must offer a guide to action that will tend to subvert rather than reinforce this subordination" (1989a, 91). What I would like to add to Jaggar's first condition is a requirement that a feminist approach to ethics problematize how an oppressed and morally damaged self is likely to arrive at the performance of correct action.[10] Within a virtue ethics framework, it is, of course, not enough to perform the right action. As Aristotle says:

> If the acts that are in accordance with the excellences have themselves a certain character it does not follow that they are done justly or temperately. The agent also must be in a certain condition when he does them; in the first place he must have knowledge, secondly he must choose the acts, and choose them for their own sakes, and thirdly his action must proceed from a firm and unchangeable character. (*NE* 1105a28–1105b1)[11]

Thus, for instance, the fully virtuous man and the "continent" (strong-willed) man may perform the same actions, but they differ in character, the fully virtuous man having the right desires as well as the right principles, and the continent man having the wrong desires but following his principles to "override" the desires (*NE* 1152a1–4). Part of the problem of continence is that it is a painful state to maintain, since one feels pain at the thought of performing the right action but does so nevertheless. The morally damaged agent described by Card—one who lacks an integration of desires and principles and is internally conflicted—is akin to Aristotle's case of continence (or incontinence, depending

9. A later version of these conditions appears in Jaggar 1991; however, the condition to which I refer is essentially unchanged.

10. I am not claiming that Jaggar herself fails to problematize the way that someone's emotional constitution relates to her principles or to the actions she is led to perform; in fact, Jaggar addresses this issue extensively in Jaggar 1989b. Rather, I am pointing out that a feminist ethical theory that meets her criteria for adequacy (and here I have mentioned only the first of her conditions) by guiding feminists to correct action could do so without giving attention to the possible conflicts between disposition and principles.

11. All references to Aristotle are to the translations in Jonathan Barnes, ed., *The Complete Works of Aristotle: The Revised Oxford Translation* (Princeton, NJ: Princeton University Press, 1984). Many quotations from Aristotle contain gendered terms: "the good man," "his character," etc. It becomes tiresome and distracting to follow the feminist convention of inserting a [*sic*] after each of these "errors," which are indications of Aristotle's sexism, so I refrain. This should not be taken, however, as endorsement of Aristotle's treatment of gender. Abbreviations of Aristotle's works are as follows:

DA: *On the Soul (De Anima)*
EE: *Eudemian Ethics*
NE: *Nicomachean Ethics*
Poet.: *Poetics*
Pol.: *Politics*
Rhet.: *Rhetoric*
Top.: *Topics*

on the outcome of the conflict between desires and principles) and in a similarly painful state; it is this psychic pain that is not taken into consideration by feminist ethical theories that prescribe actions based on feminist principles without attention to character.

It will be illustrative here to look at some actions that might be prescribed by feminists within an action-centered framework and to consider what it might take to perform these actions, if one's character has been formed under oppression. Suppose that among these prescribed actions are the following:[12] within feminist organizations, make decisions using cooperative rather than hierarchical procedures, aiming at consensus; help to undermine the power of misogynist and racist beauty norms by refusing to conform to these norms; engage only in those forms of sexuality that do not draw upon and reinforce a pornographic imagination; and carry out organized resistance in the form of demonstrations, political education, or direct actions aimed at changing structural features of the society that are oppressive. What will it take for these actions to be carried out by one who has a competitive disposition, or by one who has internalized a body aesthetic according to which an unadorned female and/or dark-skinned body is ugly and dirty, or by one who responds sexually only to images of domination, or by one who is excessively fearful and unassertive, lacking the courage and confidence to stand out, to risk being fired or arrested or abandoned by those upon whom she may depend to confirm her worthiness? It is quite probable that the prescribed actions either will be quite difficult (if not completely out of reach) for those whose characters have been damaged in the above ways or that, if the actions are possible, they are achieved through the compromise of continence. Then, even if the prescribed action is performed, the agent is faced with having to stand behind or take responsibility for the conflicted self who performs it. For instance, a feminist might steadfastly refuse to mark herself with the signs of femininity, simply enduring her own painful thought of herself as ugly in her lack of femininity, if she is unable to change the internalized misogynist aesthetic. Although she performs the "correct action" according to at least some feminist prescription for action, she is left conflicted (and not fully "virtuous") and in this way is barred from really flourishing. A prescription for action, then, ignores the need for a consideration of how the character of the agent who is to carry out the actions may interfere with the success of the project, where success will involve not only performing the action, but doing so in such a way that one is not pained by its performance. This sort of a failure of a feminist ethicopolitical project will be particularly evident when the project is conceived as part of a politics of personal transformation, for in this case transformation of desires and thus of character is understood as intrinsic to the project.

In contrast to an action-centered approach, an agent-centered approach to, for instance, feminist ethicopolitics will have a consideration of character built

12. I do not intend for the items in this list to be exhaustive, nor for them to stand as some sort of universal feminist prescriptions. They are meant to serve only as possible examples.

in. Let me suggest, then, an alternative to Jaggar's conditions for adequacy, by reframing her conditions within a virtue ethics (and eudaimonistic) approach: any adequate moral theory must promote human flourishing. An adequate *feminist* moral theory will pay particular attention to systemic barriers to human flourishing that have been created by conditions of oppression (including, but not limited to, the oppression of women). Since one cannot flourish if one's virtue is diminished by the fact that one's inclinations are at odds with one's own liberatory ideals, an adequate feminist moral theory will have to either address the question of how to undo the moral damage that causes this conflicted state or will have to acknowledge that not all moral damage can be reversed and instead consider what it means to engage ethically under damaging conditions. Since part of examining the systemic barriers to flourishing under oppression will involve looking at how moral damage is inflicted on and reinforced in the characters of those who are constituted under conditions of oppression, thereby preventing, or making more difficult, or making painful, the actions that are characteristic only of those who have not suffered such damage, it will involve asking questions about systemic, constitutive, intrinsic, bad moral luck.

V

I am now in a position to ask whether the practices that can be described as part of the politics of personal transformation enable one to do what a virtue ethics framework suggests for feminist ethics, namely, to examine the systemic barriers to human flourishing created by conditions of oppression, including those barriers that are tied to the morally damaged characters of the oppressed. At first glance it seems as if the politics of personal transformation has indeed presupposed a model of feminist ethics that is better described as agent-centered than as action-centered. A feminist politics of personal transformation may begin by giving an account of flourishing and a corresponding set of virtues or character traits that will either enable one to resist oppression (since oppression is understood to interfere with flourishing) or to flourish as one would if one had already escaped oppression. It then suggests a transformation into a self that can dependably and without internal conflict enact such resistance or such flourishing. Thus, the politics of personal transformation avoids the problem of an action-centered approach by recognizing that change in character is necessary for resisting oppression and for becoming a self for which one can unproblematically take moral responsibility.

However, while those engaged in the politics of personal transformation recognize the need for changing character, they tend not to recognize the complexity of carrying this out, particularly in the light of moral luck, which makes it clear that the transformation of character is not entirely within one's control. As Card points out, when one takes responsibility for the transformation of one's character, one cannot act as an autonomous agent whose actions result solely from her will. One cannot simply will one's character to change.

This point is central to Sandra Bartky's argument in "Feminine Masochism and the Politics of Personal Transformation" (in Bartky 1990) where she observes that the politics of personal transformation has tended to proceed on the false assumption that a feminist-oriented change in character is at least largely a product of the will and that it can follow from feminist consciousness-raising. To illustrate this claim, Bartky explores the case of someone who suffers from what in Card's terms could be described as a lack of integrity, in this instance, a lack of integration between desires and principles. Bartky begins with the question: "What to do . . . when the structure of desire is at war with one's principles?" (1990, 45) and tries to answer the question (or reveal it as unanswerable) by telling the story of a woman whom she names "P.," where P. is "a feminist, who has masochistic fantasies" (1990, 46). Her description of P.'s situation resonates with Card's account of a self who has been morally damaged and who becomes a "site of seriously warring inclinations, moods, likes, and dislikes elicited by the double-binds of oppressive institutions" (Card 1996, 42). Bartky writes:

> A person may experience her own sexuality as arbitrary, hateful, and alien to the rest of her personality. Each of us is in pursuit of an inner integration and unity, a sense that the various aspects of the self form a harmonious whole. But when the parts of the self are at war with one another, a person may be said to suffer from self-estrangement. That part of P. which is compelled to produce sexually charged scenarios of humiliation is radically at odds with the P. who devotes much of her life to the struggle against oppression. (1990, 51)

Not only is P. in this painful state of conflict and lack of integration, but her distress is augmented by the fact that she feels shame at being in such a state, at having desires that "are not worthy of her" (1990, 52). Given the state that P. is in, she is clearly motivated to change her character or, more specifically, her sexual desires. P. tries every possible avenue of change, with no success. Among the least helpful models for change is that presented by a feminist politics of personal transformation, which Bartky points out relies upon a voluntarist theory of sexuality. She writes:

> The view is widespread among radical feminists . . . that female sexuality is malleable and diffuse and that a woman can, if she chooses, alter the structure of her desire. . . . [This] sexual voluntarism has two sources; first, the fact that for many women, thoroughgoing and unforeseen personal changes, including the rejection of heterosexuality for lesbian sexuality, have often accompanied the development of a feminist politics; second, a theory of sexuality that relies heavily on Skinnerian-style behaviorism. While it is a fact that many women (and even some men) have been able to effect profound personal transformations under the influence of feminist ideas, a theory of sexuality I believe to be both false and politically divisive has taken this fact as evidence for the practicability of a willed transformation of self. (1990, 55)

Because P. is unable to change her desires, it seems that her options are to be either strong-willed or weak-willed (continent or incontinent); if she is strong-willed, she will abide by her principles, repressing her sexual desires and refusing to indulge them, which may require forgoing sexual satisfaction altogether; and if she is weak-willed, she will indulge the desires but feel the troublesome lack of integration of her desires and her principles and the accompanying shame. While of course continence is usually taken to be superior to incontinence, it is really not clear that either option better enables flourishing for P.; both produce terribly painful psychic states. What is unavailable to P. as an option is full virtue, that is, having both the "correct" desires and the "correct" principles; this would require the transformation of desire that P. has discovered to be impossibly difficult and that a feminist politics of personal transformation, with its voluntarist account of character change, has failed to enable.

Part of the failure of a feminist politics of personal transformation, then, is that it recognizes the need but not the difficulty, or even impossibility in some cases, of the transformation of character.[13] According to the voluntarist account of character change employed by a politics of personal transformation, one would never experience a serious and unalterable conflict between desires and principles, for one could always simply choose to desire in accordance with one's principles, at most retraining oneself along a behavioral model. To allow moral luck a place is to necessarily reject this voluntarist account of agency in favor of the claim that although one is the "morally relevant center of agency" (Card 1996, 28) for one's own character, this does not imply that one can effectively will one's character to assume a particular shape. To repeat Williams's insight, "[O]ne's history as an agent is a web in which anything that is the product of the will is surrounded and held up and partly formed by things that are not" (1981b, 29).

Through its theoretical commitment to voluntarism, the politics of personal transformation is unable to admit the full extent of moral damage that can be done through systemic, constitutive, bad moral luck. When such luck is intrinsic to a project, as it always is in the case of a politics of personal transformation, the project must fail. As Bartky points out, the politics of personal transformation has not included a complex enough understanding of how oppression works in interfering with flourishing. Bartky makes this point powerfully:

> Those who claim that any woman can reprogram her consciousness if only she is sufficiently determined hold a shallow view of the nature of patriarchal oppression. Anything done can be undone, it is implied; nothing has been permanently damaged, nothing irretrievably lost. But this is tragically false. One of the evils of a system of oppression is that it may damage people in ways that cannot always be undone. (1990, 58)

While I would not suggest giving up on the possibility of creating the sorts of practices that might effectively change character when it interferes with living well or flourishing, Bartky does seem to be right in claiming that, for now, feminism lacks "an effective political practice around issues of personal

13. See Homiak 1999 for a feminist (and Aristotelian) discussion of the malleability of character.

transformation" (1990, 61).[14] Not wanting to admit to this lack, feminists may continue to theorize as if the means of transformation were readily available. Even Card, who clearly is focused on the force of bad moral luck in the formation of a damaged character, seems to pass fairly easily into finding a solution for undoing moral damage and achieving integrity, implying only that under unfavorable conditions, the achievement of moral responsibility becomes *harder* and demands more conscious work. She writes:

> Potentialities for becoming responsible may be realized without much self-consciousness in a moderately favorable environment. . . . What develops without much self-consciousness under moderately favorable conditions may be stunted or damaged by oppression or abuse. The development of responsible agency then may require the deliberate construction of friendly space and a monitoring of what is permitted inside. (1996, 47)

I believe, however, that this sketch of how character can be transformed cannot be taken to solve problems like the one that Bartky presents through the story of P. Instead of only trying to find a way *out* of situations where the self is damaged and barred from flourishing, I propose developing an ethical theory intended specifically for those who are *in* such situations: those who have suffered irreversible damage, who endure inescapable oppression, and who will continue indefinitely to face (and accept or turn away from) the demands of resistance.

VI

Oppression can be seen as interfering with flourishing in two ways. The first and most obvious way is that it creates circumstances external to the oppressed agent (whether that agent be virtuous or not) that limit options so that every way one turns one runs into barriers that make it difficult or impossible to gain or be granted freedom, material resources, political power, and respect or social recognition of personhood—all of which are needed to live well.[15] In response to

14. One feminist theorist who has tried to develop practices of self-transformation—in this case, specifically, practices of self-recovery for black women—is bell hooks. Her aim in hooks 1993 is to connect psychological healing with political analysis that is attentive to systemic sources of damage.

15. This description echoes Marilyn Frye's in "Oppression" (in Frye 1983), where she writes:

> The experience of oppressed people is that the living of one's life is confined and shaped by forces and barriers which are not accidental or occasional and hence avoidable, but are systematically related to each other in such a way as to catch one between and among them and restrict or penalize motion in any direction. It is the experience of being caged in: all avenues, in every direction, are blocked or booby trapped. (1983, 4)

She uses the metaphor of a bird in a birdcage: one cannot see the relationship between the wires of the cage—and thus understand why the bird does not just fly free—unless one steps back and takes a "macroscopic view" (1983, 5).

this first way in which oppression interferes with flourishing, political resisters must fight for structural changes to remove the barriers, and indeed, these are the sorts of changes that (radical) resistance movements do focus on. While I certainly think that fighting for structural changes is of primary importance in the struggle against oppression, what I have focused on here is tied to the second way in which oppression interferes with flourishing, something that is less often attended to by oppositional communities, perhaps because it cannot be addressed solely through structural changes. The second way in which oppression interferes with flourishing is that it gives rise to moral damage in the oppressed agent; one way that it does this is by creating inclinations that conflict with liberatory principles, thus barring the possibility of full virtue. Both of these ways in which oppression interferes with flourishing are forms of bad luck, in that both arise from something at least in part beyond the control of the agent; the first way could be described as systemic, incident luck and the second as systemic, constitutive luck.

For Aristotle, bad *incident* luck does interfere with flourishing, but according to him, one may still morally evaluate someone in a context of bad luck; in fact, in such a context, one evaluates a person precisely by seeing how she/he responds to bad luck. In Aristotle's words:

> Now many events happen by chance, and events differing in importance; small pieces of good fortune or of its opposite clearly do not weigh down the scales of life one way or the other, but a multitude of great events if they turn out well will make life more blessed (for not only are they themselves such as to add beauty to life, but the way a man deals with them may be noble and good), while if they turn out ill they crush and maim blessedness; for they both bring pain with them and hinder many activities. Yet even in these nobility shines through, when a man bears with resignation many great misfortunes, not through insensibility to pain but through nobility and greatness of soul. (*NE* 1100b22–32)

One can still look for the virtues that "shine through" bad luck and that aid one in living as well as possible under bad circumstances. Aristotle suggests that one should consider someone to be good if he makes the best of what is given:

> For the man who is truly good and wise, we think, bears all the chances of life becomingly and always makes the best of circumstances, as a good general makes the best military use of the army at his command and a shoemaker makes the best shoes out of the hides that are given him. (*NE* 1101a1–5)

Others have developed the idea, consistent with what Aristotle has said here, that there could be a response that is especially called for when facing the consequences of bad incident luck. Bernard Williams has in mind a case where an agent's intentional actions (such as driving a lorry) in combination with bad luck (such as having a child run into the street at just the wrong moment) cause something terrible to happen; Williams speaks approvingly of the regret that the agent may feel in this case. The regret is of a special kind, different from the regret of a spectator, and to signal this Williams calls it agent-regret, in full recognition of the fact that the agent did not *voluntarily* commit the regrettable action. Even without complete control, the agent has become responsible for the action, and this sense of responsibility is what is acknowledged by the presence of agent-regret, accompanied, perhaps, by a desire to make any reparations that are possible (Williams 1981b, 27–29).[16]

Rosalind Hursthouse describes the appropriateness of this regret explicitly in terms of how it affects the evaluation of an agent as virtuous, for she is interested in framing moral dilemmas, including tragic ones (the encountering of which can be thought of as one variety of bad luck) in virtue-ethical terms. The presence of regret or pain that one may experience upon enacting what—apart from the circumstances that offer no better alternative—would be a reprehensible action is an indication that one is not acting viciously. Hursthouse notes that in situations where no good option is available, "the charitable, honest, just agent... does not act callously, dishonestly, unjustly, that is '*as* (in the manner) the callous, dishonest, unjust agent does.' She acts with immense regret and pain instead of indifferently or gladly, as the callous or dishonest or unjust one does" (1999, 73–74). When the virtuous agent must engage in an act that she could not *choose* and that is truly terrible, she, unlike one who lacks the relevant virtues, also suffers from what she must do; a feeling of pain becomes part of what characterizes the particular virtue—justice, for example—when it is exercised in the context of a tragic dilemma where the just agent may have to, say, sacrifice one life in order to save another. In fact, the suffering—characterized as sorrow, a feeling of being haunted, or a lack of peace with oneself—can be so profound that Hursthouse believes that while the agent's virtue is revealed by these responses, her/his life is marred or ruined (1999, 74–77). What Hursthouse has described, then, may be the virtues—with their component emotions—appropriate for facing the very worst sorts of moral luck, but they are not virtues that, as virtues ordinarily do, contribute to the agent's own well-being; they contribute instead to her/his distress.[17]

Margaret Urban Walker also suggests that there are virtues that are possible and necessary specifically for withstanding and responding to moral luck; she calls these "the virtues of impure agency," by which she means the virtues of the agent who has moral responsibility for things beyond her control. The virtues of impure agency are thus virtues that arise within what Walker describes as "a distinctive field of assessments of ourselves and others, in terms of how we regard and respond to... [the] interplay between what we control and what befalls us" (1993, 241). Within this field, she claims, "we expect ourselves and others to muster certain resources of character to meet the synergy of choice and

16. Compare Williams's account of agent regret to Rawls's (1971) belief that a rational plan of life is one that one cannot later regret having followed. In Rawls's framework, one could never feel agent-regret for that over which one did not have complete control.

17. In the second half of this book, I develop an analysis of virtues of exactly this sort: those that burden the agent by their lack of a connection to flourishing.

fortune, which is especially burdensome in the case of bad moral luck" (1993, 241). While the virtues appropriate for responding to bad moral luck may include virtues that are also called for elsewhere, Walker finds that there are some virtues that the very context of bad luck creates the need for; she proposes integrity, grace, and lucidity, which together help one to comprehend or survive the realization that one's moral life is subject to luck and that one's moral possibilities are limited, and to do so without losing one's "moral center" (1993, 241–242). By describing situations of bad moral luck as burdensome, Walker seems to refer to the fact that they require virtues that are especially formidable to achieve; that is, it is the burden of accepting a challenge rather than the burden of experiencing pain, such as the pain that is present in the regretful and sorrowful responses that Williams and Hursthouse describe. There is indeed a challenge posed by the necessity of reckoning with the vulnerability that all humans live with simply as a result of our susceptibility to luck; as Walker has so aptly noted elsewhere, "the moral of moral luck is that we have to learn to be moral without hoping, or worse pretending to be noumenal" (Coyne [Walker] 1985, 24), and this is certainly a harder—because riskier—task than just exercising one's will in the right way. It is thus the fact that bad moral luck is *luck*, rather than (just) the fact that it is *bad*, that gives rise to these distinctive and difficult virtues.

I will adopt the idea from Aristotle, Williams, Hursthouse, and Walker—each with their different points of emphasis—that there are virtues that are praiseworthy precisely because of how they shape one's response to bad moral luck. Because I am interested in theorizing a specific variety of bad moral luck—namely, the bad luck of moral damage under oppression—I would like to extend or revise the idea in two ways that I think serve to adapt it well for this project.

First, as I have been doing throughout the chapter, I want to broaden the discussion from incident luck to constitutive luck, since what is at issue here is the (perhaps irreparably) damaged self. Aristotle does not consider the case of bad constitutive luck, since he shies away from claiming that a morally bad character may be due to bad luck, maintaining instead, and in spite of his knowledge that character formation begins early in childhood (*NE* 1103b24–26, 1104b11–12, 1105a2), that bad moral states are voluntarily incurred, though they may not always be voluntarily reversed, since they may, like the moral damage that Bartky discusses, be beyond repair (see *NE* 1114a12–22). Others have also avoided the issue of constitutive luck because it suggests the troubling notion that since the agent is thoroughly constructed, there is not only a lack of control due to luck, but there is also a lack of any self who by being outside of the reach of luck could even have any control. However, I do not think that pointing to one specific and identifiable way in which a self is constituted by forces beyond her/his control, as I am doing when I name oppressive social forces as a causal factor in moral damage, runs the risk of destroying the idea of agency. Instead, it makes clear that this aspect of a self's character (a result of bad constitutive luck) is an appropriate object of whatever emotions are also appropriate for responding to bad incident luck. I believe that the set of responses ranging from regret (agent-regret) to sorrow—that things must be as they are—may properly be experienced by an agent reflecting on her/his own damaged self. In the case of the agent who meets with bad incident luck and is led to commit a terrible action, the agent regrets or is pained by what she/he *did* or had to *do*. In the case of a self whose character has been constituted under the adverse conditions of oppression and who has been damaged accordingly, the agent may regret or be saddened that she/he had to *become* or *be* morally limited in a certain way (and regret whatever unfortunate choices or actions have arisen out of these limitations). While Williams uses "agent-regret" to indicate that the regret is felt by someone who takes responsibility for the object of regret, when one experiences agent-regret over one's own character, there is a double sense of connection between the regret and the agent: the regret is both *of* a responsible self and *about* that very self.

Second, for the purpose of finding the virtues suited specifically for responding to the bad luck of moral damage under oppression, it will be essential to determine what allows one not only to make the best of bad circumstances or to come to terms with one's susceptibility to risk, but also, since the luck under question is systemic rather than natural or accidental luck, to resist or refuse to accept the bad luck as given. While situations of nonsystemic bad luck may just call for special virtues having to do with bearing or enduring the bad luck commendably as well as taking responsibility for its results, in the case of systemic bad luck—since the source of the bad luck can be identified and potentially altered through social or political action—the special virtues that are called for will also be those that help one to protest or even eliminate the systemic source of bad luck. Thus, in addition to agent-regret, I suggest that the self who has sustained moral damage under oppression may properly experience anger about this damage and may be angry *at* the sources of the damage. Unfortunately, as necessary as anger may be, anger also can function as a burden on its bearer, especially when the level of anger that is called for is great.[18]

I am proposing, then, that a mixture of anger and agent-regret will be called for to reflect an understanding of the bad luck of oppression and to act in light of—and in resistance to—it. Since luck creates agents who take responsibility for their characters and the results of their choices in the complex ways that acknowledge the mixture of control and lack of control, the best responses will be ones that demonstrate this complex taking of responsibility. The dual responses of anger and agent-regret at the damage that systemic bad luck inflicts registers a protest to this damage while recognizing both that others (other agents or social systems) are responsible for it (thus the anger) and that oneself is responsible for it (thus the agent-regret). To only feel anger would be to refuse the sort of complex responsibility that properly belongs to the impure agent.

Of course, one's own character will not be the *only* result of systemic bad luck about which one might appropriately be both regretful and angry. While I have focused on constitutive luck, situations of bad incident luck are also, for systemic

18. In chapter 5 I explore at length how anger may burden the politically resistant self.

reasons, pervasive under oppression. Some bad incident luck directly harms the victim of oppression; other bad incident luck places a victim of oppression in a dilemmatic position where she/he may be forced to commit an action that would otherwise never be chosen. Oppressive circumstances often present severely limited options that create moral dilemmas, including tragic ones, and being faced with such dilemmas can be described as cases of bad incident luck, for as Hursthouse has pointed out, if one emerges at all from such dilemmas one does so with one's life marred (and thus ultimately the incident will also have its effects on one's self). Consider, for instance, being faced with the alternatives of staying with a partner who is abusing one's children but who keeps one financially secure or leaving and subjecting oneself and one's children to poverty. Or consider being the victim of an attempted rape and having the options of being raped or killing one's attacker in self-defense. A mark of virtue, here, will be a capacity and a tendency to feel agent-regret, in addition to anger, that one has to enact either option. But this "virtue" is one that may itself be distressing to the agent, and so could in fact be an added harm attributable to oppression.

There is one other disposition that seems to capture a quality that one must have in order to navigate the complexities of taking responsibility under conditions of systemic bad moral luck. It can be described as a willingness to engage in a self-reflective understanding (and perhaps acceptance) of the limitations on the moral health of a self under oppression, including the resistant self. This disposition helps one to not assign *too* much responsibility (to oneself or others) when it is not deserved. It helps one to say, "This is the best I (or she, or he) can do under the circumstances of bad luck." That is, it allows for a recognition that there are many equally acceptable answers to the question of how one ought to live, a question that will have no *one* right answer as long as it is applied not to some imagined ideal circumstances, but to the circumstances one finds oneself in, for when faced with no good choice, different virtuous agents may well act differently. As Hursthouse points out:

> It must be . . . a thesis in virtue ethics that two virtuous people cannot, in the same circumstances, act differently, each thinking that what she does is right and what the other does is *wrong*. But to insist on that is a far cry from insisting that the two must always act as one. If they agree on what is good and evil in each choice, and believe that each is a choice of the good, though not of the best, it seems that they can, consistently with their virtue, act differently. (1995, 63)

Taking responsibility and fully "standing behind" one's own (or others') imperfect characters and choices—and counting this as a virtue under oppression—may permit members of oppositional communities greater room for moral disagreement with each other, without the condemnation that follows from denying a place to luck.

2

The Damage of Moral Damage

I

Within any eudaimonistic theory that is concerned with the possibilities for human flourishing and with the role of the virtues in contributing to or constituting such flourishing, the fact that someone has been morally damaged will be of grave importance, for moral damage interferes with flourishing. In the previous chapter I relied upon the concept of moral damage, emphasizing the role of bad systemic luck in inflicting this damage and the consequent vulnerability of the oppressed to being damaged and arguing that because of the difficulties of overcoming moral damage, there is a need for moral theory that ponders the situations of those who must carry on within the bounds of some moral limitations.

It is time to raise some complications. To begin with, it seems that—to the extent to which one can distinguish between beneficiaries and victims of oppression at all—it is primarily the people occupying dominant rather than subordinate positions in systems of oppression who should be understood as morally damaged; after all, the character traits that allow one to actively dominate others, or even to be passively satisfied with benefiting unfairly from overprivilege, could accurately be described as character flaws or vices. I believe that in fact both beneficiaries and victims of oppression (and all those who occupy the ambiguous social positions created from a field of intersecting oppressions) are morally damaged and thus prevented in this way from what could truly be called a flourishing life, but I will wait until the next chapter to explore how those tending in the direction of dominant positions may be said to fail at flourishing.

I am concerned here with a second complication: those whose aim is to oppose the injustice indicated by moral damage in the oppressed do so against a background in which this damage has already been scrutinized, for conservatives have long been not only proclaiming the moral deficiencies of the oppressed but also using the alleged fact of the existence of such deficiencies for pernicious ends; most notably, moral damage in the oppressed has been utilized as a way of "blaming the victim." Given this history, portraying a group as flawed exposes that group to the political and social danger that the shortcomings will be used against them, as evidence of an inherent or at least permanent or semipermanent inferiority.

When analyzing the problems that face an oppressed people, it is essential to avoid the mistake of characterizing those people *as* the problem, a thought that is captured in W. E. B. Du Bois's repeated posing of the question: "How does it feel to be a problem?" (1969 [1903], 43). Following Du Bois, Lewis Gordon remarks, "[W]e must study even dehumanized human subjects in a humanistic way in order to recognize the dehumanizing practices that besiege them" (1999, 24). While it is indeed my aim here to theorize about dehumanization without *engaging* in dehumanization, it may not be enough to have good intentions. Even when one's goal is to identify the systemic sources of moral damage and even when one emphasizes that finding moral damage in the oppressed only serves to further demonstrate the injustices of oppression, in a context of entrenched prejudices one's words can easily be transformed into precisely what Du Bois meant to caution against: turning those who suffer from a problem into the problem itself. Any liberatory project of exposing moral damage thus runs a risk of misinterpretation and misuse. And yet, simply denying damage—perhaps even taking "vices" of the oppressed and glorifying them as virtues[1]—can be problematic, too. Hence, despite the strategic dangers of exposing moral damage in various oppressed groups, I am unwilling to relinquish the project. Nevertheless, if the project of revealing and examining the moral damage of oppressed people is so dangerous, those who—like myself—insist on its importance had better have both some pretty good reasons for persisting in the project and some decent idea of how to avoid the likely pitfalls.

II

I will begin by giving an initial sense of why the concept of moral damage may be useful for understanding and resisting oppression (despite its appearance of reinforcing oppression by blaming the victim), by seeing how the concept suggests revisions to a neo-Aristotelian virtue ethics framework that links moral excellence with human flourishing. I believe that creating a revised or critical virtue ethics through the addition of the idea of moral damage can help to explain one of the less-obvious ways in which oppression interferes with flourishing.

1. I would not argue that it is never useful to perform this transvaluation, only that one should not do so in a way that makes one unable to ever treat damage as damage. Douglas Glasgow, for instance, performs what might be a useful transvaluation. Using the term "survival culture" to describe the so-called black underclass in positive terms, he argues that the character traits of this culture should be considered virtues given their utility in the situation. He writes, "[N]otwithstanding its reactive origin, survival culture is not a passive adaptation to encapsulation but a very active—at times devious, innovative, and extremely resistive—response to rejection and destruction. It is useful and necessary to young Blacks in their present situation" (1980, 25). These traits may qualify as what I will later call "burdened virtues."

For Aristotle, certain "external" goods are necessary for flourishing (*NE* 1099a31–1099b8, 1101a14–16, 1153b14–21; *Rhet.* 1360b20–30),[2] but he envisions these goods or the lack thereof as resulting from accidental or natural events, such as being born of high or low status, having friends or children who die, or encountering misfortunes in old age that ruin one's prosperity. Having an analysis of oppression as a structural phenomenon requires seeing social or systemic forces as responsible for the fact that members of some social groups are deprived of these external resources. Hence it requires expanding Aristotle's list of the things that typically interfere with flourishing to include those things that regularly, and in a patterned way, arise as barriers to flourishing under conditions of oppression. Since oppressions vary widely depending on the social, political, and economic differences at play, the list may expand in a variety of directions. It must include, for instance, lack of access to resources that are distributed unfairly in an oppressive system, such as housing, education, health care, or, more generally, income and especially wealth. There are also resources that are not the sorts of things that can be captured under what Iris Young calls the "distributive paradigm" (1990, chap. 1), for some of the forces of oppression and domination cannot be remedied simply by instituting a fairer system of distribution. Young points out, for instance, that different oppressed groups may experience their oppression in quite different forms: they may be exploited, marginalized, made powerless, subjected to cultural imperialism, and/or targeted for violence (1990, chap. 2). All of these could be described as ways in which oppression creates external conditions that prevent flourishing. Adverse external conditions are probably the most readily visible and forceful obstacles to flourishing.

Despite Aristotle's crucial acknowledgment that certain external conditions must obtain for a person to flourish, his primary focus is on a consideration of the features of character that enable flourishing. Since, for him the "human good [is] activity of soul in conformity with excellence" (*NE* 1098a16–17), it is only the virtuous/excellent man who attains this good. That is, Aristotle links moral excellence with living the good life; one cannot be said to have reached *eudaimonia* without a virtuous character.

It is difficult, at first glance, to see how the claim that one must be virtuous to attain the good life will be helpful for understanding any additional way (besides the deprivation of external goods) in which oppression interferes with flourishing. Instead, the claim seems to place the blame on oppressed people themselves for being unable to flourish: the inability is attributed to their own lack of virtue. The linking of virtue to flourishing, then, seems to directly summon a chorus of victim-blaming in which one hears that, for instance, women are overly emotional, blacks are prone to violence, Jews are stingy, the poor lack self-discipline, and so on, and that these vices are what bring on the particular hardships faced by members of these groups.

2. Not all virtue ethicists agree with Aristotle's position on this; Socrates and the Stoics present virtue as sufficient for flourishing.

This is where it is useful to turn to the concept of moral damage, the concept that I utilized in chapter 1 and that emphasizes the role of systemic bad luck in shaping the characters of members of subordinated groups. That is, in order to make progressive use of the linking of virtue to flourishing, one needs to assert that the underdevelopment of the virtues can itself have structural or systemic sources rather than, for instance, sources in what is inherent, biologically given, or simply accidental. There is injustice already at work in the formation of character; the fact that something is based on character does not imply that it is not also rooted in an oppressive social system.

Aristotle lacks any way of seeing that the social and political positioning of people such that they have unequal chances for developing the virtues is itself an injustice. Clearly, for him, some people do have a better chance of being virtuous than others; to begin with, one must be a citizen male and must have the sort of leisure time necessary for practicing the virtues, and all of this can take place only within a correctly constituted and good *polis*, and even then, one does not fully develop all virtues unless one is ruling and thereby able to develop the virtues associated exclusively with ruling (*Pol.* bk. II, chaps. 4–5). But there is, for Aristotle, no injustice in this inegalitarian state of affairs where some are better positioned than others for becoming virtuous; as long as all those who are equals are treated equally, it is perfectly just that unequals be treated unequally and given unequal opportunities for developing the virtues (*Pol.* 1280a11–13).

The concept of moral damage can potentially fill in this gap in Aristotelian theory by emphasizing not only that people are unequally situated for becoming virtuous, but also that there is injustice in this arrangement. This is exactly what is argued by Claudia Card who, rejecting the Kantian assumption that "the same basic character development is accessible to everyone" (Card 1996, 4), observes that "different combinations of circumstances . . . provide opportunities for, stimulate, nurture, or discourage the development of different virtues and vices, strengths and weaknesses of character" (1996, ix).

Moral damage bears a relationship to what has commonly been understood as the "psychic damage" suffered by the oppressed. There is a fairly long history in the United States of blacks being portrayed (and in some cases portraying themselves) as psychically damaged, a history that I will discuss at more length in the next section. Additionally, beginning early in the second wave of the women's liberation movement, feminists have described women's "psychological oppression."[3] One way in which psychic damage comes about is from the internalization of oppression; the oppressed may come to believe about themselves, for instance, that it is their own inferiority that accounts for their

3. One of the sections in Robin Morgan's (1970) collection *Sisterhood Is Powerful* is thus entitled "The Invisible Woman: Psychological and Sexual Repression"; Sandra Bartky's "On Psychological Oppression" (in Bartky 1990, but originally published in 1979) draws parallels between the psychological oppression of women and what Frantz Fanon refers to as the "psychic alienation of the black man" (Fanon 1967, 12; quoted in Bartky 1990, 22).

subordinate position. As Sandra Bartky writes, "[T]he psychologically oppressed become their own oppressors; they come to exercise harsh dominion over their own self-esteem" (1990, 22). When conceived as an internalization of external messages or forces, the psychic states characteristic of the psychologically oppressed are clearly a product of systemic—social, political, and economic—phenomena, though they certainly may be perceived as having their origins in internal, even biological, deficiencies. Indeed, psychological oppression helps to keep the oppressed subordinated in part by obscuring the systemic sources of their troublesome psychological traits, thus making the oppressed appear, even to themselves, as responsible for their own condition.

The sense that one is responsible for one's own damaged state—and even for one's own subordination since some kinds of damage help to keep one subordinated—is only compounded when one is described not only as *psychologically* damaged but also as *morally* damaged. Even while it might be clear that someone or something else is responsible for inflicting psychic pain on me (that is, that it is beyond my control and thus a matter of luck to me), if I am described as having *character* flaws, it seems that it is I who am morally responsible for my deficiency, not to mention for any reprehensible actions that proceed from my flawed character. This may be connected to the fact that, as Bernard Williams has argued, the "morality system" (primarily deontology)—as distinguished from ethics more generally—has focused heavily on the concept of moral obligation and on assigning moral blame for failures to fulfill such an obligation. Leaving no room for luck, such a system can only see the violation of moral obligations as voluntary (and reprehensible) acts of the will. A moral deficiency in this system is necessarily blameworthy (Williams 1985, chap. 10). In a virtue ethics framework, there need not be this separation of the psychological (which is clearly subject to luck) and the moral.[4] In pointing to a psychic—or moral—trait as damaged, one need not emphasize the issue of responsibility for the trait, but rather one can inquire about the tendency of the trait to hinder its bearer's well-being. Any psychological trait that can be labeled "damage" will in fact count as a moral trait, that is, a character trait, precisely because in calling it a form of damage one is making a normative judgment about it, in this case a negative judgment, based on the trait's tendency to interfere with flourishing. So while some psychological traits may be morally neutral, a damaged psyche represents a lack of a virtue (if not the presence of a vice), a lack of a trait that could help one toward flourishing. For instance, all of the following are possible forms of both psychic and moral damage: a tendency to feel guilt or resignation instead of anger when one is wronged, a disposition to feel persistent hopelessness, a habit of manipulating or lying to others, a lack of self-confidence.

A virtue ethics framework, in connecting living a good life with moral excellence, will count psychic damage that interferes with flourishing as moral damage. However, when this shift from characterizing the oppressed as

4. Or rather "ethical," if one employs Williams's distinction between morality and ethics (see Williams 1985, chap. 1).

psychically hurt or damaged to characterizing them as morally damaged takes place in a context shaped by a system of morality that is focused on responsibility and blame and that evaluates actions as if they issued from an unconditioned will, disturbing questions of moral responsibility will arise, and the victims of oppression will be saddled with blame. The concept of constitutive moral luck ought to help remove this blame, for if moral damage can be seen to result from luck, then it will be understood to be beyond an agent's own control despite the fact that it affects the agent in a morally relevant way. Characterizing the moral damage of the oppressed as a product of bad, constitutive, systemic moral luck—as I did in chapter 1—is meant to convey the notion of a different, more-complex relationship of responsibility for that damage. This characterization of moral damage implicates oppressive systems as the sources of the bad, constitutive moral luck that adversely affects the characters of the oppressed, but it also does not deny that the person who is morally damaged in this way retains moral responsibility for herself, despite her lack of complete control in the formation of her own character.

This complex sense of having and not having moral responsibility for one's own character allows the oppressed person to preserve moral agency by retaining moral responsibility, and yet it does not blame the oppressed agent in a way that would simultaneously excuse all systemic or oppressive forces from responsibility. For example, consider a case of rape, which is a prime site for victim-blaming: many girls and women have been socialized to have character traits that potentially contribute to their vulnerability to rape, traits such as passivity, fear of fighting back, and lack of clarity and/or a sense of legitimacy about their own sexual desires.[5] If a woman chooses a strategy of submitting to an attempted rape rather than taking what she perceives to be the risks of resisting it, she will typically be blamed for the rape. The most obvious rebuttal here is that the rapist is the one responsible for the rape (and, of course, one could talk about the rapist as a morally damaged person). But there is also a second point to be made: one can implicate the gender system that contributed to the woman's vulnerability by affecting the formation of her character into someone who is afraid or unable to fight back, that is, into someone who is in this specific way morally damaged.[6] One can recognize the moral wrongdoing of an oppressive system for being the source of moral damage without portraying the morally damaged, oppressed person as lacking in agency just because she lacks complete control over the constitution of her character. The woman is still morally responsible for her own character and her own choice, for as the concept of moral luck implies, we can be moral agents responsible for some things over which we do not have control.

Nevertheless, even if it is possible to make *conceptual* sense of why a morally damaged character in an oppressed person should not be taken as evidence that

5. On this last point, see Tolman and Higgins 1996.

6. See Snow 1994 for a discussion of whether and when rape victims may appropriately be blamed or blame themselves. Snow characterizes the self-blame of rape victims as a case of agent-regret, though oddly, since she removes the concept of agent-regret from the context of luck.

the oppressed are to blame for their own oppression, in fact, historically, images of psychic and moral damage in the oppressed have been taken and continue to be taken in exactly this way, thus making it strategically risky to try to explore psychic or moral damage for liberatory purposes. A review of a piece of this history will be helpful here, so I will devote the next section to this, beginning with Daryl Michael Scott's historical account of the "image of the damaged black psyche," which presents a clear-cut case of damage imagery being used to the detriment of an oppressed group.[7]

III

Scott's *Contempt and Pity: Social Policy and the Image of the Damaged Black Psyche, 1880–1996* chronicles the changing historical contexts in which damage imagery has been employed by social scientists studying and reporting on black Americans. He contends that despite the association of the use of damage imagery with conservatives and blatant racists, such imagery has actually been used by both racial liberals and conservatives, often at cross-purposes. He argues, however, that this entire range of uses of damage imagery should be regarded with suspicion: "I believe that depicting black folk as pathological has not served the community's best interest. Again and again, contempt has proven to be the flip side of pity. And through it all, biological and cultural notions of black inferiority have lived on, worsening the plight of black people" (1997, xviii).

Scott's focus is on *psychic* damage, for his thesis is that in the late nineteenth century, "as personality replaced moral character as the key to success" (1997, xiii) and psychological well-being surfaced as an issue worthy of attention, it became possible to conceive of a person as being wronged by being hurt psychologically. As this "therapeutic ethos" increased in strength even more after World War II, humanitarian concern grew for the psychological health of subordinate groups. Scott explains, "[L]iberals used damage imagery to play upon the sympathies of the white middle-class. Oppression was wrong, liberals suggested, because it damaged personalities, and changes had to be made to protect and promote the well-being of African Americans" (1997, xiii). This liberal use of damage imagery played a primary role in, for instance, the argument against segregation used in *Brown v. Board of Education*, in which Chief Justice Earl Warren opined that "segregated children suffered damage to their psyches that made an equal education impossible" (1997, 135). However, argues Scott, the liberal use of damage imagery depends upon evoking pity, an emotion that presupposes one's own superiority to the object of pity:

> Liberals proceeded as if most white Americans would have been willing to grant black people equal rights and services only if they were made to appear

7. See also Walker 1998 (123–125) for a feminist argument against portraying the oppressed as morally damaged.

> psychologically damaged and granted a special status as victims. In so doing, they militated against their efforts to eliminate white supremacy. As they assaulted its manifestations in the law, they reinforced the belief system that made whites feel superior in the first place. (1997, xiii)

While the pity of white liberals presents a significant drawback to employing damage imagery for bringing about policy change, a further problem emerged when liberals split around the question of what sorts of changes were needed to address the damage. By the late 1950s social scientists theorizing about the "underclass"—a term introduced by Gunnar Myrdal (1944) to refer to an economic, and not a specifically racial, group—were divided into the "pathologists," who focused on curing individual pathological responses to poverty, and the "structuralists," who insisted that fundamental changes in social, economic, and political institutions would effectively end the phenomenon of psychic damage (Scott 1997, chap. 8). While for a time it seemed that these two schools advocated changes that were at least compatible with each other, their incompatibility emerged with Oscar Lewis's (1961) introduction of the "culture of poverty" theory, according to which the poor developed a pathological culture that was passed down through the generations and became self-sustaining (Scott 1997, 142). Whereas pathologists had previously been able to see institutional changes as helpful for addressing individuals' suffering, the culture-of-poverty theory suggested that since the pathology would perpetuate itself regardless of changes in social structure, such changes would be misguided. As Stephen Steinberg has noted, for advocates of the culture-of-poverty thesis, "the aim of social policy becomes one of reforming the poor rather than changing society. That is, instead of instituting the sweeping changes that could redistribute income, the focus of social policy becomes indoctrinating the poor with middle-class values" (Steinberg 1981, 109). This conservative side of the pathologists' position alarmed the structuralists, who at that point "recognized that notions of severe damage, particularly permanent damage, cast doubt on the efficacy or desirability of state intervention" (Scott 1997, 143).

As the term *underclass* became more and more automatically understood to refer to a *black* underclass, and as it became clearer that portraying this underclass as pathological would fuel the conservative claim that blacks had no one but themselves to blame for their plight and therefore had no basis for claiming special treatment, reparations, or assistance from social programs, it became strategically more dangerous to attempt to use damage imagery to bring about progressive, antiracist change. Nevertheless, in 1965 Daniel Patrick Moynihan, in his *The Negro Family: The Case for National Action* (otherwise known as the Moynihan Report) tried to support a plan of action—to be initiated by President Lyndon Johnson as preferential treatment programs—by relying on damage imagery. However, he made the same assumption as Lewis had in his culture-of-poverty theory, namely, that the pathological condition of blacks was being perpetuated by blacks themselves and would continue regardless of structural changes. Although Moynihan conceded that "not every instance of social pathology afflicting the Negro community can be traced to the weakness of family structure," he did argue:

> Nonetheless, at the center of the tangle of pathology is the weakness of the family structure. Once or twice removed, it will be found to be the principal source of most of the aberrant, inadequate, or anti-social behavior that did not establish, but now serves to perpetuate the cycle of poverty and deprivation. (Moynihan 1965, 30)

Moynihan contended that it was because of bad character formation in black families that there existed within the black community high rates of crime and delinquency, welfare dependency, unemployment, poor academic achievement, and in turn, more "unstable"—which largely meant "female-headed"—black families.

Moynihan recognized that white racism was originally responsible for creating the situation that blacks were in and even attributed the development of the black family structure to injustices perpetrated by whites under slavery and reconstruction; however, he did not believe that white racism had a significant role in perpetuating the situation of inequality. All responsibility for that had been shifted to blacks themselves. Thus Moynihan concluded: "Three centuries of injustice have brought about deep-seated structural distortions in the life of the Negro American. At this point, the present tangle of pathology is capable of perpetuating itself without assistance from the white world" (1965, 47).

Although it was probably not Moynihan's intention, the content of the Moynihan Report served as perfect evidence to bolster the conservative, racist image of blacks as inferior, an image that was used, for instance, to explain the behavior of blacks in the 1965 Watts riot. Scott points out that "released at the moment of the riots, the Moynihan Report was viewed by conservatives as an expression of their own views on black social and personal pathology" (1997, 157). That is, damage imagery, intended by liberals to support antiracist measures and improve the condition of blacks, had quite the opposite effect. Furthermore, even if it had not been coopted for straightforwardly conservative purposes, it still would have retained a paternalistic edge. As Scott puts it: "The racial liberals who sought to manipulate the paternalistic tendencies of whites may not have been racists and the dupes of racists, but many were all too willing to exchange black dignity for something other than justice, for social policies that reinforced white America's age-old belief in black inferiority" (1997, 185). Thus, in the wake of the Moynihan Report, there arose a near-consensus on the Left to avoid all damage imagery and to condemn its use as racist.

The dangers of trying to utilize damage imagery in liberatory projects have only intensified since the 1960s, because more recently neoconservatives have reinvigorated such imagery and put it to use in their attacks on affirmative action and, more generally, in their arguments against government or social responsibility for improving the conditions that many blacks face. Governmental programs aimed at helping blacks are, they claim, the primary source of the new damaged black psyche; according to them, preferential treatment is actually causing, rather than ameliorating, psychic problems, such as low self-esteem, and is actually giving rise to character deficiencies, such as "criminality" and "dependency" (Scott 1997, chap. 10). Some neoconservatives point to what they see as the failures of governmental aid programs as evidence that insufficient attention has been given to what they see as the root of the problem: character flaws. Glenn Loury, for instance, laments the fact that other blacks do not share his own conviction that Moynihan had been right all along; Loury complains that thirty years after the Moynihan Report, "to invoke such terms as 'values,' 'character,' or 'social pathology' in speaking about the poor (black or otherwise) is still to invite the charge of blaming the victim or, if the speaker is black, of being an Uncle Tom" (Loury 1995, 258). Loury even goes on to express his disapproval of the fact that Moynihan himself has retreated from his former position and is no longer willing to condemn female-headed households or to show sufficient respect for "old-fashioned virtues" (Loury 1995, 260).

Neoconservative talk of "family values," along with the rise of other segments of the right wing, such as the religious Right, have shifted the language used in the discourse on damage. Scott focuses on the image of *psychic* damage because during much of the twentieth century concern with damage was represented primarily as an issue of psychological health; however, there is now a movement back toward an explicit focus on character and moral virtue. Unfortunately, because a focus on character is almost entirely associated with the right wing and because that discourse consists principally of a defamation of the characters of people of color, gays and lesbians, women, and poor people, it is extremely hard to imagine a critical or liberatory application of an analysis of character. Moving beyond Scott's analysis to a focus on the right-wing discourse on character reveals the perils of this discourse.

James Wilson, a neoconservative political scientist and policy advisor, provides in his 1991 book, *On Character*, a particularly clear example of this neoconservative discourse on character. In his schema, social problems are attributed to individual character deficiencies, and these character deficiencies are racialized. Wilson's thesis is that "a variety of public problems can only be understood—and perhaps addressed—if they are seen as arising out of a defect in character formation" (1991, 11). The public policy questions that he sees as most tied to character include crime and welfare. His primary focus is on crime, and he identifies "a persistent and wanton proclivity to criminality" as that which "almost any of us would regard as a defect in character" (1991, 5).[8] Criminality, he believes, results from the absence of what he considers to be the most important aspects of good character, namely, empathy and self-control, arguing that almost no criminals have both empathy and self-control. Since Wilson assumes that character formation depends upon what takes place within the family, the question of how to reduce crime becomes, for Wilson, the question of how "a government [might] remake bad families into good ones" (1991, 21), where presumably those families that do

8. Wilson defines criminality itself as a character trait; he takes criminality to be

> not an occasional violation of the law but a persistent and high rate of participation in illegal or disorderly actions. Criminality in this sense refers to a personality disposition—a character trait—that makes some people less likely than others to resist the temptations presented by criminal opportunities, less likely because they are impulsive or self-centered. (1991, 43)

not adequately teach self-control and empathy are the bad families. Wilson advocates the development of experimental programs aimed at improving how families instill proper values in children, commenting, "[I]f we discover that these ideas can be made to work on a large scale . . . then we will be able to reduce crime by, in effect, improving character" (1991, 21).

Welfare dependence can also be explained, according to Wilson, as a matter of character deficiency: those on welfare have the wrong values and therefore do not feel appropriate shame at the dependence itself nor at the actions—such as having children out of wedlock—that may have led to it. Wilson's argument here is that changing incentives in the welfare system has changed people's behavior and their character for the worse; thus, the task at hand will be to investigate a "way of using either obligations or incentives to alter character so that people who once thought it good to sire or bear illegitimate children will now think it wrong" (1991, 17).

While Wilson argues that there has been a moral decline in the United States in general ever since, as he puts it, an "ethos of self-control" began to be replaced by "an ethos of self-expression" (1991, 28), not surprisingly he remarks that "Black Americans have been especially vulnerable" (1991, 35) to this degenerate ethos. While he concedes that some of this vulnerability can be attributed to what he calls "exclusion from economic life" and thus from respectability, the primary problem according to him is to be found in what he perceives to be a defective black culture. He writes:

> The folk culture of urban blacks . . . was and is aggressive, individualistic, and admiring of semiritualistic insults, sly tricksters, and masculine display. This popular culture may have been a reaction against the repressive and emasculating aspects of slavery; whatever its origin, it was not a culture productive of a moral capital off which people could live when facing either adversity or affluence. (1991, 36)

Perhaps even more disturbing than Wilson's explicit claim that black Americans have culturally acquired defective characters—a blatant reiteration of the culture-of-poverty theory—is the fact that in the current political climate, he actually has no need to make this explicit reference to blacks in a discussion of either crime or welfare; both are code words with so thoroughly racialized meanings that a discourse on the degenerate character of criminals or welfare recipients functions as a masquerade for a more directly racist—and less socially acceptable—discourse in which blacks get directly cited as the prime example of a morally deficient population. In the context of a racist society in which blacks are stereotypically associated with both crime and welfare, a complicated racial project actually takes place through a color-blind discourse purportedly about crime reduction or about welfare reform. In the course of this project, an image of "the criminal" and "the welfare recipient" as morally degenerate characters is formed, and the vices of these characters are associated with blacks in general (particularly, black men in the case of crime and black women in the case of welfare), who already stand as the stereotypical criminal and welfare recipient. Both the criminal and the welfare recipient embody socially despised characteristics, characteristics that are attributed not just to specific, actual people who commit crimes or who receive public assistance, and not even just to "criminals" and "welfare recipients" in some generalized way, but rather to *blacks* in this generalized way, for in the imagination shaped by this racialized discourse, blacks stand in for both the (generalized) criminal and the (generalized) welfare recipient. Public fear (in the case of crime) and resentment (in the case of welfare) are generated toward these morally degenerate characters and thus toward blacks in general. Finally, public policy that addresses that fear and resentment seems reasonable and justified; if it involves harsh treatment of the criminal or the welfare recipient, such treatment is justified since it was brought on by those characters' own moral degeneracy and furthermore is necessary to protect the upstanding members of society against violence or against having to support the undeserving with their own hard-earned money.

Angela Davis, for instance, points out that "crime," and thus "the figure of the 'criminal'—the racialized figure of the criminal—has come to represent the most menacing enemy of 'American Society'" (1997, 270), thus justifying what amounts to disregard for the lives of those whom the figure signifies. Since the figure of "the criminal" is taken as a character type—and "criminality" as a vice—any empirically grounded correlation of a specific racial group with high rates of crime is taken to reflect solely on the character traits—perhaps culturally acquired—of that racial group, not on the many ways in which the continued forces of structural racism set up targeted racial groups for actual or imagined involvement in crime. Thus when crime statistics reveal high percentages of blacks to be in the criminal justice system, the data serve as evidence of black moral degeneracy (Davis 1997, 268).

The discourse on welfare is closely tied to the one on crime; gender analysis of both discourses reveals that the welfare recipient is the female counterpart to the male criminal; the full stereotypical picture of the welfare-recipient-as-criminal is of a black, single, teenage mother. As Davis points out, "[T]he current liberal-conservative discourse around welfare criminalizes black single mothers, who are represented as deficient, manless, drug-using breeders of children, and as reproducers of an attendant culture of poverty," and she notes that "the woman who does drugs is criminalized both because she is a drug user and because, as a consequence, she cannot be a good mother" (1997, 275). The black, single, welfare-dependent mother is also considered to be responsible for the black male criminal, since it is in the deficient, female-headed household that the black male child develops his vices.[9]

9. For an example of the racialized discourse on welfare, see Patricia Williams's commentary on a series run in the *Washington Post*, "on the trials and tribulations of a welfare mother named RosaLee who seemingly had committed every sin the Bible could think of, including, of course, having many children by many different men, setting up her boyfriend to be killed, spreading AIDS, teaching her children to steal, and cheating the welfare system" (1995, 8). As Williams points out, such discourse—and the examples of it are plentiful in the mainstream media—gives the false impression that cases such as those of RosaLee are typical ones, portraying the case "as generally representative of a 'culture' of black pathology whose cure could only come from blacks themselves" (1995, 8).

There are clear policy implications to portraying blacks—with exceptions made for the middle class—as the morally degenerate exemplars of such vices as criminality and dependency, for in the current conservative context such a portrayal is not used to show the injustices of racism and other structural forms of oppression, but rather is used to demonstrate either that the moral deficiencies inhere in blacks or actually result from governmental attempts to end inequalities. Either way, the implication is that there are no injustices to blacks as a group that need to be rectified.

Shelby Steele makes this position explicit; by contrasting psychological and moral problems—which he locates in the individual—with social or systemic problems, he is able to site the source of blacks' problems within individual blacks, claiming that "if conditions have worsened for most of us as racism has receded, then much of the problem must be of our own making" (1990, 15). He believes that blacks' desire to blame "the system" for their problems is not based on there still being an actual system of racism that truly oppresses blacks; rather, the desire can be explained psychologically as a quest for innocence, the innocence that comes with being a victim. Such innocence, according to Steele, excuses blacks from the responsibility for changing their circumstances and protects blacks from their fears of failing, because all failure can be blamed on racism. Convinced that "from this point on, the race's advancement will come from the efforts of its individuals" (1990, 16), Steele focuses on the need for black individuals to change their own characters, something that requires what Steele calls "moral effort" (1990, 16). According to Steele, theories that point to the ways that structural racism victimizes blacks fail to recognize the role that this moral effort on the part of blacks could play; that is, they fail to recognize the "margin of choice" that he insists is always present. For instance, Steele cites the argument that black students have poor academic performance because they "internalize a message of inferiority that they receive from school and the larger society around them," but instead of acknowledging the ways in which educational and other institutions do function systemically to undermine blacks' sense of intellectual competence, Steele redirects attention to the part that individual blacks play in accepting the messages of inferiority, insisting that "the relevant question in the 1990s is why they *choose* to internalize this view of themselves" (1990, 27). He asks, "Why do they *voluntarily* perceive themselves as inferior?" (1990, 27–28; emphasis added). Steele thus simultaneously puts the responsibility for character change entirely on individual blacks and employs an account of character change that is fully voluntaristic; one can change if one wants to, and one can do so regardless of external conditions. His account leaves no space for implicating the oppressive social systems that cause moral damage.

IV

In this increasingly conservative climate (and a climate in which it is only the conservatives who are talking about character), it becomes more likely, regardless of the intention of the theorist, that an examination of the ways in which oppression produces damaged people will be used against the oppressed group and, as Steele has used it, against the notion that structural changes must (still) be fought for. It thus becomes risky in practice to raise the issue of moral damage with the intention of using it for liberatory ends, and it remains risky even if one can make conceptual distinctions between different ways of attending to moral damage. Indeed, the conceptual distinctions are not hard to make; one can distinguish between the conservative victim-blaming stance, the liberal pity-evoking approach, and a critical position. One can point out that (unlike the conservative position) the critical position locates the source of moral damage in the continuing force of systems of oppression and rejects the individualist and voluntarist notion that one can simply will one's own character to change, and (unlike the liberal position), a more radical critical position is not concerned with appealing to the sympathy of the mainstream for reforms that will ameliorate damaging conditions, but rather is primarily concerned with understanding moral damage in order to develop collective practices within communities of resistance that will effectively address or repair the damage, both for the sake of the individuals who suffer from the damage and for the sake of better enabling members of the community to pursue liberatory projects, especially those projects that aim at fundamentally transforming the structures of society.[10]

10. It is interesting to note that "self-help" strategies including those aimed at repairing moral damage were formerly associated with radical politics, such as the Black Power movement. Such strategies made sense in the context of separatist politics, where autonomy from a dominant group was taken to be a prerequisite for developing an alternative set of values and learning to incorporate oppositional beliefs into the selves who thereby could enact their resistance to dominant values and practices. The conservative implications—that the government need not provide any form of support for members of a disadvantaged group as long as the group itself was taking responsibility for changing—were not anticipated precisely because they are in no way entailed by a separatist self-help strategy. See, for instance, Charles Hamilton's 1992 afterword to his and Stokely Carmichael's 1967 *Black Power.* Hamilton reflects on the fact that

> some Black Power advocates of an earlier time were frankly naïve in assuming that their *political* movement ["closing ranks" among Blacks and engaging in practices of self-help, including a "pride" politics aimed at changing Blacks' self-conceptions] would be inevitably an economically liberal one. . . . They assumed that the liberal position was obvious and correct and would be continuing precisely because their mass constituencies still needed so much in the way of vast governmental support. Such support had always been understood as necessary and frequently forthcoming in times of severe economic need. (Hamilton 1992, 209)

The assumption that a self-help strategy would be automatically paired with governmental redistributive measures was mistaken, and a segment of the Black Power movement split off to develop black capitalism:

> Black Power advocates on the left saw the conservatives as equating Black Power with Black Capitalism. This meant simply another version of exploitation of the masses, replacing white capitalists with black capitalists, and not really addressing the fundamental problems of an economic system that would leave most black people on the bottom of the socio-economic ladder. (1992, 210)

While both the left-wing and right-wing branches that developed out of Black Power pursued a separatist politics that, in the language I have been using, aimed at addressing moral damage in black people, they disagreed fundamentally on the interpretation and implications of that politics.

However, these distinctions among various approaches to understanding moral damage notwithstanding, in light of the empirical evidence of how damage imagery has functioned in the political arena (historically and in contemporary times), one might be led, for purely strategic reasons, to simply refuse to discuss the ways in which moral damage may be a significant aspect of oppression.

I am wary of the conservative context that is currently shaping the use of the concept of moral damage; I am also wary of the liberal use of damage imagery to evoke pity or sympathy from dominant groups in an attempt to have them show concern for the oppressed. But I worry about the agendas of potentially radical communities of resistance being influenced so strongly by the fear of cooptation by either conservatives or liberals. Specifically, I worry when radicals become unable to attend to questions of moral damage simply because every instance of recognizing moral damage appears to take sides in a contest for explaining subordination, where one might *either* point to character deficiencies *or* to institutionalized or structural forces, a binary that leaves no room for seeing damage to character itself as resulting from structures of oppression and no room for challenging these structures and *additionally* tending to damage already inflicted. Stephen Steinberg, for instance, seems to think that one cannot simultaneously attend to moral damage and work to change structural causes of oppression. Because he takes any sort of attention to character to indicate an allegiance to the conservative victim-blaming stance, he leaves no conceptual space for a radical version of a character-based ethics. It is out of this conceptual vacuum that Steinberg is forced, for instance, to understand Cornel West's concern with "the profound sense of psychological depression, personal worthlessness, and social despair . . . widespread in black America" (West 1993, 12–13) to necessarily imply—despite ample evidence to the contrary—that West does not locate the problem in systemic racism. Steinberg goes so far as to charge West with "substitut[ing] a vapid and utterly inconsequential 'politics of conversion' for a genuine political solution" (1995, 132).

But Steinberg's own solution does not pay attention to the difficulty of repairing damage, suggesting instead that damage will be undone automatically when conditions change. Insisting on structural explanations for all differences of character between social groups, he argues that character change will correspond neatly to structural changes, claiming that "individuals and groups who encounter a favorable structure of opportunity respond accordingly, and exhibit high motivation, zeal for work, and other virtues that we associate with success" (1995, 14). Steinberg starts from an assertion that an oppressive system causes damage—an important assertion to make, given the conservatives' denial of it—but infers from this that removal of the oppressive forces will simultaneously undo the damage. While it may well be that favorable external conditions are necessary—or at least very helpful—for the development of certain virtues, it does not follow that such conditions are sufficient, especially once damage has already been done. It therefore does not follow that it is sufficient for the Left to focus *exclusively* on structural changes. If Steinberg were right that changing external conditions alone would undo moral damage, there would be no need for liberatory struggles to include any attention to the issue of moral damage.

A liberatory politics that recognizes the depth of damage under oppression and that insists on addressing it along with working for structural changes will still need to be careful not to fuel the conservative and liberal misuses of this acknowledgment of moral damage. First, it will be key to constantly reiterate the point that structures of oppression caused and continue to cause the damage and that the location of responsibility for selves constituted through systemic bad luck is complex. Second, it will also be important to realize that mainstream accounts of the virtues may be wrong in precisely the same way that status quo social arrangements corresponding to those virtues are wrong, and that therefore what are considered to be the virtues that subordinated people characteristically lack may not really be praiseworthy traits at all. For instance, the "virtue" of being able to command others with authority will be rejected when one rejects a hierarchical social arrangement where some give orders and others obey. Similarly, one must not take for granted that what gets labeled "damage" under dominant values are really undesirable traits. For instance, a greater inclination to express emotions—more typical of women than of men—should perhaps be seen as a praiseworthy trait rather than as a liability. Third, while one might need to make a general point that a subordinated group is likely to have members with certain forms of moral damage, it is essential to avoid stereotyping on the basis of such a claim. For example, acknowledging that there are higher rates of drug addiction in poor communities of color than in middle-class, white communities (and analyzing the systemic reasons for this) is necessary in order to mobilize the community to struggle against the underlying causes of addiction and to properly create resources for recovery for those who suffer from addiction. However, acknowledging these higher rates of drug abuse must never lead to the stereotypical assumption that any particular poor person of color is an addict. Because of the history of the use of damage imagery for pernicious ends, those attempting to reveal moral damage for liberatory ends will need to keep a constant vigilance for the many threatening pitfalls.

V

Nevertheless, I do believe that radicals need to examine moral damage—for purposes other than those of the conservatives and the liberals—and that a critical virtue ethics framework is useful not only because of the way that it makes conceptual space for such an examination, but also because it enables a more extensive inquiry about the relationship between character traits and flourishing, an inquiry that only suggests itself once one is willing to admit that all is not well with the selves or characters of subordinated people. Some of the negative consequences of ignoring moral damage should be clear. For instance, I have argued in chapter 1 that moral damage may interfere with the ability of an oppressed person to carry out the actions suggested by her/his own liberatory principles or at least to do so without internal conflict. Moral damage may also be directly destructive of the damaged self; feelings of hopelessness and an internalized belief in one's own inferiority are examples of forms of damage that may not only retard resistance but also cause great pain or an immediate lack of well-being for their bearer.

A further reason for communities of resistance not to ignore moral damage is that the damage may lead one to act oppressively toward others. Card's attention to the question of moral responsibility under oppression is motivated in part by her insistence that "although it is morally problematic for beneficiaries of oppression to hold its victims responsible for bad conduct," particularly when such conduct was chosen by a self who was morally damaged by oppression, "victims have responsibilities of their own to peers and descendants" (1996, 41). She is thinking, here, of the ways in which "women's oppression and childhood abuse are intertwined historically," such that "both are morally damaging, and the damage of one can apparently lead to that of the other" (1996, 41). Thus, there are cases, for Card, where it would be inappropriate to blame someone for acting out of a morally damaged character, but where one still must be able to demand that the person take responsibility for her character and her actions. Card writes: "Overcoming and resisting our own oppression require us to *take* responsibility for situations for which others could not reasonably hold us responsible . . . , despite our complicity" (1996, 41).

Seeing the deleterious effects of failing to attend to moral damage may be enough to motivate one to insist on acknowledging moral damage despite the strategic risks. However, I am further motivated by seeing what sorts of projects—both theoretical and practical—suggest themselves once moral damage is recognized. I place the projects within a critical virtue ethics framework, where the damage in question can be specifically construed as damage to the virtues. This framework, by maintaining the simple point that even Aristotle endorses, namely, that flourishing requires external goods as well as the right character, can assert, contrary to the conservative understanding of the role of character, that social, political, and economic systems create the most formidable barriers to members of oppressed groups' ability to flourish. Then, taking as a given the need for structural changes, the critical virtue ethics framework permits one to proceed to raise a number of questions about the relationship of character (with its likely damage) to flourishing.

Examining this relationship is useful, I would contend, because doing so will reveal otherwise hidden harms of oppression (and I value awareness of these harms whether or not such awareness puts one in a position to successfully prevent or repair harm). While structural barriers to flourishing are readily visible without the help of a virtue ethics framework, multiple, more-subtle ways in which flourishing is prevented under oppression come into view when one uses this framework to link moral excellence with flourishing. Lacking some virtues as one does when one suffers moral damage—or, as I will argue in later chapters, having to develop virtues that are disconnected from flourishing—can be understood as a real deprivation created by oppressive conditions.

What becomes possible once it has been acknowledged that oppression gives rise to moral damage is the philosophical project of sorting through potential virtues and vices to try to determine which traits will promote flourishing,[11] and the practical project of learning how to cultivate the desired traits and overcome the destructive ones. I have little to say about the practical project (but hope others have much to say about it), for it requires answering largely empirical questions.[12] It may call for the work of social scientists (wary as one must be of how oppressed groups have been dealt with by social science) who can research questions of how the self learns new habits of desire, emotion, and action. Or, it may be that people working together in activist communities can be the ones to develop political practices that will bring about personal or character transformations along with structural changes, under the assumption that character will not necessarily change automatically with structural changes. Since character traits do tend to be constructed and reconstructed socially, it may be through collective practices that there will be the most potential to reverse moral damage. To give just one such example, consider the women's martial arts movement, which since the beginning of the second wave of the women's liberation movement has been politicized as it is linked to work against violence against women. This movement has not only consisted in women training in self-defense and martial arts (and thus learning a set of skills, a discipline, and an art form), but also in these women developing certain traits associated with this training, traits such as a sense of self-worth, assertiveness, resistance to violation, physical courage, and integrity of the body/self.[13] Indeed, there have been many attempts within the feminist movement, with its commitment to making the personal political, to link personal transformation with fundamental changes in social and political systems, though as I argued in chapter 1, these personal transformations have frequently not proceeded successfully, since many feminist political projects have overestimated the degree of control that one can have in bringing about personal transformation.

I have quite a bit more to say about the philosophical project than about the practical one. This project involves the normative evaluation of character, that is, judging which character traits will count as virtues and which as vices. If an account of moral excellence—tailored for the conditions of surviving and resisting oppression—were produced, it could serve to map out the more practical project; or, if such an account proves elusive (as I think it does), this too sheds light on the insidious effects of oppression, for oppression can be seen to complicate the appraisal of character traits by muddying any potentially praiseworthy trait.

11. Card, noting that oppressive circumstances may give rise both to special insights and to forms of damage, writes that "a challenge for feminist moral philosophers has been to distinguish the insights from the damage" (1996, 8).

12. Martha Nussbaum's 2001 *Upheavals of Thought* is an example of a book that undertakes both the normative task of evaluating certain traits (understood in a complicated way as emotions), such as compassion, and the nitty-gritty work of outlining—on the basis of much empirical research—how those traits might be fostered in a democratic citizenry.

13. One source for further information is the Web site of the National Women's Martial Arts Federation, which also has links to many women's/feminist martial arts schools: http://www.nwmaf.org/. See also Bar On 2001 for a consideration of what may be problematic about the sorts of habits learned by women training in the martial arts.

A virtue ethics framework might seem to suggest that one could identify a virtue by determining which traits tend to contribute to or be constitutive of human flourishing. This approach actually oversimplifies the relationship of virtue to flourishing in several ways. Flourishing, at least for Aristotle, is defined in terms of virtue (*NE* 1098a16–17), which in turn is understood as excellence of a specifically human function (*NE* 1097b22–1098a15). Avoiding the sticky issue of a human function, adopting a conception of flourishing from some other source, and working from there toward a list of virtues is going about the process backward.[14] Because it is not the case that virtue is both necessary and sufficient for flourishing, this reversal poses an additional problem: there may be virtues that fail to lead to or constitute flourishing (at least under some conditions), and these virtues may be missed by merely searching for the traits that are connected with flourishing. One possibility for addressing this additional difficulty is to designate as virtues those traits that *under favorable conditions* would tend to enable flourishing; other possibilities will emerge later in the book.

This leaves the problem of what conception of flourishing should guide one in the search for corresponding virtues. I will not try to argue for a conception of flourishing.[15] What I will do instead is to adopt a general conception of flourishing from what is implicit in the goals of liberatory movements (such as feminist movements and movements for racial liberation) and use this conception of flourishing as a guide, though one that becomes quite complicated, for analyzing the relationship between virtue and flourishing under oppression and examining some potential virtues under these conditions. To explain this move, I need only point to the fact that searching for the virtues suited for

14. Aristotle does not take a conception of flourishing, or *eudaimonia*, as given by what (certain) people already believe or know (as I will do in order to have a working conception of flourishing), but he does arrive at a list of the virtues in this way, using as a starting point the values of those who have been "brought up in good habits" (*NE* 1095b5–6) and creating some problems of circularity (how does one know which are the good habits and therefore know which are the well-brought-up people with whom one ought to consult?).

15. Trying to present a conception of human flourishing opens up a range of thorny possibilities stretching between two poles, both of which I want to avoid: the first pole is marked by the endorsement of a universal account of human flourishing, and the second consists of a relativist or subjectivist acceptance of just about any version of flourishing that someone might adopt for her/himself. Martha Nussbaum does not shy away from the first pole, endorsing what she believes to be a universal account of human flourishing. Her approach, which she calls the "capabilities approach," lists human capabilities (that is, opportunities for functioning) for which she believes all nations should provide support, and she uses the list to argue that governments should be politically pressured to provide guarantees that each and every citizen shall be enabled with each of the capabilities. Many items on her list are quite broad and would be hard to reject as universally desirable, but they also may be difficult to implement in practical ways without losing the universality that they do have. Despite Nussbaum's embrace of universal goods, her overall aim is a liberal one: she uses an account of human nature that assumes that humans engage in choices as autonomous individuals (though highly influenced socially) and privileges the preservation of an individual's capability to *choose* to develop and maintain certain human functions. Nussbaum thus believes that she allows for plurality despite the universality of her account of human functions, since no individual is required to develop a particular function. See Nussbaum 1999.

surviving and resisting oppression requires a specific account of human flourishing to a no-greater extent than committing to any particular form of social or political change does. Those fighting oppression must already hold certain implicit beliefs about what a flourishing or good life is. Without some notion of what is a greater rather than a lesser degree of flourishing or, put differently, a better rather than a worse sort of life, one would not have any basis for objecting to oppression; one would not struggle for social changes if one did not believe the changes to be for the good. To oppose some specific forms of oppression one must be able to claim, for instance, that one lives better when one is not in fear of police brutality than when one is; that it is preferable for one to believe one deserves love than for one to believe one is beaten because one is bad; that self-chosen, meaningful work contributes more to flourishing than mind-numbing, repetitive labor does; that a good life is not marked by the overwhelming loss of loved ones through racial or ethnic persecution; or that the disintegration of self that occurs under torture destroys rather than enhances one's life.

The normative work of evaluating character—if one bases this evaluation on a determination of which traits contribute to or constitute a particular conception of flourishing—demands no more of an endorsement of values than the normative work of maintaining political commitments does, whether one manifests this commitment in theoretical arguments or in practice through activism. However, conceptions of human flourishing are not always made explicit or visible within communities that work for liberatory changes, and so the search for corresponding virtues may seem like an importation of values rather than simply an identification of the character traits whose moral worth is already implicit in the liberatory goals of the community.

In the context of communities whose commitments are to fighting oppression, investigation of any character trait may take the form of asking about its consistency with the liberatory aims of the community. What complicates matters is an ambiguity in how a trait is to be connected to the liberatory goals of a community of resistance or to the conception of flourishing implied by those goals. One might ask, for instance, does the character trait help its bearer to engage in liberatory struggles, the purpose of which is to eventually enable a good life for all? Or, alternatively, one might ponder, does the character trait help its bearer to live well now (or to contribute to others' living well now), in the context of continuing oppression, where living well is itself understood in part by the same liberatory values that one wishes ultimately to be able to live out more fully? Because the answers to these two sorts of questions often diverge, there may be a set of traits whose moral status remains problematic precisely because of the context of oppression in which the trait is evaluated. The last three chapters of this book will explore the implications of there being such traits, suggesting that this indicates that there is a sort of moral trouble created by oppression and the demand for resistance.

3

The Ordinary Vices of Domination

I

This chapter departs from a focus on the victims and resisters of oppression to address the implications of thinking of members of dominant groups as morally damaged by the same oppressive structures from which they are meanwhile thought to benefit. From Socrates' insistence (contra Thrasymachus) that the unjust cannot be happy, to the more contemporary wisdom that "money don't buy you love," there is a history of suspicion about the goods that social, political, or economic power can bring. Does privilege that is conferred on a person because of her/his social positioning really bring the wonderful and coveted things that one might expect it to, and does it bring the ultimate good, namely, does it enable a person to flourish, to lead the good life? If members of groups that are structurally positioned to exercise power do in fact have serious moral flaws, this ought to stand in the way of their own well-being. Perhaps what they have, then, is not truly privilege, for if they cannot lead flourishing lives, what good are the so-called advantages that they have?

Socrates' belief that the unjust cannot lead the good life constitutes a core assumption of virtue ethics. As Aristotle more fully argues, flourishing depends upon virtue; *eudaimonia* is an "activity of soul in conformity with excellence [virtue]" (*NE* 1098a16–17). Due to its central place in ancient Greek ethics (and perhaps also due to its implausibility in contemporary times), the claim that the "wicked" cannot flourish has been much discussed in the literature on virtue ethics.[1] I am interested here in a very particular, contextualized implication

1. Joel Feinberg is a defender of the claim that the wicked can indeed flourish or, more precisely, the wicked are not at all harmed by their wickedness as long as they themselves do not desire a better character and their wickedness does not work against any of their other interests. That is, he rejects the idea of a "purely moral harm." He writes: "If a wicked person has no ulterior interest in having a good character, and if such a character is not *in* his [*sic*] (other) interests, then his depraved character is no harm to him (*pace* Plato *et al.*), and even if he becomes worse, he does not necessarily become worse off" (1984, 66).

of it: if the claim is correct, then members of structurally privileged groups can only flourish if they are morally good.

However, although the privileged may enjoy especially ample opportunities to develop certain virtues,[2] it is at the same time hard to conceive of the privileged as morally good, because the so-called privileges that are under consideration here are those that result from *unjust* social positionings, positionings that depend upon systems of male dominance, white supremacy, class divisions under capitalism, norms of heterosexuality, and so on. Although to some extent one might unwillingly and hence innocently be a recipient of the privileges that come with one's position—and thus one might argue that the beneficiaries of injustice need not themselves be unjust—in many cases it takes having some vicious characteristics in order to maintain oneself in a position of dominance. I will be focusing on those who, in order to stay secure in a dominant position, at least exhibit a culpable passive acceptance—if not a positive endorsement—of their unjust privileges.

These people—who display what I will call the *ordinary vices of domination*—could include a wide range of types, for there are several forms of domination and different levels and kinds of privilege associated with them (and of course many individuals are members of both dominant and subordinate groups). I will focus only on those who, while displaying the vices associated with their form(s) of dominance, are commonly understood to be leading the good life. So, for instance, violent men who batter or rape women, or racist whites who form hate groups and terrorize people of color on the street clearly take advantage of their positions of dominance and exhibit vices such as cruelty, indifference, contempt, and arrogance, but they are not widely believed to be flourishing people: their own lives are generally thought of as degraded and twisted, probably as a result of past or present pains of their own.[3] In contrast, those enjoying unjust economic advantage are popularly believed to be living the good life, regardless of the moral flaws that lead them to accept, develop, or maintain their unjust position; this group could include anyone from the wealthy capitalist who exploits the labor of working people while remaining unsympathetic to the hardships of their strenuous, unsafe, or deadening working conditions, to the hard-working but fulfilled and well-rewarded member of the

2. This claim is consistent with work of Claudia Card's that I have been drawing on in the previous two chapters, for she argues that the moral luck arising from conditions of oppression may make certain virtues easier for beneficiaries of oppression—and harder for the oppressed—to develop. For instance, she points out that the virtue of "liberality" is generally not available to those without means to carry it out (1996, 4). She also recognizes, though, that privileged people are likely to develop certain vices (see, for instance, 53). (On liberality, notice that Aristotle does permit the poor to be called liberal: "There is . . . nothing to prevent the man who gives less from being the more liberal man, if he has less to give" [*NE* 1120b9–10]; however, the larger-scale getting-and-spending virtue, magnificence, is a virtue that is unattainable by the poor: "A poor man cannot be magnificent, since he has not the means with which to spend large sums fittingly; and he who tries is a fool, since he spends beyond what can be expected of him and what is proper, but it is *right* expenditure that is excellent" [*NE* 1122b26–29]).

3. Thanks to Steve Scalet for this point.

middle or upper class who resists redistributive measures that would equalize wealth. Other forms of privilege may also be thought to support the good life, despite (or even because of) the ways that the privileged exhibit vices associated with their particular type of dominance. For instance, the sexist or misogynist who uses women for sexual/emotional "service" but keeps himself free from responsibilities may be seen as leading the good—unencumbered—life of the bachelor; furthermore, he may sexually harass or discriminate against women in the workplace or fight against measures to equalize women's status without these injustices being seen as detracting from his own well-being. Ordinary white people may arrange their lives so as to avoid contact with people of color—for instance, by choosing a segregated residential area—and rationalize policies that further disadvantage people of color without the vices associated with these forms of racism being seen by other whites as detracting from the racists' capacity to live the good life. Thus many groups of people thought to be living well clearly exhibit moral vices (such as callousness, greed, self-centeredness, dishonesty, cowardice, in addition to injustice) or at least the absence of certain specific moral virtues (perhaps compassion, generosity, co-operativeness, openness to appreciating others). Some people's moral deficiencies will be less blatant; their lack of respect for those whom they take to be their social inferiors may be less purposeful, but absence of conscious effort to resist animating the role of dominator will still result in similar character traits (perhaps in milder versions), as these are the traits they are socialized to have as they learn to occupy positions of privilege.

The case may be a bit different with those members of privileged groups who engage in active and committed resistance to the structures that confer their privileges. Those who become critical of their own social privilege may try to change not only structural sources of oppression but also their own characters. They may or may not have any success in this latter project, for just as I argued in chapter 1 that the politics of personal transformation often fails because character change is subject to luck and cannot simply be willed, the privileged who try to unlearn habits of domination may have similarly unmalleable characters. The white raised as a racist may later learn not to actually cross the street or clutch tightly to her/his belongings upon seeing a black person approach, but still be unable to rehabituate her/himself to not feel fearful.

In oppressively structured societies, a large proportion of the population will display the vices such as those that I listed; hence one may think of them as the ordinary vices of domination. Recognition of this fact must shift the discourse in virtue theory, because much of virtue ethics literature speaks as if most people are basically virtuous. For instance, Rosalind Hursthouse, in the context of considering the relevance of the point that it is difficult to convince the "wicked or the moral sceptic that the virtues benefit their possessor," makes the following remark: "Few of us (by which I mean myself and you, my readers) are likely to be steeped in vice or to be genuine moral sceptics. Thereby *we* believe many things we know we couldn't convince *them* of, but we do not reject those beliefs as implausible just because of that" (1999, 174–175; emphases added). Other theorists simply do not contextualize their analyses of character at all and instead of thinking about real, common cases of injustice or other vices (for instance, as they occur when supported by structures of oppression), they portray such cases as unusual or even bizarre, or as merely hypothetical; one theorist, for instance, gives someone the symbolic name "Unscrupulous" instead of concretizing virtue and vice in any actual society.[4] Given the pervasive injustice of oppression and given the high level of participation in maintaining structures of oppression and the difficulty of unlearning traits associated with domination even for those who become critical, I see unjust and other vicious people as fairly ordinary. In questioning whether privileged, dominating people with the ordinary vices associated with their domination can flourish, I am not talking about marginal or extraordinary cases—those few who are socially rejected because their injustices are socially recognized as unacceptable. Hursthouse slips into implying that *we* (virtuous ones) should think about vice in others; in contrast, I am asking some of my readers (and myself) to examine friends, neighbors, colleagues, family, and even self.

If virtue theories are correct to assume that moral virtue is necessary for flourishing, then those exhibiting the ordinary vices of domination, despite appearances to the contrary, are far from ever attaining the good life. However, this is an odd claim to add to a theory of oppression, which one would expect to explain how the *victims* of oppression—rather than its beneficiaries—are denied a shot at the good life. I have proposed in the previous chapters that under a virtue ethics framework, one can conceive of the conditions of oppression as creating systemic barriers to flourishing, namely, barriers that the *victims* of oppression run into; while these barriers consist primarily of external, structural features of the society, a virtue ethics approach suggests that there are also barriers to flourishing that become internal to the victims of oppression. That is, oppressed people typically experience systemically based moral damage because conditions of oppression may stunt the development of some of the virtues; lacking these virtues, they are thereby prevented from flourishing. As I argued in chapter 2, this description of oppression does not entail blaming the victim; rather, under this description, one of the harms of oppression is that it is psychologically—and characterologically—damaging to oppressed people, which in turn diminishes their possibilities for leading a flourishing life. For instance, the lack of opportunity to develop the character trait of (appropriate) confidence—a typical problem of gender oppression—may stand in the way of a woman's pursuing challenging and meaningful lines of work or other projects, and engagement in such projects may be partly constitutive of a flourishing life. The same trait may also be necessary for becoming a strong resister of injustice. For a more general example, consider the fact that facing daily disadvantages and experiencing oneself as always in struggle while others enjoy the ease of

4. See Hooker 1996. Within the virtue ethics tradition, an exception to the tendency to portray vice as uncommon is Kekes 1998 (though he is motivated in his claims by quite different concerns than I am); outside of the neo-Aristotelian virtue ethics tradition, see Shklar 1984 for a discussion of the significance (especially for liberal tolerance) of "ordinary vices."

gliding through a life of open opportunities might give rise to virtues such as courage and perseverance and properly directed anger, but it could and often does instead give rise to what are arguably vices: bitterness, resentment, a tendency toward hopelessness or despair. It is helpful for understanding how oppression operates to recognize how members of structurally subordinated groups are harmed by enduring conditions that make the development of certain virtues particularly difficult.

If people who are in positions of social, political, or economic dominance *also* are unable to flourish because of a lack of moral goodness, then the claim that the oppressed are especially harmed by being morally damaged loses some of its force. Oppression seems to equally, though in quite different ways, affect everyone's chances at developing the virtues and—if one accepts the connection between virtue and flourishing—thus negatively affects everyone's chances at leading the good life. Oppression certainly harms its victims in ways that it does not harm its perpetrators because oppression entails the denial of the external conditions for a good life to its victims. Virtue ethicists can recognize this by acknowledging the obvious fact that it is not *only* and not even primarily because of moral deficiencies that one is denied the possibility of flourishing. For Aristotle, favorable external conditions—such as access to sufficient material goods—are also necessary for flourishing (*NE* 1099a31–1099b8, 1101a14–16, 1153b14–21; *Rhet.* 1360b20–30). The oppressed are clearly denied favorable external conditions in a way that members of dominant groups are not. Nevertheless, if a virtue ethicist wants to contend—as I have suggested—that the oppressed are also especially harmed by being characterologically disabled from flourishing, and if it turns out that oppression also prevents dominators from developing (other) important virtues and therefore interferes with their flourishing, then one reaches a counterintuitive conclusion: according to this line of thinking, oppression is similarly harmful in this particular respect to its victims and to its perpetrators.

II

It seems to be a mistake to maintain that oppression operates in this way; reaching such an unexpected conclusion suggests that the premises may be false and must be reexamined: perhaps it is wrong to assume that virtue is required for flourishing, or perhaps virtue is indeed necessary for flourishing but the people exhibiting the ordinary vices of domination are not really leading the good life. One difficulty in deciding whether virtue and flourishing are indeed connected, or whether any particular person is really flourishing, comes from a lack of clarity about what is meant by human flourishing or by the good life. What I will argue is that if the traits exhibited in association with maintaining privilege are really vices, then their bearers cannot be said to flourish in anything like the ancient Greek understanding of the term (nor, I will suggest, in accordance with a conception of flourishing consistent with liberatory goals); however, the contemporary meaning of the word *happiness* is quite unlike *eudaimonia* or flourishing, and the contemporary context permits "happiness" without moral virtue.[5] Given this, it turns out that members of dominant groups are in fact beneficiaries of oppression, in the sense that they get to be vicious and still lead "happy" lives. Thrasymachus's world has, so to speak, materialized. So I will return briefly to the disagreement between Thrasymachus and Socrates.

Thrasymachus and Socrates differ on the question of whether it is through justice or injustice that one can be happy, because they disagree fundamentally about whether happiness is attained alone or in harmony and unity with others. Their visions of the relation of the ruler to his/(her) subjects reflects this difference: for Socrates, the ruler is analogous to a doctor, whose craft is aimed at the advantage of the patient's body (which is that over which the doctor rules), or a ship's captain, who performs his craft by concerning himself with the advantage of the sailors (again, his "subjects"); the ruler's well-being is tied up with that of others. Thrasymachus, who assumes a ruler may act tyrannically, securing his own advantage and taking pleasure in this, analogizes the ruler to a shepherd, who does not fatten his sheep for the sake of the sheep (*Republic* 341c–343d).[6] The key disagreement here is about whether the ruler's success is achieved in opposition to or in harmony with the ruled; if success depends on such harmony, then even a powerful person requires others' flourishing in order to flourish him/(her)self. In a second argument with Thrasymachus, Socrates points out that the unjust would be unable to cooperate with others in pursuing a common end; so, for instance, even a band of robbers would be unable to achieve its (unjust) aim, since each member of the band would undermine the others through injustice. He concludes that "wherever [injustice] is found in city, family, camp, or in anything else, it first renders the thing incapable of cooperation with itself owing to faction and difference, and secondly an enemy to itself and to its opposite in every case, the just" (*Republic* 351d–352a). Furthermore, the same internal strife that injustice gives rise to can occur within a single individual, ruining that person's chance at accomplishing his/(her) ends (*Republic* 352a). There must be harmony and unity within a collective—such as a *polis*—to succeed and flourish, and, as the individual soul reflects the *polis*, there must be harmony and unity within the individual, too.

Aristotle has his own way of insisting that flourishing depends on a certain sociality. Aristotle asserts that "man is by nature a political animal" (*Pol.* 1253a2–3) and that the *polis* is "a creation of nature" (*Pol.* 1253a2), because humans have a natural tendency to congregate together, and this implies that the human good—*eudaimonia*—can only be achieved through sociality. Indeed, what is attainable in a *polis* is not just "the bare needs of life"; rather, the

5. See Annas 1998 for an interesting discussion of the relation between virtue and *eudaimonia* and on the differences between the ancient Greek conception of *eudaimonia* and the modern conception of happiness.

6. Socrates has a reply to this: it is not *as* a shepherd that one concerns oneself with fattening the sheep; one has this concern when thinking *as* a guest at a feast, or *as* a merchant who stands to profit from the sale of the sheep (*Republic* 345d).

polis "continu[es] in existence for the sake of a good life" (*Pol.* 1252b29–30; see also *Pol.* 1278b19–27). The human good, which Aristotle argues must be self-sufficient, is characterized not as "sufficient for a man by himself, for one who lives a solitary life," but rather as being for a collective of people: "parents, children, wife, and in general for his friends and fellow citizens, since man is sociable by nature" (*NE* 1097b8–11); having this good (*eudaimonia*), one lacks in nothing, as long as one has it not just for oneself, but for others as well. Aristotle's discussions of friendship reflect and highlight similar assumptions: friendship is "most necessary with a view to living" (*NE* 1155a4–5), and it is clear that "friends ought to live together, that all wish this above all things, and that the happiest and best man tends especially to do so" (*EE* 1245b9–11); one would choose to have friends no matter what other goods one had in one's life. As Aristotle puts it:

> Surely it is strange, too, to make the blessed man a solitary; for no one would choose to possess all good things on condition of being alone, since man is a political creature and one whose nature is to live with others. Therefore even the happy man lives with others; for he has the things that are by nature good. And plainly it is better to spend his days with friends and good men than with strangers or any chance persons. Therefore the happy man needs friends. (*NE* 1169b17–21)[7]

For both Plato and Aristotle, then, the good life is attainable only within some collectivity such as a *polis*. The connection between moral virtue and human flourishing is strengthened in light of this belief, because any one person's moral virtue is understood in the context of a collectivity that depends on the virtue of its members in order to flourish as a whole. And, in turn, belonging (as a member in good standing) to a strong, flourishing *polis* is partly constitutive of leading a good life for any particular member of the *polis*. This is one of the key ancient Greek assumptions in support of the central claim of virtue ethics that one must be good to lead a good life.[8] One's goodness secures one a proper place in the *polis*; it is only within the *polis* that one's life can be assessed, and the assessment depends upon the (good) *polis*'s (correct) understanding of what it is to be good and what the good life is. For instance, one might be judged to be flourishing *as* a good citizen, or even further, *as* a good man. This is an objective assessment: a man might, for instance, believe himself to be happy/flourishing when he is not.[9]

7. There is of course much debate over whether Aristotle believes that the very best life is the contemplative life, which he portrays as a life of solitary contemplation (see *NE* bk. X, chaps. 7–8). I will not enter into that debate here.

8. Another Aristotelian assumption—that I do not focus on here—is that humans have a function tied to their rationality and that virtue is the excellent performance of this function; virtue and *eudaimonia* are linked because *eudaimonia* is an activity in accordance with the excellent (virtuous) performance of this function.

9. See Aristotle, *NE* bk. III, chap. 4, where he notes that some people aim not at the real good, but at an apparent good, usually because they mistakenly confuse the pleasurable and the good.

III

Contemporary theoretical developments of virtue ethics frequently focus on whether it is really the case that one must be good in order to lead a good life. Indeed, separated from the ancient Greek context, the claim that flourishing requires virtue seems quite implausible. These contemporary approaches often ignore or explicitly reject the assumption that the good life can only be achieved collectively and pursue the question of whether moral goodness is "good for" the individual by asking whether moral goodness is *beneficial* to a self-interested individual, an individual who is also assumed to subjectively determine what will count as happiness in an assessment of her/his own life.[10]

Indeed, this seems like the only available approach now that conditions of and assumptions about life have changed so dramatically from the ancient Greek context.[11] In a context such as the contemporary United States or other pluralistic liberal democracies, there is no single, unified, harmonious polity to map a route to flourishing. Individual lives are fragmented into pieces as people move from work environments to home to neighborhoods to places of consumption where they may be anonymous; the virtues for home life may not only be achievable in the absence of the virtues for work life, and so on, but they may actually conflict with each other. The society itself is also fragmented into multiple, sometimes overlapping, sometimes clashing groups; these different "communities of sense" may hold opposing or at least divergent conceptions of what the good life is. The state itself cannot endorse the view that there is a human end or purpose (*telos*) given by nature or by any god, and those people who do believe this are compelled (or are supposed to be compelled) to keep this as a matter of private religion, and they do not have their belief collectively upheld in the public sphere. Under these conditions, a person's life cannot be assessed as a whole, and there is no objectively determinable good life for a person's life to be measured against. Given all this, the link between virtue and flourishing (in the ancient Greek sense) would be difficult to support. Furthermore, the life of virtue involving the pursuit of an objectively determinable good, if carried out in a contemporary context, would require undermining the

10. Very clear examples of this are Sumner 1998, which I analyze below, and Hooker 1996. (Hooker distinguishes between asking whether moral virtue is *instrumentally* beneficial to an agent and whether it is *constitutively* beneficial; nevertheless, he is still concerned with benefits to a self-interested individual.) Also see Driver 1996, Taylor 1996, and (for somewhat of a contrast) Hursthouse 1999 (chap. 8). Phillips 1964–1965 is critical of the approach of asking whether justice (or any virtue) is beneficial or profitable, given the reliance of this approach on using nonmoral justifications of moral claims; his critique focuses on the argument given by Philippa Foot in "Moral Beliefs" (in Foot 1978).

11. The key text to see for a full discussion of the differences between the ancient Greek context and the modern context that are relevant for virtue and flourishing is MacIntyre 1981. MacIntyre also makes important distinctions within an ancient Greek context, for instance, between a Homeric and an Aristotelian world. Because I am not developing any detailed account of ancient Greek flourishing here, I am only noting some differences between ancient Greek and modern/postmodern understandings of the relationship between virtue and happiness.

protection of democratic freedoms;[12] such freedoms are premised on the notion that the good is not objectively determinable and that individuals must be permitted to exercise choice (within some limits) in what ends to pursue and how to pursue them.[13]

Instead of trying to resurrect a strong link between virtue and flourishing, some contemporary virtue theorists try instead to demonstrate a link between some of the virtues and a *subjectively* determined account of happiness or of a good life. Wayne Sumner, for instance, argues along these lines, first emphasizing a division of the virtues into "self-regarding" virtues (such as prudence), which clearly benefit the agent, and "other-regarding" virtues (generosity, fidelity, etc.), which seem not to. I will return in the next sections to a fuller consideration and ultimately a rejection of this division. It is a division that Sumner must presuppose because his aim is to find a way of linking the other-regarding virtues to happiness; he assumes that a link between self-regarding virtues and happiness will not be contested in the same way. "Happiness," for Sumner, refers to what he calls the "*prudential value* of a life, namely, how well it is going *for the individual whose life it is*" (1998, 21). He creates room for the link by stipulating that "a condition of someone's life counts as an intrinsic source of well-being for her just in case she authentically endorses it, or finds it satisfying, for its own sake" (1998, 30) and by arguing that if one of the other-regarding virtues satisfies this criterion, then it is tied to happiness in more than just an instrumental way. Sumner does have a concern with this account: an evil agent may endorse one of the vices as a source of happiness, and because happiness is for Sumner subjectively determined, it seems one would have to accept that vice as a real path to happiness. However, Sumner dismisses this problem because he is for the most part convinced that the evil agent's endorsement of a vice would not be *authentic* (and thus the vice would not count as an "intrinsic source of well-being") because it would either be mis/uninformed about the "facts" of the agent's own life, or it would be externally manipulated (through indoctrination, etc.), both of which Sumner claims would undermine its authenticity: "self-assessed happiness counts as well-being only when it is authentic—i.e., both informed and autonomous" (1998, 34).

For Sumner, as for many contemporary virtue ethicists, the "evil agent" is an unusual type, someone whose views are not widely endorsed. As I pointed out earlier, however, oppressively structured societies are characterized by pervasive injustice; broad segments of the society, namely, all those who uphold their unjust social privileges, will tend to animate the ordinary vices of domination. Thus, as distinguished from Sumner, I am not particularly concerned with idiosyncratic cases of, say, greed or infidelity in abstract persons, but rather with the case of members of privileged groups—who lack moral virtue in ways associated with the exercise of their dominance—and the possibilities for their flourishing. Sumner

12. This fact has led some feminists to critique communitarian thinking. See Friedman 1993 (chap. 9).

13. See John Rawls's (1993/1996 and 2001) concept of political liberalism that attempts to balance an overlapping consensus in the political realm with individuals' or groups' privately held comprehensive doctrines.

argues that the vicious will not tend to characterize themselves as morally good and their own lives as good lives or that they will do so only in ways that can be dismissed as based on an inauthentic self-assessment (inauthentic because of a lack of relevant information or a lack of autonomy). However, I believe that the people I am concerned with—those who maintain themselves in unjust social locations—will actually have a structurally supported tendency to believe in their own virtue and in the goodness and happiness of their lives, and it will be quite difficult to credibly dismiss these beliefs as inauthentic in the sense that Sumner means.

There are several forms of support that unjustly privileged people (especially those who uncritically accept their own privilege) have for thinking of themselves as good and of their lives as happy; I will return to comment on these after first turning to an examination of the implications of the distinction between self-regarding and other-regarding virtues.

IV

The tendency in contemporary virtue theories to rely on a distinction between self-regarding and other-regarding virtues seems like it further reflects an abandonment of the ancient Greek idea of collective flourishing, where self and other are understood as interdependent.[14] The distinction, however, is not entirely absent from Aristotle's thought, though it never leads him to question that self-concern can be morally praiseworthy nor to question the connection between the so-called other-regarding virtues and flourishing.[15] It is precisely because of the

14. For a clear statement of the distinction between self-regarding and other-regarding virtues, see Von Wright: "One way of marking the distinction between [self-regarding and other-regarding virtues] is to say that self-regarding virtues essentially serve the welfare of the agent himself, who possesses and practices them, whereas other-regarding virtues essentially serve the good of other beings" (1963, 153). Von Wright notes that the distinction is not challenged by the fact that self-regarding virtues may *accidentally* benefit others and other-regarding virtues may *accidentally* benefit the agent (1963, 153). Also see Philippa Foot, who remarks briefly on the distinction in "Virtues and Vices" by noting that while virtues are beneficial, "we must ask to whom the benefit goes, whether to the one who has the virtue or rather to those who have to do with him?" (1978, 3), perhaps picking up on her own consideration of the issue in "Moral Beliefs," where she addresses the apparent problem that "while prudence, courage and temperance are qualities which benefit the man who has them, justice seems rather to benefit others, and to work to the disadvantage of the just man himself" (1978, 125). Here she is able to answer that justice *is* beneficial to the agent precisely because of humans' equality and interdependence (pointing out that "if a man only needed other men as he needs household objects, and if men could be manipulated like household objects, or beaten into a reliable submission like donkeys, the case would be different" [1978, 129]), but she is not led to reject the distinction between self-regarding and other-regarding virtues altogether (see Foot 1978 for both "Virtues and Vices" and "Moral Beliefs").

15. Plato, however, does question this connection: otherwise there would be no Thrasymachus. This makes it clear that the question was quite thinkable within the ancient Greek context and that answering the question the way Plato ultimately does—by arguing that a trait such as "justice" which seems to benefit others actually benefits oneself—required defense. See Brink 1997 for a unique interpretation of how Plato (and Aristotle) cement the link between other-regarding virtues and an agent's own well-being.

centrality, for Aristotle, of the relationship between moral virtue and flourishing that other-regarding traits, if they are to be considered moral virtues, must be necessary for flourishing. In contrast, with few exceptions, current considerations of virtue not only accept the distinction between self-regarding and other-regarding virtues, but also assume that morality itself is only concerned with other-regarding virtues or actions. The popular belief is that self-concern is not moral and that concern for others *is* moral but will not necessarily contribute to one's own well-being. The demands of morality and the pull of self-interest are seen as opposed.[16] Consider, for instance, Brad Hooker's presupposition that for a virtue to be a *moral* virtue, it must be other-regarding. He states: "the traditional problem of reconciling virtue with self-interest focuses . . . on other-regarding virtues" (1996, 142), and further notes that "the potential for conflict between self-regarding virtue and self-interest is fairly slight. . . . The focus on *moral* virtue leads to a focus on other-regarding virtue, since morality is (at least primarily) concerned with how one treats others" (1996, 142f.).

There is a way in which the distinction between self-regarding and other-regarding virtues seems initially appealing for the purpose of responding with a neat solution to the problem I outlined earlier in this chapter (namely, that the beneficiaries of oppression are apparently harmed by oppressive structures, since the vices tied to their domination bar them from the good life); after all, isn't it the mistreatment of *others* that is the mark of the vices of domination? The distinction thus suggests an interesting possibility: it might be applied to distinguish between the way that oppression affects the characters of members of dominant groups and those of members of subordinate groups. Perhaps what I have called the ordinary vices of domination are all failings of other-regarding virtues, such as justice, compassion for others, generosity, and so on. In a parallel fashion, perhaps the moral damage done to oppressed people can be characterized as damage to their capacities to be sufficiently self-regarding. Thus if

16. Obviously, ethical egoism is a theory that rejects the belief that self-concern is not moral. However, egoism is seldom seriously defended. As Rogers 1997 points out, it might be *because* egoism violates the requirement that morality be about how one treats others that it is so implausible. Rogers argues for a rejection of the distinction between self-regarding and other-regarding virtues, commenting about the "self-other model" that "on this view, an action has no moral worth unless it benefits others—and not even then, unless it is motivated by altruism rather than selfishness" (1997, 1). Her focus is on critiquing the idea that morality is other-based. Jean Hampton's 1997 discussion of egoism is of interest to feminists. She rejects the view that self-concern is not moral, after having pointed out that the view that morality is limited to other-regarding concerns is something "that most contemporary moral philosophers take for granted" (1997, 21). She writes: "Moral action and moral regard are taken to be other-regarding. . . . Self-interest is generally taken to be outside the province of the moral" (1997, 21). One of her points about egoism is that it can teach the lesson that "our own selves are valuable" (1997, 48). This has not been seen as morally significant to theorists who assume that agents believe in and promote their own self-worth. Hampton rightly remarks, "Probably because most philosophers have, up until now, been males from relatively privileged social positions—a background that encourages people to think well of themselves—there has been virtually no recognition of how difficult it can be for some people to believe in their own worth" (1997, 48).

I were to accept the distinction between self-regarding and other-regarding virtues, then I could concede that oppression has the effect of diminishing virtue (or opportunities to develop virtue) in the characters of both oppressors and oppressed, without thinking of this effect as homogeneous.

Suppose I were to go further and, severing the tie between moral virtue and flourishing, classify the other-regarding virtues as moral but not beneficial (to the agent), and the self-regarding virtues as beneficial but outside of the realm of the moral. Then I could accept the notion that it is only a lack of self-regarding virtues, and not a lack of other-regarding virtues, that is "unprofitable"; this would enable me to hypothesize that oppressed people, because their opportunities to develop self-regarding virtues are limited, are prevented from flourishing, while privileged people, who tend to develop self-regarding virtues but underdevelop other-regarding virtues, can thereby aim unhindered—albeit in a morally reprehensible way—at the good life. Accepting all this, I could have my neat solution to the problem: if lacking self-regarding virtues interferes with flourishing, then I could point to this as one more way in which members of oppressed groups (and *not* members of dominant groups) are harmed in their quests for good lives.

I have two claims to examine, though, before I will be in any position to proclaim the success of the neat solution. The first is primarily an empirical claim, namely, that the distinction between self-regarding and other-regarding virtues maps nicely onto the characterological differences between members of dominant and subordinate groups. The second claim is that lacking the other-regarding virtues does not interfere with flourishing while lacking self-regarding virtues does. I will examine them in turn.

Clearly, at least some self-regarding virtues (such as confidence, self-esteem, proper pride) are battered under oppression, and the absence of these virtues makes it extremely hard to live well in the case of the oppressed. Racism, gender subordination, and class divisions (accompanied by elitism) do serious damage to those of the self-regarding virtues that are largely about the way the subordinated self views her/his own capacities; in a society that sees one as inferior, it is difficult not to come to see oneself this way too and to question one's capacities, one's worth, or even one's beauty. Such "self-hate" has been a widely discussed and influential concept in black liberation movements, though many are critical of the use of the concept.[17] The idea of this sort of damage was articulated fully by Kenneth Clark in 1951: "As minority group children learn the inferior status to which they are assigned, they react with feelings of inferiority and humiliation; they lose self-esteem. As a consequence of being almost universally regarded as inferior, they become confused concerning their own personal worth."[18] The Black Power movement drew heavily on Clark's

17. See chapter 2, and Scott 1997.

18. In Witmer and Kotinsky 1951, 48–49; quoted in Scott 1997, 96. See also Clark 1955, especially "The Negro Child and Race Prejudice" (chap. 3); and Clark 1965, especially "The Psychology of the Ghetto" (chap. 4), which begins: "It is now generally understood that chronic and remediable social injustices corrode and damage the human personality" (63).

observations; Stokely Carmichael and Charles Hamilton noted, for instance, that "born into this society today, black people begin to doubt themselves, their worth as human beings. Self-respect becomes almost impossible" ([1967] 1992, 29). Furthermore, the theory that oppression—or discrimination—results in self-hate has profoundly affected policy decisions; for instance, the *Brown v. Board of Education* opinion formulated by Justice Earl Warren (which drew on Clark's writing) referred to the fact that "Negro" children's sense of inferiority under segregation interfered with their learning.[19] The belief that self-degradation results from oppression has also been adopted by the (second wave) feminist movement, under which the phenomenon has come to be known as the *internalization of oppression* or *psychological oppression*.[20] Self-hatred that may have roots in oppression could also erode a virtue vaguely akin to what Aristotle would call *temperance* (partaking in an appropriately moderate way in certain physical pleasures), because such self-hatred can lead to self-destructive habits of eating (overeating or starving oneself), using alcohol or drugs for escape or numbing, purposely creating physical pain (for instance, cutting or burning oneself) to deflect from emotional pain, or engaging in any of the other myriad ways of destroying the body. Because the self-regarding virtues have in modern times been disconnected from moral discourse and attached instead to the concept of psychological health, these traits may appear as psychological rather than (moral) characterological traits (and this may in part mask the ways in which processes of subordination entail moral and not just psychic damage); understood as psychological traits, they stand out as psychological *problems*, precisely because they interfere in recognizable ways with a person's capacity to be happy.

There is another, related set of self-regarding virtues that may be absent in oppressed people, in this case because of an excess of a competing other-regarding trait, an excess which is commonly cultivated in subordinated peoples as a part of servility. These sorts of traits may also be tied to the phenomenon of self-degradation because they can stem from seeing others as more worthy than oneself whenever self-regarding and other-regarding aims conflict. Thomas Hill's insightful analysis of servility in "Servility and Self-Respect" is helpful here. He looks at patterns of servility in three cases, giving portraits of "the *Uncle Tom*" (a black man who "accepts without question the idea that, as a black, he is owed less than whites" and acts accordingly, displaying gratitude for the little he receives and never complaining that whites are prioritized); "the *Self-Deprecator*" (whose problem is "not a sense of racial inferiority but rather an acute awareness of his own inadequacies and failures as an individual" and a belief that "his failings warrant quite unrelated maltreatment even by strangers"); and "the *Deferential Wife*" (who claims to believe that women are equal to men, but meanwhile "believes that the proper role for a woman is to serve her family" and does so by deferring to her husband and "tend[ing] not to form her own interests, values and ideals; and when she does, she counts them as less important than

19. See Scott 1997, 133–136.

20. For a classic feminist essay on this phenomenon, see Sandra Bartky, "On Psychological Oppression" [1979], in Bartky 1990; Bartky draws on Fanon 1967 [French, 1952].

her husband's") (1973, 88–89). The first and third cases clearly relate servility to structures of oppression. The examples together suggest that servility consists in "the absence of a certain kind of self-respect" (1973, 97). In the language of virtue ethics, servility is thus a vice because it is a deficiency, a case of inadequate self-respect and belief in one's own worth. In Hill's Kantian language, the problem with servility is that it violates a duty to oneself: "at least one sort of respect for persons is respect for the rights which the moral law accords them. If one respects the moral law, then one must respect one's own moral rights; and this amounts to having a kind of self-respect incompatible with servility" (1973, 98).

Servility as a character trait can result from the internalization of stigmatization and status hierarchies based on race, gender, and other social groupings. Servility in Hill's account requires either that one believe that one lacks certain rights or that one place relatively little value on them; either of these problems can arise from conditions of oppression.[21] Furthermore, one might also believe oneself to be worthy but, given the external demands of one's position, be unable to insist on respect and justice from others. That is, one may be required to exhibit what appears to be servile behavior, without having the accompanying beliefs that would qualify one as having a character trait of servility. In this case the burden of serving others is not only bad in itself but also carries the danger that one will, through constantly displaying excessive other-regarding care, come to develop the belief that one's own self is less worthy; that is, one risks becoming servile.

While all subordinated peoples may be vulnerable to the threat of losing their sense of self-worth and becoming servile, for some women there is an additional factor: some women's only basis for thinking of themselves as good or valuable is their capacity to nurture and care for others, and this makes these women particularly susceptible to developing the trait of being self-sacrificial, which is one aspect of servility.[22] The group of women who are at risk here are those whose self-affirmation takes place only or primarily in the family, particularly if they are heterosexual women who are socially expected to serve and care for their male partners as well as their children.[23]

Many of these points about the "feminine virtues" such as self-sacrifice have been made by feminist critics of (feminist) care ethics. Nel Noddings's (1984) version of care ethics stands out as blatantly promoting what can be seen as self-sacrificial traits, since the "one-caring" becomes engrossed in the "cared-for," moving out of her own self and into the experience of the other's desires, fears, or

21. One could describe the beliefs typical of the servile person without using the language of rights. For instance, under an Aristotelian account, if justice entails distributing to each his due amount, then believing one should give oneself less than is appropriate is as problematic as the vice of giving oneself an unfairly large share.

22. For early essays on women's self-sacrifice and altruism, see Tormey 1973–1974; and Blum, Homiak, Housman, and Scheman 1973–1974.

23. Notice that under slavery and to some extent under the pressures of a certain kind of paid labor (labor that while not fulfilling in itself meanwhile takes women away from their families), women are denied the affirmations offered by their potential role as nurturer in their families and are not compensated by being valued elsewhere.

suffering. Noddings describes the ethical ideal of caring as specifically feminine and portrays ethical caring as arising from what she calls *natural caring*, the primary example of which is a mother caring for her child. Noddings has been a clear target for feminists who have recognized self-sacrifice as detrimental to women and who think of mothering as a problematic model for other sorts of ethical relations.[24] When ethics is seen as limited to the realm of concern for others, women may be seen as occupying the moral high ground relative to men, but there is a cost: they are unable to pursue their own interests as long as their interests conflict with that of others. This compulsory sacrifice is one of the harms of oppression. As Susan Moller Okin puts it, "in virtually all human societies, women do far more than men to promote the day-to-day material and psychological flourishing of others, and . . . this promotion of the flourishing of others is not infrequently done at the expense of some aspects of their own flourishing" (1996, 227).[25]

To summarize: oppression that is internalized into self-hate produces a tendency toward deficiency in certain self-regarding traits (those concerned with how one perceives and experiences the self's worth, capacities, etc., and those that have to do with preserving rather than destroying one's own physical and emotional health); and, when self-regarding and other-regarding interests conflict, subordinated peoples who are likely to have developed the trait of servility will manifest a deficiency in those self-regarding traits that help one to promote one's own needs and desires.

But these empirical facts by themselves do not confirm in its entirety the claim that I was assessing, a claim that breaks down into four parts: (1) that subordinated people tend not to exhibit self-regarding traits, (2) that dominant people do tend to exhibit self-regarding traits, (3) that dominant people do not tend to exhibit other-regarding traits, and (4) that subordinated people do tend to

24. See, for instance, Hoagland 1988 (chap. 2).

25. Even those who reject the usual depiction of self-regarding and other-regarding virtues may miss out on the fact that false beliefs about the value of one's self may lead to failures of the self-regarding virtues. Among theorists who question the distinction between self-regarding and other-regarding virtues, Taylor and Wolfram's (1968) version is interesting because they actually retain the distinction but shift the criteria for calling a virtue self- or other-regarding. Beginning with an account of the distinction such as the one Von Wright makes, they argue that the self-regarding virtues "are not logically connected with the pursuit of self-interest. . . . they differ from the other-regarding virtues, so far as self-interest is concerned, only in the fact that they are not logically connected with benefiting others: a man can, though he need not, display them in his own interest" (1968, 244). They suggest that instead of a distinction based on who is benefited, one can base the distinction on how one accounts for why an agent fails to have a virtue: they attribute failings of self-regarding virtues to weakness of the will, not to false beliefs about what is right. "If we analysed cases of so-called weakness of will we should find that in each case the agent had displayed a self-regarding failing, while cases of so-called wickedness would turn out to be cases of an other-regarding failing" (1968, 247–248). Given their new distinction, they surmise that it is worse for everyone if someone lacks the so-called self-regarding virtues, for

> if on most occasions it is to someone's own interest to benefit others rather than harm them, then the strong-willed man who does not care about others will in fact mostly benefit them, while the weak-willed man who wants to benefit others will not often succeed in doing so if on most occasions it takes strength of character; and he is likely to make a mess of his own affairs as well. (1968, 248)

exhibit other-regarding traits. Even if one grants part 1 of the claim and agrees that oppression corrodes the capacity to be self-regarding in the ways I have discussed, the remainder of the posited match between self/other-regardingness and dominant/subordinate groups is not confirmed by evidence.

First, the experience of social privilege may diminish the opportunity to develop a different set of self-regarding traits. There are things that the privileged never learn because they never engage in the associated practices: the habits of hard work and the capacity to fully value or treasure the fruits of one's labor are arguably beneficial self-regarding traits that very wealthy people tend to lack (especially if they do not actually perform any labor).[26] If courage comes through practicing courageous acts (facing the possibility of pain for a good or noble end), people who are protected throughout life will not tend to develop this self-regarding trait; many men, socialized to not express some of their own emotions, are likely to be unable to identify or even experience a full range of emotions, and this emotional incompetence could count as a lack of an important self-regarding trait.

Second, it is also false that members of privileged groups lack other-regarding traits. They *do* develop other-regarding virtues, though they often exercise them toward other privileged people by, for instance, being compassionate, generous, and so on toward other members of their race and class. Or, they exercise them in exchange for recognition; charity, when it is not anonymous, works this way. One of Elizabeth Spelman's (1991) criticisms of feminist care ethics is about the lack of attention given to the question of who the recipient of "women's" care is. Many privileged women exhibit their caring tendencies only toward other racially and economically privileged people (often their husbands or children). The maintenance of their racial or class privilege depends on their not extending this care (as an equal, not as a "benefactor") to less-privileged people. Still, they cannot be said to not be other-regarding, though the fact that they exhibit their other-regarding virtues within a limited circle is important, and I will return to it later.

Third, and perhaps the most disturbing fact about how self-regarding and other-regarding traits appear in relation to members of dominant and subordinate groups, there is a phenomenon that has to do with what Nietzsche has called "slave morality," the morality of those who out of their powerlessness become resentful and vengeful toward the powerful, embracing the virtues of equality and justice in order to rein in their dominators' power and freedom. As implied by Wendy Brown

---

Taylor and Wolfram's proposal demonstrates a different way that systemic influences on character are ignored. They argue that failures in attaining self-regarding aims can only be accounted for by an insufficiency in the strength of will necessary to do so. However, internalized oppression that creates in the oppressed false beliefs in their own inferiority or worthlessness may account for many failures of self-regarding virtues. Consider courage, for example: many women have been taught that they are incapable of fighting physically or that fighting back would only make their assailant angrier or even that a woman's fighting is "unbecoming." These (false) beliefs, and not weakness of the will, may hold them back from displaying physical courage when attacked. Taylor and Wolfram do not acknowledge that agents who fail to display self-regarding virtues may suffer from these systemically distorted beliefs.

26. Of course, Aristotle does not consider this as a virtue, but this very fact probably reflects his elitism: it is not a typical virtue of leisured gentlemen.

in her application of this Nietzschean analysis, when disfranchised groups articulate their experiences in terms of an injured identity—including, perhaps, as conveyed through the idea of moral damage under oppression—they become tied to their very suffering. It is the basis upon which they have any claim to having been morally wronged by the powerful: "Insofar as what Nietzsche calls slave morality produced identity in reaction to power, insofar as identity rooted in this reaction achieves its moral superiority by reproaching power and action themselves as evil, identity structured by this ethos becomes deeply invested in its own impotence" (1995, 70). While an (over)attachment to an injured identity may only be detrimental to one's own self, the vengefulness that it fuels undermines the possibility of many other-regarding traits. Thus the demand for justice and equality appear to be other-regarding but deceptively so; as long as the demand stems from Nietzschean *ressentiment*, it aims to inflict injury (from below). Someone who under oppression has become bitter, resentful, or vengeful cannot be said to display the other-regarding virtues.[27] Other aspects of powerlessness also interfere with the development of other-regarding virtues. For instance, as Hoagland has noted, "the power of control can be exercised from the subordinate position," and women, when subordinated, have used the "feminine virtues" to do just that: "female agency involves manipulation and cunning" (1988, 85).[28] Claudia Card, in noting that "feminist thinkers are understandably reluctant to address publicly women's reputation for lying, cunning, deceit, and manipulation," writes:

> But, *are* these vices, one may ask, if they are needed for self-defense? They are surely not virtues, even if they are justified from the point of view of justice. Those who tell just the right lies to the right people on the right occasions may have a useful and needed skill. But it does not promote human good, even if it is needed for survival under oppressive conditions. (1996, 53)

I agree: these are not virtues; they are failures of other-regarding virtues, and they are typical of subordinated people who believe, perhaps rightly, that they have no alternative ways of exercising control.[29]

To conclude this consideration of the allure of the distinction between self-regarding and other-regarding virtues: it is clear that, despite the empirical evidence that oppression does in some specific ways seriously damage the capacity of subordinated people to be self-regarding, the division of kinds of virtues does *not* map easily onto a division of people into the privileged and the disadvantaged.

27. See McFall 1991 for a (qualified) defense of bitterness, and Potter 2001 for a consideration of whether being unforgiving should be considered a vice, even in the case of those who have been abused. Marguerite La Caze 2001 points out the value of both envy and resentment, arguing that they can enable recognition of injustice.

28. Hoagland is drawing on Card 1985.

29. Aristotle does not recognize how one may exercise control or take vengeance from below (what did he think of Medea?) and wrongly asserts that "we feel comparatively little anger, or none at all, with those who are much our superiors in power" since "no one grows angry with a person on whom there is no prospect of taking vengeance" (*Rhet.* 1370b12–15).

V

There was a second claim that the neat solution depended upon, namely, that only the self-regarding virtues are necessarily "good for" the agent. As I pointed out earlier, those virtue theorists who make use of the distinction between self-regarding and other-regarding virtues are skeptical about the connection between the other-regarding virtues and flourishing because they reduce the concept of flourishing to the quite different notion of benefit or the fulfillment of self-interest and focus on how other-regardingness may be detrimental to one's self-interests. Although I would be willing to concede that other-regarding virtues such as having a sensitivity and a disposition toward caring about others' suffering may in some way stall one's pursuit of a narrowly understood self-interest (though quite often these other-regarding virtues instrumentally promote one's self-interest, too) what I will not concede is that such self-interest can be equated with a concept of flourishing—if it is to have any resemblance either to the ancient Greek concept or, I will argue, to an account of flourishing consistent with liberatory goals. Thus I will have to reject the claim that other-regarding virtues do not help one to flourish.

It is helpful to return to Aristotle for some guidance on how to think of the other-regarding virtues as contributing to one's own flourishing and on how to think of the self-regarding traits as morally praiseworthy. While some theorists have wanted to claim that Aristotle makes no distinction akin to the one between self-regarding and other-regarding virtues, this is not entirely accurate. He *does* have some ways of talking about what might be called other-regardingness as distinguished from self-regardingness. What he does *not* do is match this distinction up with a split between what is moral and what is beneficial (for the agent): both kinds of virtues are both.[30]

There are at least two contexts in which Aristotle makes extensive remarks about the distinctiveness and moral praiseworthiness of what might be called other-regardingness: *Rhetoric* book I, chapter 9, and *Nicomachean Ethics* book V.[31]

30. See Wilkes 1980:

> The essential thing to realize is that Aristotle—and Plato—wrote in a time when the distinction between the moral (other-regarding) and prudential (self-regarding) virtues had not yet been framed, and, perhaps even more importantly, that they would have denied any reality or importance to the distinction had it been explicitly presented to them. (1980, 354)

Wilkes's point is partially that Aristotle (and Plato) did not equate moral virtues with other-regarding virtues, but she makes this point without noting and accounting for the fact that Aristotle does specially pick out some traits as other-regarding.

31. These are in addition to his discussions of friendship, which could also be used as Aristotelian sources for thinking about self- and other-regardingness. I am not focusing on friendship in part because concern for a friend is so clearly a limited kind of other-regarding concern, as a friend is very close to one's self (especially for Aristotle). See Julia Annas's 1993 discussion in her chapter on "Self-Concern and the Sources and Limits of Other-Concern" (chap. 12), where she does focus on Aristotle's treatment of friendship.

Much of the actual praise for other-regarding virtues appears in the *Rhetoric* where it seems that Aristotle does value other-regarding virtues more highly than those that do not immediately express concern for others. What he says in this context must be read in light of the fact that it represents Aristotle's report of popular understandings more than his own view, since his purpose in these passages is to explain how to give one's audience a particular picture of one's own or someone else's character. Nevertheless, Aristotle does at least demonstrate his familiarity with, if not his endorsement of, the view that benefiting others is particularly praiseworthy: "If virtue is a faculty of beneficence, the highest kinds of it must be those which are most useful to others" (*Rhet.* 1366b3–4). Noble actions are

> those in which a man aims at something desirable for someone else's sake; actions good absolutely, such as those a man does for his country without thinking of himself; actions good in their own nature; actions that are not good simply for the individual, since individual interests are selfish[,] . . . all actions done for the sake of others, since these less than other actions are done for one's own sake; and all successes which benefit others and not oneself; . . . and good deeds generally, since they are not directed to one's own profit. (*Rhet.* 1366b35–1367a7)

In addition, he says, "[T]hose qualities are noble which give more pleasure to other people than to their possessors; hence the nobleness of justice and just actions" (*Rhet.* 1367a18–20).

Because of these remarks, one cannot claim that Aristotle has no notion at all of the difference between a virtue that benefits the self and one that benefits others. However, merely noting this difference and even recognizing that benefiting others is especially noble does not commit Aristotle to removing self-beneficial traits from the list of moral virtues or to seeing benefiting others as detracting from one's own well-being; on the contrary, according to Aristotle, the more noble a virtue is, the better it leads one to *eudaimonia*. Part of what would muddy any distinction Aristotle might draw between self-regarding and other-regarding virtues is precisely that benefit to the self could include "moral benefit": that is, one gains by being more noble. Thinking of benefit in this way clearly depends upon Aristotle's being committed in advance to the connection between virtue and *eudaimonia*. Thus, when considering the virtuous man who, in displaying the trait of (distributive) justice, gives to himself less than his share, Aristotle points out that "he perhaps gets more than his share of some other good, e.g. of honour or of intrinsic nobility" (*NE* 1136b22–23).[32] What seems to be an other-regarding act blurs into one that is ultimately good for the agent himself: in acting particularly honorably or nobly, the agent gains in moral goodness and therefore also in his capacity for *eudaimonia*.

There are further ways in which the discussion of justice is illuminating of Aristotle's view of the role of other-regardingness. Aristotle thinks of the virtue of justice in two senses: a general sense and a more particular sense which is restricted to the correct distribution of goods or to rectification. The general sense has to do

32. A similar point is made by Nancy Sherman; see Sherman 1993, 287.

with abiding by the laws, because all that is unjust will be forbidden by law (assuming good legislators). Good laws aim to make the citizens virtuous and in part do so by "commanding some acts and forbidding others" (*NE* 1129b23). This general sense of justice, then, is a sort of a meta-virtue for Aristotle, in that abiding by the laws—if the laws are good—consists of acting virtuously in every realm; thus Aristotle concludes that "this [general] form of justice . . . is complete excellence [virtue]." However, he quickly qualifies this because he does not mean even this general sense of justice to cover *all* the virtues, but only those that—long after Aristotle's time—have come to be called the other-regarding virtues. With the added stipulation, Aristotle's claim is that "this [general] form of justice . . . is complete excellence [virtue], not absolutely but in relation to others" (*NE* 1129b27–28). Thus while Aristotle does not use the term *other-regarding*, his use of the term *justice* in the general sense is meant to mark off and be an umbrella term for those virtues that are exercised not in regard to oneself but rather in relation to others; this is indicated when Aristotle says, "what, as a relation to others, is justice is, as a certain kind of state without qualification, excellence [virtue]" (*NE* 1130a13–14). Furthermore, justice is difficult to achieve and especially praiseworthy precisely because it "does what is advantageous to another": "the best man is not he who exercises his excellence towards himself but he who exercises it towards another; for this is a difficult task" (*NE* 1130a4–9).

What Aristotle offers, then, is a way of acknowledging the difference between self-regarding and other-regarding virtues and of noticing how difficult it is to exercise those that are other-regarding—and also how these virtues merit special praise—without ever having to conclude either that the self-regarding virtues are therefore not moral virtues at all or that the other-regarding virtues are not ultimately beneficial for the agent. What allows Aristotle to do this is his assumption that virtue and *eudaimonia* are tied and that the sociality and interdependence of humans makes *eudaimonia* impossible to achieve outside of a social collectivity (such as a *polis*). While the self-regarding and other-regarding virtues can sometimes be distinguished, both, in that their presence strengthens the *polis* and a good *polis* in turn sustains the good life for all its members, are necessary for anyone's flourishing: "if *all* were to strive towards what is noble and strain every nerve to do the noblest deeds, everything would be as it should be for the common good, and every one would secure for himself the goods that are greatest, since excellence is the greatest of goods" (*NE* 1169a7–11). Some of Aristotle's virtues are best thought of as "social virtues," namely, virtues that further the good of a social collectivity and thereby further the good of all members of the collectivity, including oneself and others.[33]

33. I do not mean, here, to refer just to the virtues that are displayed in social intercourse (such as amiability or friendliness, sincerity or truthfulness, and wittiness), though these are social virtues too. See *NE* bk. IV, chaps. 6–8. See Sherman 1993 for a discussion of what she calls the "virtues of common pursuit"; Sherman also points out that many of Aristotle's virtues mix self-regarding and other-regarding aims, naming even those that appear to be most other-regarding (liberality, magnificence, and magnanimity) as having self-regarding elements, such as (in reference to liberality) "being a good steward of one's acquisitions and expenditures" and "not being negligent about what one materially requires for a non-depraved existence" (1993, 286).

Aristotle provides what was needed to firmly reject the second premise that my neat solution depended on: it is *not* the case that only the self-regarding virtues are necessary for flourishing. One can make this claim, following Aristotle, without having to pretend that no distinction can ever be drawn between self-regarding and other-regarding virtues. What one must accept, though, is that those virtues that are or appear to be other-regarding turn out to ultimately also be beneficial for the agent, assuming with Aristotle that the well-being of any agent depends upon the well-being of a social collectivity.

The neat solution falls apart (on two counts now) and cannot provide an explanation of how members of dominant groups seem to get to lead the good life. The theoretical commitments of a neo-Aristotelian virtue ethics seem to entail accepting that because oppression deprives members of both dominant and subordinate groups of certain (different) virtues, ultimately everyone suffers. But this conclusion fails to explain how the moral damage done to *victims* of oppression can be thought of as a harm in a different and more profound way than that done to its beneficiaries, and it fails to account for the happiness that privileged people seem to have an easier time attaining. So does virtue ethics have anything special to say about how oppression harms those who are subordinated (besides what can be obvious to both virtue ethicists and others, namely, that oppression deprives certain people of external opportunities and resources)?

VI

Looking again—this time more critically—at Aristotle will yield some clues about how one can exhibit the ordinary vices of domination and still manage to lead the good life.

I have rejected, following Aristotle, the separation of virtue and flourishing that permits one to question whether the other-regarding virtues are "good for" the agent, and I have done so because I agree with Aristotle that humans are social beings who depend upon the well-being of a social collectivity for their own well-being. For Aristotle, not just any collectivity will serve to fulfill the social needs of humans. It is only in a good *polis* that one can become properly trained in virtue, have the right opportunities for its practice and exercise, and have others with whom to share the joys of the good life. According to Aristotle, it is not simply sociality—for a *polis* can be a bad one—but what I will call a *successful sociality* that is required for flourishing.

I must, however, depart from Aristotle in making a judgment about what will count as successful sociality. According to Aristotle, a *polis* is a good one—providing what will count for Aristotle as successful sociality—just in case it supports the virtue and therefore potentially supports the *eudaimonia* of its members ("potentially," because its members must also be able to meet their material needs and have not too much bad luck). Aristotle's version of eudaimonism ensures that other-regarding virtues will be cultivated and practiced, but it ensures this in part because the pursuit of one's own *eudaimonia* requires contributing to the maintenance of successful sociality, which in turn requires benefiting the others who comprise one's community.[34] Whether it is in loving one's friend and wanting what is good for one's friend for one's friend's sake, or whether it is in a more general contribution that one makes to the virtue and well-being of all of one's fellow citizens, one engages in other-regarding virtues as a part of the overall moral virtue that must accompany the "activity of the soul" that is *eudaimonia*.

However—and this is where I become critical of Aristotle—there is no built-in requirement for the social collectivity (the *polis*) to be inclusive, and Aristotle's is notoriously exclusive: citizen-class women, all slaves, for the most part all foreigners, and perhaps landless laborers are all excluded (*Pol.* bk. I, chaps. 4–7, 12, 13; bk. III, chap. 5; 1280a32–34). Man is a political animal—but his political nature can be fulfilled in an exclusive *polis*; successful sociality can be exclusive sociality. The flourishing of one does not require the flourishing of all; it just requires the flourishing of some particular others. What Aristotle's eudaimonism really guarantees is that the leisured adult Greek males will concern themselves with each other, because they must do so in their pursuit of flourishing, but it does nothing to extend morality beyond this circle; one does not tarnish one's virtue by directing it only at certain specified others. This eudaimonism does not collapse into psychological egoism—since concern for others' well-being is quite central for these virtuous Greek gentlemen—but it can, without violating the requirement for what Aristotle considers to be a successful sociality, be compatible with sexism, class divisions and economic exploitation, xenophobia and nationalism, pernicious ethnocentrism, and that which, since modernity, can be called racism. It is compatible with an utter lack of concern for the well-being of those who have relatively little social, economic, and political power.

The pursuit of happiness engaged in by contemporary members of dominant groups works—at best—similarly. While they cannot be completely vicious and still be said to lead the good life (though they may, as I have explained, be "happy"), they can, if they develop other-regarding virtues and exercise them in relation to an exclusive circle of others positioned like themselves, indeed live well even while lacking other-regarding concern for those who occupy the positions of subordination in their society.[35] In order to be said to flourish (in the

34. One might argue for a different connection between other-regarding virtues and one's own *eudaimonia* under Aristotle's version of eudaimonism, a connection that does not emphasize (though is compatible with) Aristotle's assumptions of human sociality. William Prior (2001) argues that "reason is the crucial link between virtue and *eudaimonia* in Aristotle's theory. . . . since a good life is essentially characterized by excellence in rational activity, every act that makes excellent use of reason, every virtuous act, contributes essentially to the good life of an agent" (2001, 330). With respect to an other-regarding virtue such as justice, Prior observes that "in order to act justly, we must first determine rationally what justice requires. This use of our rational ability contributes intrinsically to our *eudaimonia*, and so benefits us. The *phronimos*, in reasoning out the demands of justice in a particular situation, contributes to his own *eudaimonia*" (2001, 331).

35. They can also be fairly indifferent toward far-away strangers in general, regardless of privilege. Notice that Aristotle's conception of interdependent community is based on a small *polis*, which is not only exclusive but is also simply limited in size or population.

ancient Greek sense) they must have both self-regarding and other-regarding virtues, and their other-regarding virtues must help to sustain a social collectivity that they are a part of—but because the link between virtue and flourishing is mediated by the assumption that humans are by nature sociable and this sociality can be satisfied alongside exclusion, their other-regarding virtues do *not* have to be directed toward everyone. They can have the sociality that is required for their own virtue and well-being without extending their concern beyond others who are structurally positioned like themselves (and further, they can have many of their material and emotional needs met through exploitation of those whose well-being they can be indifferent to). I noted earlier that while members of dominant groups do not entirely lack the other-regarding virtues, they often noticeably direct them only to others who share their privilege (or, in the case, for instance, of white women whose other-regarding concern is focused on white men, others who exceed their own level of privilege). This suggests that it will not be enough to worry about whether an agent exercises both self-regarding and other-regarding virtues, because one should not be satisfied, as Aristotle is, with an agent whose other-regarding virtues are directed only toward an exclusive circle of others.[36]

Aristotle would not agree with the claim that I made at the beginning of this chapter, that there is a certain group of people who exhibit what I have been calling the ordinary vices of domination. That is, he would not believe that the activities of domination and the character traits that correspond to these activities are necessarily vicious. For instance, since justice, for Aristotle, entails treating equals equally and unequals unequally (*Pol.* 1280a11–14), there is no vice of injustice committed when some people (such as the slaves or the wives of citizens) are denied material goods or economic opportunities. In general, because Aristotle believes that it is right to treat certain others (women, slaves, etc.) as less than fully human, the traits that I have called the ordinary vices of domination are *not* vices for him. Those who dominate—who turn out for Aristotle not to be doing anything bad at all—are not examples of vicious people flourishing and thus pose no challenge to the relationship between virtue and flourishing. The vices (that do interfere with flourishing) are those that erode the sort of sociality that is necessary for flourishing, but for Aristotle, unequal treatment of much of the population does not constitute such a vice.

Thus, while I have borrowed much from Aristotle, now I need to depart from him to be rid of the unacceptable aspects of his conception of *eudaimonia*; I need to turn instead to a conception of flourishing implicit in the liberatory goals of communities that are struggling against oppression. This conception of flourishing, I suggest, should maintain Aristotle's assumption that the health of a social collectivity is key for any individual member's well-being. But there will need to be an added stipulation to Aristotle's version of eudaimonism in order for it to serve the purposes of liberatory politics: one must stipulate that the pursuit of one's own flourishing cannot qualify as morally praiseworthy (and what one attains cannot

36. See Annas 1992 for a consideration of which of the ancient eudaimonistic theories might accommodate a wider-reaching other-concern than Aristotle's theory does.

count as flourishing) unless one is engaged, as part of that pursuit, in promoting the flourishing of an inclusive social collectivity. Many questions will arise about how an inclusive—and democratic—polity can best function, and these questions may best be settled by using concepts imported from outside of a eudaimonistic framework.[37] I call my addition a "stipulation" because I do not think that there is a way to argue for inclusivity from within every possible eudaimonistic framework; one needs a eudaimonistic framework to be informed by a particular conception of flourishing in order to yield inclusivity from the principle of pursuing one's own flourishing.[38] Aristotle's eudaimonism, while ensuring other-regarding concern, falls short of requiring that this concern be for an inclusive population.

The idea that is captured by the slogan "no one is free while others are oppressed" is regrettably false: those who are not oppressed may find their happiness (or their freedom) by simply not noticing the others. In fact humans are *not* actually dependent on a sociality that is inclusive of everyone; interdependent community can be constructed to support the flourishing of those within it, disregarding or even undermining the flourishing of those excluded. Because I believe that this is the sort of interdependent community that Aristotle had in mind, a form of eudaimonism like Aristotle's—without the stipulation I suggested above—is not enough to ensure that morality will include attention to subordinated people.

To highlight the contrast: under Aristotle's eudaimonism, morality consists in using practical reason to pursue one's own flourishing, given that doing so will require developing virtues including those that contribute to the well-being of some particular others. My claim is that this morality is not good enough. Rather, moral goodness requires a pursuit of not just my own well-being, and not just the well-being of those whose well-being I depend on, but also the well-being of those whose very lack of well-being may have been a condition of my privileges. If one finds oneself living the good life while others' lives are systemically set up to be wretched, it is a mistake to think that moral goodness lies just in the pursuit of one's own flourishing.

VII

I am ready now to return to my earlier claim that unjustly privileged people—or at least those who are uncritical of their privilege—are structurally enabled

37. I find Young 2000 promising for addressing these questions.

38. Others have also considered whether one can derive a requirement for inclusivity or justice from eudaimonism. Brink 1997 contends that "there are good eudaimonist reasons for recognizing a more inclusive common good than Aristotle does" (1997, 150). His argument rests on claims about "interpersonal self-extension" that he conceives as parallel to the continued personal identity of a single self through time; that is, one extends oneself by investing oneself in or contributing to the projects of others, no matter how distant those others may be. I do not find his argument to be convincing but will not argue the point here. See also Brink 1990. See Nelson 1996 for a consideration of whether eudaimonism—focused on the question "how should a person live in order to achieve a happy life?" (1996, 247)—can by itself yield a requirement for justice.

to think of themselves as good and to think of their lives as happy lives. I pointed out earlier that if one thinks about vice as limited to marginal members of society, one might imagine—as Sumner does—a formal mechanism to prevent these vicious people's traits from counting (at least subjectively) as traits that contribute to happiness. But my focus on members of dominant groups uncovers a class of people who, precisely because of their dominant positionings and their acts of exclusion that parallel those of Aristotle's leisured Greek gentlemen, are able to have their character traits—which include what I have referred to as the ordinary vices of domination—appear as acceptable or even good and to have their lives count as good lives. I have in mind two specific ways in which exclusion enables the privileged to exhibit the ordinary vices of domination (injustice, cruelty, lack of compassion, greed, etc.) and yet still be happy (or one would even say they flourish, if one rejects the stipulation for inclusivity that would rule out describing their lives as flourishing and if one rejects the classification of their traits as vices). First, they are especially enabled to believe in their own moral goodness no matter what their actual character traits may be, and second, they are able to hold a conception of the good life that is consistent with the sort of life they lead and find widespread *intersubjective* agreement to confirm their sense of what the good life is.

Believing in one's own moral goodness regardless of its actual absence is facilitated by what I think of as a "meta-vice," namely, indifference or, more specifically, indifference to the (preventable and unjust) suffering of certain others.[39] People actively occupying unjust positions of power tend to exhibit selective indifference to suffering—selective because as I pointed out earlier they may be able to feel compassion for certain others, typically others positioned in some ways like themselves. But they cannot allow themselves to be moved by the situations of those whose suffering is tied, directly or indirectly, to the very positions and privileges they actively work to maintain. Being moved in this way would disrupt their sense of themselves as morally good. Thus the husband who does not believe his wife's "second shift" taking care of the children and the household constitutes an unfair level of extra work must remain indifferent to her exhaustion; the advocates of punitive welfare reform policies must avoid facing the realities of how anguishing it is to have to put one's child in inadequate care or even leave one's child dangerously unsupervised while one works a minimum-wage job. There are structural features of an oppressive society that help privileged people simply not to notice the problems that disadvantaged people face. For instance, as Iris Young has pointed out, residential racial segregation prevents those who live in predominantly white neighborhoods from perceiving in any detailed way how their quality of life differs from that of the residents of predominantly black or Latino neighborhoods. Young writes:

39. I extensively consider the phenomenon of indifference in the next chapter.

> The very same process that produces . . . relations of privilege . . . obscures that privilege from those who have it. In order to see themselves as privileged, the white people who live in more pleasant neighbourhoods must be able to compare their environment with others. But this comparison is rarely forced upon them because those excluded from access to the resources and benefits they themselves have are spatially separated and out of sight. (2000, 208)

The freedom from noticing the suffering that their own advantages depend on enables indifference.

Indifference of the sort I have been describing is a vice that facilitates other vices, for it permits its bearer to think of her/himself as a good person by masking the effects of her/his unjust, cruel, callous, dishonest, and so on actions. If a remaining link between virtue and well-being lies in the fact that *thinking* of oneself as a morally good person contributes to one's own happiness, then it will be important for members of privileged groups to be able to sustain an image of themselves as good.

Believing oneself to be living a good life is also—in the absence of the ancient Greek reliance on an objective account of what the good life is—going to be partly constitutive of actually living a good life. Contemporary virtue theorists tend to accept that the modern conception of happiness is simply subjective and accept a life that is self-assessed as a good life to actually be a good life. I contend that—without being led to abandon democratic freedoms in search of a commonly held and publicly enforced conception of the good—one can still aim to have accounts of happiness or of a good life that are supported by *intersubjective* agreement within some community of sense (and this is in part why I recommend identifying and articulating the sense of flourishing implicit in liberatory politics). Members of dominant groups tend to find this intersubjective agreement easily, for their communities of sense can readily include only others similar to themselves in the relevant respects. Their views are reflected by the versions of bourgeois ideology that permeate the societies they live in. Sumner portrays vicious agents as relying only on their own subjective sense of how good they are and what a good life they are leading—or perhaps finding their subjective sense informed or confirmed by sources that are clearly illegitimate from the point of view of most members of society. However, members of dominant groups find their own conceptions supported by wide—and powerful, dominant—segments of society. These views cannot easily be dismissed as "inauthentic" (without offering in their place an objective account of the good), though it might be fruitful to try to use—as many feminist theorists have—complicated arguments about epistemic privilege in order to try to show that dominant beliefs are inauthentic in Sumner's sense: either lacking correct factual information or lacking autonomy from coercively imposed ideologies.[40]

40. For a critique of the use of the concept of epistemic privilege, see Bar On 1993.

Not only do members of dominant groups experience widespread intersubjective agreement about what the good life is, but this agreement has a certain character to it. The ideology that undergirds this conception of the good life is one that promotes meritocracy and competitive individualism and sees "success" as the attainment of self-interested rather than collective goals. An important feature of this intersubjectively supported account of the good life is the belief that—contrary to what the bumper sticker wishfully declares—some *can* be free while others are oppressed. Even if one assumes as Aristotle does that sociality is required by humans—and especially if as an individualist one rejects the implications of this assumption—one can believe that flourishing takes place alongside (or even through) exclusion.

VIII

Even without fully depending on the concept of epistemic privilege, one can still note that there are certain epistemic requirements for being able to live well despite—or because of—one's vices. Both being able to think of oneself as morally good and being able to sustain the intersubjectively confirmed understanding of the good life as one that does *not* depend on the flourishing of all requires an epistemic isolation; knowledge cannot be gained from outside of the boundaries of groups of people similarly committed to maintaining their privilege.

This claim is consistent with, for instance, Charles Mills's description in *The Racial Contract* of the epistemological contract that he sees as part of the overall racial contract that the supporters of white supremacy endorse. Those who are "signatories" to the racial contract (and who become its beneficiaries on account of the whiteness that they assign to themselves) must agree to maintain an ignorance about the racial order: "one has to agree to *mis*interpret the world . . . *on matters related to race, the Racial Contract prescribes for its signatories an inverted epistemology, an epistemology of ignorance*" (1997, 18). Similarly, María Lugones has observed that white feminists often maintain an epistemology of ignorance about their own place in the racial order; specifically, she points out that white feminists are afraid of knowing the selves they are in the eyes of women of color and afraid of identifying with these selves precisely because doing so would undermine their sense of themselves as morally good. She writes, "[Y]ou do not expect us to show a self that is good, decent, sensitive, careful in your attending to others. . . . You know a self that is decent and good and knowing your self in our mirror frightens you with losing your center, your integrity, your oneness" (1991, 42). The epistemology of ignorance, to use Mills's phrase, contributes to the well-being of members of privileged groups both because it allows them to believe themselves to be more virtuous than they are (which is important if having an image of oneself as morally good is partly constitutive of happiness), and because it facilitates the illusion that all is well in the world, that the good life can be achieved by some, consistent with the deprivation of others.

Thus, one can live well while others suffer, and one can have one's sense of well-being affirmed by the intersubjective agreement of others who like oneself reject the requirement for inclusivity. But this is an agreement that I would argue ought to be refused. What to recommend in its place is harder to say. In conjunction with the stipulation that the sociality that enables flourishing must be an inclusive sociality, I would like to suggest the cultivation of a (meta-) virtue that would stand opposed to the (meta-)vice of indifference: a disposition that would leave one sensitive to others' well-being or lack thereof; I say this with caution, however, for *excess* in the direction of such sensitivity leaves one in a constant state of anguish.[41] There is such great suffering to face.

41. This elusive virtue in the realm of sensitivity and attention to others' suffering is the focus of the next chapter.

4

Between Indifference and Anguish

I

Immediately after my daughter was born, I began to experience—and still do though it has become blunted and much less constant—what might be described as an excess of sensitivity to others' suffering. It was the fall of 2000, and an(other) intifada was starting up in Israel/Palestine; every night on the news there were scenes of Palestinian boys and young men being shot at, then bombed, by the Israeli Defense Force, and even more detailed portrayals of the Israelis who were killed or wounded. Watching it was anguishing: every person, especially but not only the young among them, was somebody's child, somebody's baby. I held my own newborn baby, Yuval, and envisioned in tiny flashes the terrifying and unbearable possibility that someone might hurt her. With every new report of an injury or death I moved to imagining myself as that parent, losing my baby. All that loss! The level of pain was unfathomable.

While many people, perhaps especially (new) parents, may have experiences of extreme sensitivity to others' suffering, I had never quite believed accounts of such sensitive states. Feminist theories based on supposed sensitive and nurturing dispositions of mothers seemed implausible to me, so I tended to dismiss out of hand a wide range of work, such as Sara Ruddick's (1989) on "maternal thinking" that was to be gleaned for its potential in resisting militarism, or Nel Noddings's (1984) portrait of mothers' "natural caring" for their children as a basis for a moral disposition of care. I considered these to be essentializing theories that associated women too strongly with mothering or that depended on positing enduring gender traits and in so doing ran counter to feminist aims.

In retrospect, though, I do not think that my rejection of these theories was really due (only) to their essentializing of gendered character traits, or their presupposing rather stereotypical kinds of gendering, or their assuming that women would engage in mothering and other care-taking relationships, though these are the sorts of explanations I had for discounting the theories.[1] Even if there actually are good theoretical reasons for being cautious with these theories or for engaging quite critically with them, the theoretical critique is not what interests me right now, because there is a psychologically based explanation for my failure to take these theories seriously: I used to be fundamentally unable to believe that the character trait of being extremely sensitive to others' suffering actually *existed* (gendered or not).

As it turns out, it does seem to exist. I do not want to argue here for any general connection between the disposition I am describing—some form of extreme sensitivity to others' suffering or, in its milder form, an enhanced capacity for caring or compassion—and gender, or the experience of mothering or parenting. I am still quite wary of essentializing something about gender here. But I do want to consider and worry about the moral status of the disposition in its extreme form.

A couple of years before I began to have this experience of oversensitivity to others' suffering, I had begun to be struck by the terribleness of what I think of as its opposite pole: extreme indifference to others' suffering. Encountering this other pole did not take something as special as bearing a child; all it took was reading the right book at the right time. The right book was Norman Geras's 1998 *The Contract of Mutual Indifference: Political Philosophy after the Holocaust*, and it was the right time because I had finally gained enough distance from my assimilated upbringing to be willing to associate myself with people whom I had previously thought disparagingly of as "those Jews who never stop talking about the Holocaust." Finally talking about the Holocaust meant facing the fact of the indifference of bystanders. Religious Jews can ask why God seemed to abandon the Jews during the Holocaust, but Jewish atheists like myself can only ask: why did so many other human beings stand by? And then one is led to ask the question that has become almost cliché in so many Jewish contexts: why am I and so many others standing by while other atrocities happen across the globe? Norman Geras creates a powerful effect in the way he poses this question. He draws on testimony to illustrate cases of bystanders going on about their normal lives while the Nazis carried out their exterminations, and then he moves to the present, citing case after case of torture as described in Amnesty International literature. He characterizes the background conditions for such torture as the bystander phenomenon, emblematic of what he calls a *contract of mutual indifference*. I was not only moved by his writing, I was emotionally caught; compelled by some mixture of compassion and a desire to assuage my own guilt, I sent a check off to Amnesty before the day was over. The effect lasted and before I knew it I had signed up to have monthly payments to Amnesty charged to my credit card: a steady drip that functioned to drain from me some of the pain and guilt and that perhaps ended a tiny bit of suffering

1. The theories themselves largely handle such critiques by stating that "mothers" need not be female and that many actual mothers fail to exhibit the qualities in question, or by asserting that mothering should only be taken as an instance, not necessarily a paradigmatic case, of care.

somewhere in the world.[2] Much as I knew that sending money was no substitute for political activism, I also could not stop the payments; to do so would be to enter even more deeply into the horrifying realm of indifference. Indeed, even during the course of writing this chapter a mailing came to me from Doctors without Borders and as I read the first few lines ("Dear Friend: In the Doctors Without Borders/Médecins Sans Frontières hospital in Kailahun, Sierra Leone, I am shocked into silence as Sia tells me, 'I was just a girl and very beautiful when the war found me and my family. I was raped more times than I can count'"),[3] I instantly felt the bombardment: from one side the horror at the thought of my own indifference if I threw the letter as fast as I could into the recycling bin, from the other side the anguish I expected to feel if I read the rest of the letter and let it touch me, knowing that even if I responded as fully as I could, it would never be enough.

My encounters with these two poles, namely, extreme indifference and extreme sensitivity to others' suffering, have led me to this chapter. What I intend to do here is to reflect on the uncomfortable moral status of the whole range of dispositions in the sphere of sensitivity to others' suffering. It is strikingly clear that the poles that lie at the distant points of this sphere are morally unacceptable; indifference is morally horrifying and extreme sensitivity is psychically unsustainable. Thus I should, if I am to act in my usual Aristotelian fashion, attempt to find the mean between these two awful extremes. However, what I am discovering is that there is no mean state anywhere between these two extremes that is morally praiseworthy in any simple way. I find all of the sites on this spectrum of dispositions to be troubling, though not all horrify or lead to collapse.

II

I will begin by identifying more precisely the sphere with which I am concerned. For Aristotle, distinct virtues are found within spheres of actions or feelings; the virtue is generally at a mean or intermediate point between two extremes, the *contraries*. For instance, in the sphere of certain pleasures and

2. For information on Amnesty International, see www.amnesty.org.
3. The next paragraph continues:

> In a displaced camp in Liberia, where Doctors Without Borders is running a medical clinic and a feeding program for severely malnourished children, I am drawn to a newly arrived young mother who looks like my sister. We start to talk and I see that she is not okay. She rocks back and forth holding her skeletal child in her arms, their blank eyes staring out at nothing. "We have been running from the fighters for six months," she tells me. "It has been very, very bad. I cannot tell you everything that happened to me because it will only make me cry. This is the last of my family still alive," she says, motioning to the baby. "Will he die too?" She is only 18. (From a Doctors without Borders direct mailing, August 2002)

The letter was written by Martha Carey, a volunteer. For information on Doctors without Borders, see www.doctorswithoutborders.org.

pains, one finds the contraries of self-indulgence (licentiousness) and insensibility and the mean of temperance; the sphere of anger has extremes of irascibility and inirascibility (lack of spirit) and a mean of good temper (patience) (*NE* bk. II, chap. 7). While Aristotle is quite concerned to emphasize that in most cases (though there are exceptions) the virtue is a mean, his assumption even prior to this claim is simply that within each sphere there *is* some virtuous disposition. There is some morally praiseworthy way and quantity in which to experience bodily pleasures, some morally praiseworthy type and level of anger that one should feel and on which one should act, and so on in every sphere.

I am interested in a sphere within which Aristotle did not develop specific prescriptive claims: the sphere of sensitivity and attention to others' suffering.[4] Like Aristotle's spheres, it covers both a feeling and associated actions, in this case actions of attending in some way to suffering. There are many kinds of suffering, but I am focused only on suffering that is tied to injustice (including oppression, domination, and exploitation) and that is thus necessarily a result of human actions and potentially preventable. The suffering of poverty, child abuse, violence against women, political torture, slavery, and genocide are all examples. The suffering that one goes through when a loved one dies a natural or accidental death is not the sort of suffering I have in mind. And, I am more interested in thinking about great sufferings than small ones: I suffer in a way that is tied to injustice when someone makes a sexist remark to me on the street, but this is not a great suffering. I will hereafter mean great and unjust sufferings when I refer to *suffering*.

Is there, in this sphere of sensitivity and attention to others' suffering, any morally praiseworthy disposition? I am not concerned here to ascertain that such a virtue would lie in the mean; I am worrying about the more basic question of whether or not there *is* such a virtue. Is there anywhere in this sphere that one can comfortably settle, morally speaking?

There is much suffering in the world. That simple fact—which most of us block out most of the time—will be the premise that problematizes the search for a morally praiseworthy disposition in the realm of sensitivity to others' suffering. In the face of terrible suffering—suffering that could be prevented if only human institutions were more just—one grasps for strong-enough language of moral condemnation to describe those who are completely indifferent. To use Aristotle's language, they seem to cross the line from vice to brutishness, in the sense of "those who surpass ordinary men in vice" (*NE* 1145a32). Because a deficiency in noticing and attending to others' suffering (or an excess of indifference toward it) is the more common moral failing in this sphere, one will be

4. As I discuss below, Aristotle's "pity" is the passion that is akin to—though different from, in important respects—the sensitivity to others' suffering that I am analyzing. He does include pity in a list of passions that he says ought to be felt moderately (*NE* 1106b19–23); however, he does not go on to give more detailed prescriptions for pity, as he does for the other passions (fear, anger, etc.) in this listing. Contemporary theorists who are confident that there is a virtue in the sphere with which I am concerned tend to call it *compassion*.

led, following Aristotle's methods, to search for the virtue nearer to the other pole. All the way at the other pole, what one finds is a disposition that ultimately destroys the life or at least the well-being of the agent her/himself. One finds a self so immersed in the boundless pain of others—and so exhausted with the efforts of ameliorating that pain—that no piece of the self is left free to experience joy or to flourish.

Imagine now an intermediate point. Any such point is at once too indifferent and too anguished. Suppose, for instance, that I open myself compassionately toward a moderate number of those who are suffering: I feel with them their hardships and the insult of the mistreatments they bear, and I am moved to intervene and struggle against the injustices that cause them to suffer or I at least work to directly provide them with some means of survival or healing. Suppose I do this just toward those who suffer from some particular injustice in some particular place—say, abused or neglected children in the city in upstate New York where I live. Now remember the fact that I started with: there is much suffering in the world. As I focus on these children, I turn away from an enormity of other atrocities. I ignore evidence that my government or another utilizes torture; I do not think about refugees who lack food and medicine; I pass by homeless people. I force myself into this daily indifference for my own self-protection: I must not become overwhelmed by all that need. Meanwhile, I *am* overwhelmed. That tiny number of sufferers on whom I concentrate have enough pain so that, if I open to it, I am filled with their anguish. If someone notices my constant anguish, they will urge me to use less of my energy on the needy; I should go out and enjoy myself more or focus on my family or my work. I should, it seems, know how to ignore others' suffering better. Someone else will at the same time notice how appallingly little I attend to others' suffering: am I doing nothing for prisoners' rights, nothing for immigrant workers exploited and endangered in sweatshops? Now it seems clear that I should be morally condemned for failing to act in the face of all the suffering that results from injustice. And, they will both be right: at any intermediate point in the sphere of sensitivity and attention to others' suffering, I can be characterized as both excessively anguished and excessively indifferent.

That this is the case should not be surprising, though it breaks Aristotle's model. It breaks the model precisely because of there being so much suffering in the world that one could potentially face. Ignoring any of the suffering that one could potentially attend to requires indifference, a refusal to respond to others who are in "dire need or great distress" (Geras 1998, 26), a cold turning away; it is not just that one cannot *do* anything about everyone's suffering, one cannot even sorrow for all sufferers. Turning one's back on any single instance of great suffering is morally problematic and in a world with masses of suffering people one necessarily turns one's back on many. Meanwhile, being fully sensitive and responsive to just a small portion of the suffering population requires taking on enormous pain. The background conditions of the world we live in make it impossible to escape both the horror of indifference and the psychic pain (and perhaps exhaustion) of sensitivity and attention.

In Aristotle's schema, no such background conditions are considered. His is a eudaimonistic theory, according to which the pursuit of one's own flourishing (through the use of practical reason and the cultivation of the virtues) is morally praiseworthy. As I pointed out in the previous chapter, Aristotle's assumption is that in the course of pursuing one's own flourishing, one necessarily contributes to that of others, because members of a *polis* depend on one another and on one another's virtues and well-being in order to flourish. But, as I argued there, this interdependence is limited and permits those who are fully included in the *polis* to be indifferent to the well-being of those who are excluded and to do so without detracting from their own virtue or flourishing. In part because the conditions of the world were different in Aristotle's time and in part because he ignored what took place among those excluded from or outside of his elite society, Aristotle never pondered the moral problems associated with great and far-reaching suffering.[5] If one adds to a eudaimonistic theory the requirement (that I proposed in chapter 3) that a trait that contributes to one's own flourishing will only qualify for moral praise if one's own flourishing is understood as connected with the flourishing of an inclusive social collectivity, then the present level of suffering seems to undermine everyone's potential virtue in the realm I have been discussing: if one fails to be inclusive with one's attention to suffering, one falls into indifference, but utter exhaustion of oneself would be reached before one ever succeeded at inclusion. The stipulation for inclusivity seems to present an unattainable demand, a demand felt by those who commit to pursuing only those versions of flourishing that are consistent with the flourishing of all.

In Aristotle's closed society the virtues that benefit primarily the self and those that benefit primarily others could converge: the fact of interdependence (within the *polis*) makes it odd to center the concept of self-interest or to promote the idea that politics is primarily about adjudicating between conflicting interests and claims. A contemporary radical politics may reflect similar assumptions when it rejects individualism and strives for the recognition of interdependence and the creation of public or collective goods. Radicals may be tempted to deny the relevance of the distinction between the self-regarding and the other-regarding virtues, in an insistence that the good of the self is tied to the good of others.[6] However, recognizing the atrocious level of injustice and consequent suffering in the world, and acknowledging how the self who tries to respond to this suffering can her/himself be destroyed by it, highlights a new way in which self-regarding and other-regarding virtues can diverge. Toward the pole of indifference, one sacrifices the other-regarding virtues in an attempt to preserve narrowly regarded self-interests, but toward the pole of extreme sensitivity and attention to others' suffering, while one's other-regarding virtues may peak, one forfeits important self-regarding virtues. It seems that one cannot care adequately for oneself as one

5. However, as Nussbaum (1986) has argued, Aristotle did shape his ethical and political theories on an awareness of the vulnerability of human life and human virtue to war, unjust enslavement, and political instability, and he does acknowledge that great suffering can interfere with both being good and leading the good life. See Nussbaum 1986, chap. 12, sec. 1. Nevertheless, the question of how to respond well to the enormity of others' suffering is not a focus for Aristotle.

6. For a full discussion of self-regarding and other-regarding virtues, see chapter 3.

gives oneself over to caring for all those whose lives are truly wretched. If one's own well-being is really tied up with the well-being of *all* others—as the requirement of inclusivity would suggest—then none of us will ever live well in any foreseeable future, for it is inconceivable that across the globe unjust suffering will be eradicated. It seems that the only way to attain or preserve one's own well-being—if one is lucky enough to not be among those who are victims of great injustice—is to separate one's well-being sufficiently from the plight of those who suffer. One of the special features of virtue ethics is that it does allow one to value the well-being of oneself. Other moral frameworks may see the self-sacrificing martyr as particularly laudable; virtue ethics for the most part would see the self whose life has been ruined by taking on the anguish of others' suffering as someone who has had the great misfortune of encountering conditions that make flourishing, and possibly even virtue, impossible.[7]

I have suggested that the conditions of our world require that one be either too indifferent or too anguished or both. Because every possible intermediate point in the sphere of sensitivity and attention to others' suffering is marked by indifference and anguish, I am reluctant to characterize any point as an excellent one in any unqualified sense. Every point sacrifices either the other-regarding virtues or the self-regarding virtues or both. This is not to deny that there are levels of noticing and attending to suffering that are, morally, the best possible levels to choose. Rather, my claim is that simple excellence is not possible in this sphere given the background conditions and that even the best choices fail to enable flourishing and may even fail to preserve virtue itself.

Rosalind Hursthouse's discussion of tragic dilemmas points in a similar direction. In asking what the virtuous agent does in cases where the available alternatives are all terrible ones, Hursthouse follows a line of thinking begun by others who have analyzed tragic dilemmas.[8] I draw on her work here because she frames her question more specifically in terms offered by virtue ethics. She points out that the virtuous agent may, when facing a tragic dilemma, perform the best possible (or one of the best possible) actions given the constraints of the situation, but that if the choices are truly terrible then even these actions will fail to be good and the agent will fail to act well, as one would expect a virtuous agent to act. Nevertheless, the virtuous agent, Hursthouse claims, can be distinguished from the vicious even if they both perform the same actions when

7. Aristotle does expect certain virtues to require sacrifice—even the sacrifice of life itself, and therefore sacrifice of the opportunity for further virtuous activity. The courageous soldier who dies in battle sacrifices all and yet is to be morally praised (*NE* 1117b7–15). And, in friendship a virtuous man may sacrifice nobly for the sake of his friend (*NE* 1169a18–b2). What is supposed to make these actions ultimately not sacrificial is that the agent gains moral benefit from the nobility of the actions (though it is hard to fathom what this moral benefit is like for one who has sacrificed her/his life, and even in the case of one who has not gone this far, Aristotle should recognize that the sacrifice of positively valued external goods is still significant for the possibility of the agent's well-being). See Rogers 1994, who worries about "how choosing a noble but fatal course can be intelligibly described as a choice motivated by happiness" (1994, 306).

8. See, for instance, Williams 1973.

facing terrible possibilities. As she puts it, the virtuous agent, when made to choose one terrible course of action over another, "does not act callously, dishonestly, unjustly, that is, '*as* (in the manner) the callous, dishonest, unjust agent does.' She acts with immense regret and pain instead of indifferently or gladly, as the callous or dishonest or unjust one does" (1999, 73–74). This focus on the (negative) emotions recommended for the agent who has navigated a tragic dilemma echoes other accounts. Perhaps most significant is Bernard Williams's notion of a moral remainder that trails the "*ought* that is not acted upon" (1973, 175) when there are conflicting moral oughts; this remainder typically is experienced emotionally by the agent in the form of regret, which can be extreme when there are tragic cases. As Williams writes:

> The agonies that a man [*sic*] will experience after acting in full consciousness of such a situation are not to be traced to a persistent doubt that he may not have chosen the better thing; but, for instance, to a clear conviction that he has not done the better thing because there was no better thing to be done. (1973, 173)[9]

Hursthouse adds an important point about the effect of a tragic case on a virtuous agent:

> If a genuinely tragic dilemma is what a virtuous agent emerges from, it will be the case that she emerges having done a terrible thing, the very sort of thing that the callous, dishonest, unjust, or in general vicious agent would characteristically do—killed someone, or let them die, betrayed a trust, violated someone's serious rights. And hence it will not be possible to say that she has acted *well*. What follows from this is not the impossibility of virtue but the possibility of some situations from which even a virtuous agent cannot emerge with her life unmarred. (1999, 74)

I agree with Hursthouse that if one emerges from a tragic dilemma, one does so marred, despite there having been no course of action possible that would have been better than the one that one took: "the virtuous agent's life will be marred

9. See also Williams 1981a, where he further theorizes about moral conflicts:

> In [a tragic case] an agent can justifiably think that whatever he does will be wrong: that there are conflicting moral requirements, and that neither of them succeeds in overriding or outweighing the other. In this case, though it can actually emerge from deliberation that one of the courses of action is the one that, all things considered, one had better take, it is, and it remains, true that each of the courses of action is morally required, and at a level which means that, whatever he does, the agent will have reason to feel regret at the deepest level. (1981a, 74)

See also Williams 1981b, where he introduces the concept of agent-regret. Michael Stocker (1990, chap. 1, sec. 8) discusses regret as the proper response of the virtuous agent emerging with dirty hands from certain dilemmas, and Michael Walzer (1973) suggests guilt and shame. For a feminist argument for the value of guilt and remorse when a connection is broken as a result of cases of dirty hands or other moral dilemmas, see Bishop 1987.

or even ruined, haunted by sorrow that she had done *x*" (1999, 77). But there are some consequences of this description of tragic dilemmas that are even more serious than those that Hursthouse names.

There are two points that disturb me. First, I believe that if one's life is marred or even ruined, or if one is overtaken with regret and sorrow at the thought of a terrible action that one has performed, one's character may be in jeopardy. That is, in some terrible cases, not just one's life but also one's character will have been transformed; one will be pained, regretful, and overwhelmingly sorrowful. Martha Nussbaum (1986) has discussed the ways in which Aristotle recognizes the possibility that excellent character itself can be diminished through relentless bouts of terrible luck, including encounters with those situations that force a virtuous agent into dilemmas requiring a choice between evils. While ordinary misfortunes are survivable with virtue—and even a good life—intact, truly disastrous luck destroys the opportunity for flourishing either by impeding virtuous activity or, even more seriously, by eroding good character itself.[10]

There is a second disturbing implication of Hursthouse's discussion that she does not draw out: tragic dilemmas do not present themselves only in rare and isolated incidents (though one can think of distinct cases that are stunningly devastating, such as "Sophie's choice" of sending one of her children or the other to death).[11] If my characterization above of the fact of suffering in the world is accurate enough, then we all face tragic dilemmas as a regular condition of our lives: unless we are completely indifferent (in which case we clearly lack virtue), we must always be asking ourselves whose suffering to tend to and whose to turn away from, which injustices to try to remedy and which to ignore, daily making the horrifying decision to let hundreds or thousands or millions suffer as a result of our inaction. We constantly face conditions in which we must act terribly. Thus if my first concern is valid, namely, if tragic dilemmas not only result in the marring of one's life but also in the transformation of one's character into one so pained that it cannot be called virtuous, then virtue—not to mention flourishing—is essentially always out of reach under the current conditions. It is wrong to pass painlessly through the dilemmas of attending to or ignoring others' suffering—this is the moral wrong of indifference—but to take on the pain of others and the pain or guilt of knowing how many more one has necessarily turned away from is to live a life so filled with regret and sorrow that virtue, and flourishing, are ruled out.[12]

10. See Nussbaum 1986, chap. 11, sec. v.

11. See Pakula 1982.

12. In pointing out that under current conditions of pervasive injustice and suffering there is a steady stream of tragic dilemmas with their consequent effects on the (perhaps formerly) virtuous agents who encounter them, I am portraying the world as quite different from the one Michael Stocker imagines hopefully when he remarks that dilemmas resulting in dirty hands could be eliminated if only the world were a better place:

> It does seem possible, even if humanly very unlikely, to live and act without having to suffer the losses of dirty hands. At the least, it does seem possible, even if humanly very

III

The agent who is destroyed by the demands of constantly attending to others' suffering may plausibly be said to have eliminated the self-regarding virtues to the point where her/his own flourishing is impossible. However, what can the virtue ethicist say about an agent who is sensitive and attentive to others' suffering in moderation? Such an agent can be characterized as too indifferent—for to choose a moderate level of response to great suffering is to choose to let masses of people suffer as a result of one's own failure to choose a higher level of response. But this characterization by itself seems to suggest that the agent who is moderately sensitive to others' suffering and who undertakes some limited actions to ameliorate this suffering is at least more virtuous than one who is even more indifferent. Because it seems that some compassion is better than none, one might be tempted to describe sensitivity to suffering as a virtue precisely when it does occur in moderation.

However, the trait of being sensitive and attentive to others' suffering—even in moderation—is odd as a virtue, because it is an intrinsically painful disposition. It is possible that there are ways of being responsive to others' suffering that do not entail feeling (their) pain,[13] and certainly one can engage in actions of fighting injustice without actually being sensitively attuned to the suffering that one is trying to end or prevent.[14] However, the trait I am examining *does* involve taking on the pain of others. There are several distinct reasons that it could be problematic to be pained by someone else's suffering or to allow that pain a place in politics.[15] I am looking here only at one problem with such pain, one that is suggested by the complex Aristotelian connection between virtue and pleasure.

> unlikely, that we do not create immoral situations which necessitate dirty hands. . . . The demand that it must be possible for us to be good and also innocent, and also to retain emotional wholeness, is not a demand for a conceptually or even a morally coherent morality. It is, rather, a demand for something else—a morally good world or at least not an evil or bad world. (1990, 33–34)

13. Martha Nussbaum considers whether one could have the judgments involved in compassion without experiencing the painful emotion itself. See Nussbaum 2001, 322–327.

14. Sandra Bartky (1997) argues that what may be best to motivate and accompany political activism is not a lack of sensitivity to others' suffering, but a certain kind of "feeling-with" suggested by the phenomenology of Max Scheler. Part of her concern—which I share—is that one not become so overwhelmed by the sympathetic feelings that one is destroyed (and also then deterred from political activism).

15. Bartky 1997 lays out many of the troubling possibilities. Bartky also refers to Spelman 1988 (see 178–182), who cautions against using imagination to construct in one's mind another's suffering. Spelman 1997 develops several other concerns about taking on another's suffering; many of the problems are located in the political purposes to which one can put someone else's suffering that one has made one's own. Spelman also discusses Hannah Arendt's insistence that compassion have no place in political life (see Arendt 1958 and 1963).

Aristotle's word for the emotion of being pained by another person's suffering is (translated from *eleos* as) "pity"; the term for him carries no connotations of condescension, but it is limited in some different ways, including that one can only feel it in response to someone's suffering if one fears being subject to similar suffering oneself. He writes, "Pity may be defined as a feeling of pain at an apparent evil, destructive or painful, which befalls one who does not deserve it, and which we might expect to befall ourselves or some friend of ours, and moreover to befall us soon" (*Rhet.* 1385b13–16). One can see immediately how the limitation on the scope of pity—developed further in Aristotle's discussion in the *Poetics* about the proper subject of tragedy, the "mode of imitation" that aims to "arous[e] pity and fear" (*Poet.* 1449b27–28)—makes Aristotle in one way not very helpful for my thinking about how one might respond to great and far-reaching sufferings, including sufferings that one never expects to experience oneself.[16] Furthermore, for Aristotle, pity is not especially meant to make one responsive to the person whose suffering one apprehends; rather, it turns one back to oneself and to a fear of the evil befalling oneself.[17] However, Aristotle's pity is similar in a relevant respect to the sensitivity to others' suffering that I have been trying to describe: he calls it a *feeling of pain*.

Aristotle does not ask whether or in what way being disposed to feel pity is a virtue; he names pity as one of the passions as distinguished from a faculty or a state (*NE* 1105b21–25). To think about the relationship of pity to virtue, Aristotle would have to think about the state—that is, one of "the things in virtue of which we stand well or badly with reference to the passions" (*NE* 1105b25–26)—corresponding to the passion of pity, and this he does not do when he names virtues in different spheres. Had he done so he would be led to ask how one ought to stand against pity, feeling it strongly or weakly, in relation to all other undeserving sufferers or just some particular others, and so on. When Aristotle does discuss the states in which one feels pity, he describes rather than evaluates those states, noting that pity is "not felt by those completely ruined, who suppose that no further evil can befall them . . . nor by those who imagine themselves immensely fortunate" (*Rhet.* 1385b19–22). It is rather felt by those who have survived prior evils, those who have had many years of experience, those who are especially fearful or especially educated (and thus knowledgeable about possible evils), and—perhaps most poignantly—those who love and therefore could have evils befall those they love: "those who have parents living, or children, or wives; for these are our own, and the evils . . . may easily befall them" (*Rhet.*

16. See Spelman 1997, chap. 2, for a discussion of the way Aristotle's *Poetics* guards against having certain others, such as slaves, be the subjects of tragedy: "if we are citizens we needn't pity slaves simply for being slaves nor fear developing into natural slaves ourselves; and because their faults, and the events of their lives, neither of which could ever arise above the trivial, are so different from ours, we could never be moved to pity and fear in contemplating them" (1997, 45).

17. For a critique of the self-centeredness of Aristotle's account of pity, see Carr 1999. Carr also critiques Nussbaum 1996 for adopting Aristotle's account without rejecting its self-centeredness. (However, see footnote 26 in this chapter about how Nussbaum has revised her 1996 position.)

1385b24–29). Furthermore, one only feels pity if one believes that at least some people are good and therefore undeserving of evil (*Rhet.* 1385b35–1386a2).

Had Aristotle considered the virtue in the sphere of pity, he would have run into an interesting complication (similar, as I will explore momentarily, to a complication that clouds the virtue of courage): the morally praiseworthy trait in this sphere—being disposed to feel and act on the proper sorts and levels of pity in the appropriate contexts—would involve pain, in addition to the pleasure attendant upon the thought of performing well. Even a moderate level of being sensitive to or moved by the suffering of others is intrinsically painful.

Pleasure and pain can play complicated roles in virtuous action. In simple cases, the virtuous agent feels only pleasure, namely, pleasure at the thought of carrying out the right action. For example, the liberal man gives in all the right ways (to the right people, the right amount, and so on) "with pleasure or without pain; for that which is excellent is pleasant or free from pain—least of all will it be painful" (*NE* 1120a26–28); here what is emphasized is the delight at the thought of the nobility of giving. This sort of pleasure does not admit of excess; it is always right to feel pleasure at the thought of good action. But there is also a different sort of pleasure, a sort that, if excessive or inappropriate in some other way, can lead one *away* from proper action. Sarah Broadie makes the distinction between these two sorts of pleasure as follows, using as an example the virtue of temperance:

> When Aristotle says that the temperate person delights or takes pleasure in temperate actions, meaning that they are engaged in gladly and with satisfaction, he is referring to an attitude *consequential* upon seeing the action as good or proper and as what it would be noble to do or shameful not to; whereas pleasures that can clash with the noble are felt to be pleasures independently of the rightness of pursuing them. (1991, 93–94)

In the case of pleasures that potentially "clash with the noble," the best approach is to moderate them (or eliminate them, if they are pleasures that one should not have at all) by habituating oneself to have the right desires. The temperate man, according to Aristotle, feels (the right kind of) pleasure at the thought of eating moderately and wholesomely (*NE* 1104b5–6); his most relevant pleasure is the gladness or delight that he feels at choosing properly how to eat or indulge in other physical pleasures. But ideally he also has habituated his actual tastes so that overindulging would not even bring (physical) pleasure (*NE* 1119a11–20). Pain or the threat of pain can play a role similar to that played by the kind of pleasure that may "clash with the noble," for someone may choose the wrong action in order to avoid pain, as, for instance, the coward does (*NE* bk. III, chaps. 6–7).

It is important for the virtuous agent to be habituated to feel the right pleasures because generally speaking people desire pleasure (and avoid pain) and are moved by desire, and therefore they are moved by the anticipation of pleasure and are deterred by pain: "to feel delight and pain rightly or wrongly has no small effect on our actions" (*NE* 1105a6–7). It is possible to act against pleasure by acting against one's desires; this is what the continent or strong-willed agent does. However, the better scenario is to have become habituated to have the right desires and to be able to act in accordance with these desires. Thus in the case of a typical virtue the exercise of the virtue is pleasurable both in the sense of its immediate pleasures and in the sense of those pleasures that follow from recognizing the action as excellent.

The virtue in the sphere of sensitivity and attention to others' suffering (or, for Aristotle, in the sphere of pity), then, would present a challenging case because the pain inherent in what would be the virtue in this sphere is something that ought *not* to be eliminated: the feeling of the pain is itself morally prescribed.[18] Courage presents a similar challenge in that the exercise of courage involves facing what is painful. The brave man "is fearless in face of a noble death" (*NE* 1115a32–33); in other words, he fears that which (and only that which) ought to be most feared, that is, death, and he chooses to face death despite his fear when the death is a noble one. There is pleasure in the thought of the end, namely, the noble, but there is pain in the death (or injury) itself. Aristotle remarks: "It is for facing what is painful . . . that men are called brave. Hence also courage involves pain, and is justly praised; for it is harder to face what is painful than to abstain from what is pleasant" (*NE* 1117a32–35). Recognizing that the exercise of courage is painful even leads Aristotle to acknowledge—though not fully to consider the implications of—the theoretical tension this creates; he comments: "It is not the case, then, with all the excellences that the exercise of them is pleasant, except in so far as it reaches its end" (*NE* 1117b15–16).

I am suggesting that being sensitive and attentive to others' suffering parallels courage in that both are intrinsically painful. Sensitivity and attention to others' suffering entails taking on others' pain, being pained by their pain; one's actual felt pain is part of the response to the other that constitutes the morally recommended responsive action. What, then, are the implications of there being traits whose praiseworthiness depends on and requires that the bearer of the trait experience pain? One might think that since the (most) relevant pleasure is the sort that Broadie describes as "*consequential* upon seeing the action as good or proper" (1991, 93), one should not worry so much about the immediate pains involved in sensitivity and attention to others' suffering (or in courage). However, to think this is to ignore the fact that *both* sorts of pleasure (or absence of great pain) are important for Aristotle, though in different ways.

The pleasure of doing what is right—or taking delight in the very goodness or nobility of one's action—is the pleasure that properly accompanies virtue for Aristotle; someone lacking this pleasure could not be called virtuous (even if they were to carry out the correct action). In contrast, someone experiencing physical (or other) pain *could* still count as virtuous as long as they gladly faced this pain for the sake of the virtuous action. Physical or other immediate pains

18. Some may even think it problematic in the case of this trait to feel the kind of pleasure that is consequent upon the thought of the goodness of one's own response. There is something repugnant about delighting in one's own goodness when that goodness is dependent on someone else's suffering; the suffering person becomes instrumental, a vehicle for one's own virtuous response. This is one of the concerns expressed by Spelman 1997, chap. 3.

may serve as deterrents to the exercise of virtues (such as courage or sensitivity to others' suffering), for virtues that are painful are harder to carry out; this is because, as mentioned above, people are usually moved by their desires and tend to desire pleasure and to avoid pain. Thus virtues that are pleasurable—at least to those who have been properly trained in which pleasures to feel—are easier to accomplish. But, if a person overcomes the difficulty of learning to gladly face pain for a noble end, that person may still attain the virtue. However, that a trait may count as a virtue is not all that matters for Aristotle; after all, *eudaimonia*, rather than virtue, is the end. Since conducive "external conditions"—in addition to virtue—are necessary for *eudaimonia* or flourishing, whatever affects or constitutes these conditions will matter quite a bit too. The sorts of pains that are inherent in the exercise of courage—or sensitivity and attention to others' suffering—could present impediments to flourishing, for if one does manage to cultivate and exercise the painful virtues, that very pain may constitute (and also reflect the presence of) the sort of external condition that Aristotle worried about interfering in flourishing. Aristotle contends that "those who say that the victim on the rack or the man who falls into great misfortunes is happy if he is good, are, whether they mean to or not, talking nonsense" (*NE* 1153b19–21). Those who are courageous—or, as I have been arguing, those who are disposed to be sensitive and attentive to others' suffering—are like the one who is being tortured on the rack: they may be especially virtuous, but they lack the external conditions (including the absence of great pain) needed for flourishing.

I am not claiming that there is anything problematic about having to sometimes or in small ways forgo even the best of (physical) pleasures or withstand pains in order to exercise a virtue. A good life need not be *free* from difficulty or pain. Aristotle agrees that everyday sorts of misfortunes do not bear on the goodness of a life (*NE* 1100b22–25). And, even in the case of those great misfortunes that seem like they could, "nobility shines through" (*NE* 1100b30). That is, there are virtues that specifically help one to bear such conditions, though "many great misadventures" (*NE* 1101a11) can ruin one, as it did Priam (*NE* 1100a6–8, 1101a7). However, while some level of pain may acceptably accompany a virtue, it is important that the virtues not be generally or overwhelmingly painful, because virtues enable a good life and a good life is one that includes the right pleasures. If virtues were usually painful, or if some particular virtue were especially painful *and* especially in demand, then cultivating the virtues would be such a painful endeavor that one could hardly connect virtue with the leading of a good life. If virtue were ordinarily coupled with pain, then the virtuous life would not typically be a flourishing life.

In chapter 1 I suggested that the character of those subjected to systemic bad moral luck may be morally damaged but that one might still try to identify and cultivate some virtues particularly suited for reflecting on (and carrying on within) one's own moral limitations, the very limitations that result from oppression; in this way "nobility shines through" (*NE* 1100b30) even the bad luck of oppression. Finding character traits that are intrinsically painful for the agent but that otherwise seem to be virtues—such as being disposed to be pained by another's suffering because one is sensitive and attentive to it—points now to another special set of traits related to oppression, traits whose status as virtues is murky in part because their value actually depends upon the presence of terrible conditions.

I have been suggesting throughout the previous chapters that oppression may be thought of as interfering with its victims' flourishing, both directly by creating adverse external circumstances and indirectly by undermining the possibility for some of the virtues. A third way now comes into sharper focus: some of the virtues that conditions of oppression intensify the need for—including the disposition to be sensitive and attentive to others' suffering—have a structure that is atypical for an Aristotelian virtue, that is, they are intrinsically painful (though according to Aristotle they would be salvageable as virtues because there is or should be pleasure in the "nobility" of their exercise). Given the fact of widespread and horrific suffering under conditions of oppression, it is morally wrong not to be pained, at least moderately. And yet the demand to cultivate a virtue that is intrinsically painful produces quite a burden, for as I have argued, the connection between virtue and flourishing would be hard to sustain if it were generally and not just occasionally the case that external conditions hindered virtue's power to enable the good life. If the pleasure of a virtuous action's nobility or goodness were typically accompanied by pain inherent in it, the connection between virtue and flourishing could be broken. As a result of oppression and the suffering that it causes, there is a constant pressure to exercise the intrinsically painful virtue of attending to that suffering. This pressure applies to those who are themselves oppressed—for they can still care about others who are oppressed in the same or different ways—and to those who at least in some ways escape oppression themselves. Thus, among the ways that oppression interferes with flourishing, one must include the following: it calls for certain virtues that are painful precisely because they are responses to the effects of oppression.

There is something interesting and suggestive in the fact that under conditions of oppression there is a particularly concentrated need for a disposition that seems to be a virtue but that is oddly burdened. The trait that I have been exploring—sensitivity and attention to suffering—is not alone in being burdened, though it may be distinctive in the precise burden it carries. What I think of as the *burdened virtues* include all those traits that make a contribution to human flourishing—if they succeed in doing so at all—*only* because they enable survival of or resistance to oppression (it is in this that their nobility lies), while in other ways they detract from their bearer's well-being, in some cases so deeply that their bearer may be said to lead a wretched life. There is an odd unlinking of virtue and flourishing in the case of the burdened virtues, an unlinking that is plausibly consistent with Aristotle's virtue ethics because he does not take virtue to be sufficient for flourishing. A trait may at once contribute to flourishing (because it is a virtue and conduces to a noble end) and detract from flourishing (because it undermines the external conditions for flourishing, including freedom from great pain).

When one is faced with a demand for a burdened virtue, one may accept the burden on oneself out of necessity or out of a lack of a better alternative if one is a direct victim of oppression, or one may choose to accept such a burden if one is committed to the liberatory struggles that require these particular virtues; that is, one may be compelled to maintain painful, corrosive, extremely taxing, or self-sacrificial character traits because despite their undesirability in these respects, the traits are valued as the appropriate traits in response to unjust conditions. Unrelenting anger or rage, for instance, may help the politically resistant self pursue liberatory aims while meanwhile being corrosive to the self; the demand for courage—which as I have noted, following Aristotle, is exceptional in that it is painful—may be so high for those fighting injustice that it leads them to make sacrifices, become accustomed to the threat of great losses, and perhaps consequently develop a reluctance or inability to maintain deep attachments.[19] Sensitivity and attention to others' suffering is morally prescribed under conditions where unjust suffering is widespread, but because it is both valuable and painful it, like the other burdened virtues, weighs upon the virtuous agent under oppression instead of enabling, as an Aristotelian virtue is commonly assumed to, her/his own flourishing.

I asked earlier whether there was any morally praiseworthy disposition in the sphere of sensitivity to others' suffering, anywhere that would be morally comfortable. What I have found is that there is a virtue somewhere between the poles of extreme indifference and overwhelming sensitivity. But this virtue is not a comfortable one, as it invites into one's life the pain of others. If the sufferings to which one is attentive were to be experienced firsthand, they would clearly qualify as the sorts of external conditions that could ruin an otherwise potentially flourishing life; the person who takes on these sufferings in a secondary way—and feels pain—becomes burdened too. The virtue essentially gives rise to the sort of external conditions—in this case, in the form of pain—that unlink virtue and flourishing.

Furthermore, not only is the virtue in the realm of sensitivity and attention to others' suffering burdened with pain, it is also burdened with a certain kind of guilt, something akin to Karl Jaspers's "metaphysical guilt"[20]—since the moderate position entails not just attention to some limited number of those who

19. The burdened virtues of anger and courage are discussed at length in chapter 5.

20. Jaspers writes in the context of sorting through the varieties of guilt that Germans have due to the Holocaust. Distinguishing metaphysical guilt from criminal guilt, political guilt, and moral guilt, he writes:

> There exists a solidarity among men as human beings that makes each co-responsible for every wrong and every injustice in the world, especially for crimes committed in his presence or with his knowledge. If I fail to do whatever I can to prevent them, I too am guilty. If I was present at the murder of others without risking my life to prevent it, I feel guilty in a way not adequately conceivable either legally, politically or morally. That I live after such a thing has happened weighs upon me as indelible guilt. (1961 [1947], 32)

While Jaspers thinks of metaphysical guilt as a form of guilt before God, I am certain that there is an atheist's version of it, too.

suffer but also a constant refusal to attend to the rest. Both the pain and the guilt are morally recommended and yet are burdensome.[21]

To the extent to which we live in a world where these burdened dispositions are the predominant virtues, the eudaimonistic aspects of virtue theory begin to change shape, for one who is inordinately burdened cannot flourish. One must begin to think of a revised eudaimonism as presenting the connection between virtue and flourishing as quite contingent and recognize the pervasiveness of the unjust conditions that give rise to virtues burdened with their very lack of a direct relationship to their bearers' own flourishing.

I do not know whether or not the burdened virtues should be permitted to predominate when one could choose to reject them. For those who are the immediate victims of the greatest injustices and whose lives are necessarily a constant struggle, there may be little chance of escaping the more immediate burdens of oppression. But for others, whose burdens come from taking on the pain of others, it is not clear that accepting the burden is the only choice that one could morally prescribe.

As Chris Cuomo has argued in a very different context, "feminist ethics should promote both justice and joy" (1999, 273). She points out that while feminists must advocate for "protection and vigilance in the face of racism, misogyny, and other forms of harm," this cannot be all that they do, for "joy and other fundamental affective (and less clearly chosen) aspects of being are part of what makes fighting oppression worthwhile" (1999, 273). A morality that pushes one only to accept the burdens of responding to and resisting oppression can actually amplify rather than diminish some of the effects of oppression. As the sufferings of the direct victims of oppression are taken on or experienced in a secondary way by those who attend and respond to the victims, the original harms are multiplied. I am certainly not suggesting that victims should thus be left to suffer alone in order for their suffering not to "leak" onto others. But I would like to acknowledge, also, the moral legitimacy of sometimes seeking joy in the very face of oppression. Cuomo describes her own "migration" in the direction of an ethics that centers flourishing:

> I have moved from a concern with working to eliminate oppression and harm to a more constructive interest in creating/discovering experiences, forms of communication, and expressions of being that forget oppression, resist its force and trajectory, and diminish its seemingly thorough reach. I think of this progression as a shift toward an ethic of flourishing. (1999, 278)

The insistence on joy in spite of the most terrible persecution is a theme, also, in the literature on Holocaust survivors and their children. Many survivors emerged from the camps intent upon creating new life and wanting their children's lives to be happy, free from all suffering; it was as if they could undermine Hitler's success in

21. Bartky recommends both "guilt by reason of complicity" and "guilt by reason of privilege"; in reference to both, she points out: "I am guilty by virtue of my relationship to wrongdoing, a relationship that I did not create but have not severed either" (1999, 41).

this way. Of course, a parent's demand for a child to be happy—all of the time—is itself a burden. As one child of a survivor puts it: "I had to be happy in order to make up for everything that had happened. . . . It was a tremendous responsibility. I didn't know if I could do it. It was as if each of us was making up for a lost person."[22] Nevertheless, the desire—however distorted—for there to be joy rather than additional pain in the wake of great and unjust suffering expresses something crucial: a morality that recommends only pained responses to oppression forgets that one fights oppression in order that there can be flourishing lives.

What seems like the best intermediate point, then, between complete indifference and utter anguish is a burdened disposition—one that experiences the intrinsic pains of sensitivity and attention to others' suffering—but one that seeks relief from these burdens, too: not by escaping to indifference and certainly not by taking pleasure in the suffering of others or even by insulating oneself against the pain by focusing on the pleasure of one's own attentive response to others' suffering, but rather by embracing the joys that assert themselves in spite of it all.

IV

It would be easy to slide from the moral assessment of the (burdened) disposition I have been describing into its political prescription, because there is a set of pressing political questions concerning this virtue: can it motivate people to perform actions aimed at alleviating suffering? Can it compel people to fight against injustice? The urgency of these political questions seems to push some theorists to conflate them with a moral evaluation of the sort I have been carrying out, as if the disposition can only be praiseworthy if indeed it is the one that can motivate political activism for social justice. But, I am afraid, the disposition will fail politically; this does not mean, however, that it has no moral worth. It will be essential, though, to not rely on this virtue politically, but to instead search elsewhere for a source of political motivation to struggle against injustice.

Norman Geras, the theorist whose 1998 book started me sending checks off to Amnesty International, merges the moral and political claims about indifference and attempts a moral/political argument to motivate attention to suffering and, ultimately, a socialist culture of mutual aid. Geras relies on the idea of a contract, though the one he examines is quite different from, for instance, the familiar Rawlsian one. It is actual (though only implicit) rather than hypothetical; and because the actual conditions of the world are abhorrent, this already actualized contractual relationship is one that Geras wishes to reject rather than—as in Rawls's case—one that is presented as a desideratum.[23] The

22. Quoted in Epstein 1979, 42.

23. In describing actual, undesirable conditions of our present world, Geras's account of the contract of mutual indifference is formally like Charles Mills's account of the racial contract. Both communicate something like this: "Here is the morally repugnant state of affairs that you [all those who do not do much to aid others, in Geras's account; whites who do not resist white supremacy, in

contract that Geras describes is not meant as justification of any political arrangement, of governmental authority, or of the obligations of citizens. To the contrary, Geras means for readers to recognize in his description the commitments that their own words or actions have really implied and to recoil in horror at this realization.

More specifically, Geras's aim is to "re-express . . . in the language of political theory" what has already been written about extensively in literature on the Holocaust, namely, "the moral tension set up between the enormous sufferings of some people and the blank inaction of others" (1998, 27). This tension is formulated into "the contract of mutual indifference," stated as follows:

> If you do not come to the aid of others who are under grave assault, in acute danger or crying need, you cannot reasonably expect others to come to your aid in similar emergency; you cannot consider them so obligated to you. Other people, equally unmoved by the emergencies of others, cannot reasonably expect to be helped in deep trouble themselves, or consider others obligated to help them. (1998, 28)

Geras believes that people have widely though of course not explicitly endorsed such a contract, though he acknowledges that as "a model of the world which we really inhabit," it "is exaggerated—or, better perhaps, reduced—by omission of such mutually assisting behaviour in dire misfortune as there is" (1998, 29).

While Geras suggests that it is the moral culture accompanying liberalism that feeds the tendency toward indifference and the subsequent assent to this disturbing contract, he actually seems unwittingly to share some liberal assumptions. Liberalism—characterized by Geras as focused on negative duties only, namely, duties of noninterference—allows one to blamelessly be a bystander to great suffering. But the liberal assumption that self-interest is what ultimately motivates social cooperation is evidently what Geras is depending on when he presents the contract of mutual indifference in the hopes that his audience will be moved to reject this contract. Geras's readers must, once they understand the contract of mutual indifference that they have presumably assented to, come to see themselves as possibly one day needing others to attend to their sufferings, and should then realize that to guarantee this they must themselves agree to reciprocity. The moment of apprehending that they may one day be the ones in need is quite like what takes place in Rawls's original position. Geras advocates a socialist culture of mutual aid and does so most forcefully by appealing directly to his audience's sense of horror at the juxtaposition of atrocity and comfortable or apathetic inaction (this is the aspect of his book that moved me). But as soon as Geras makes use of the device of a contract, he seems to want to motivate action on the basis of self-interest. His implicit reasoning is that one

---

Mills's account] have really agreed to, as evidenced by your words and/or actions." See Mills 1997. Carole Pateman's description of the sexual contract also presents an undesirable contract, but takes a somewhat different form (in part because she emphasizes a rejection of all contractarianism). See Pateman 1988.

must acknowledge a duty to bring aid based on the essentially self-interested desire to secure aid for oneself in case one would ever need it.

This is where Geras runs into a problem much like one that plagues Rawls's (1971) liberal theory, a liberalism that rather than just supporting negative duties also tries to motivate those who are more advantaged to recognize moral duties of aid toward those who are disadvantaged. Imagine Geras presenting his formulation of the contract of mutual indifference to a privileged member of a comfortably situated society—someone who never expects to face starvation or extermination, or to be tortured, enslaved, or subjected to state violence (and so on). This person's response to Geras's account might very well be: "Yes, I accept the risks here: I can accept the fact that if I were ever to be in a condition of great suffering and need, no one would be obligated to come to my aid; thus, I myself am under no obligation to respond to others' sufferings."[24]

Those who are positioned to harm others through their exercise of dominance or to reap benefits from their position of privilege may be especially likely to exhibit the (meta-)vice of indifference. In Geras's contractual model for thinking about indifference, the parties to the contract are unequally positioned as they enter the contract: some parties would expect, based on the conditions of their lives, to require help from others, but other parties would believe either that they will probably never be the victims of great and unjust sufferings or that they will always have private means of protecting themselves or recovering from such harm. Thus the indifference that Geras makes vivid is incorrectly characterized as "mutual." The disadvantaged may be motivated by self-interest to contract for mutual aid, but the privileged will not be motivated by self-interest to cast their lot with a population that includes others much more likely than themselves to need aid. They assess their risks for needing aid and, finding themselves at a low risk, are unmoved by its threat.

For Rawls, the parties to the original position are of course equally positioned: this can be stipulated because his contract is, unlike Geras's, hypothetical. Thus Geras encounters the problem of motivation more directly than Rawls does, but both do encounter it. For Geras, one wonders why someone who is privileged and judges her/himself to be cushioned against great suffering would ever, at least out of self-interest, not choose mutual indifference; for Rawls, one understands why parties to the original position will all agree to some sort of mutual aid (as expressed in the difference principle)—they all fear being the one at the bottom of the heap—but one does not know why those who are privileged would agree to commit themselves to that which would be chosen only by these hypothetical parties.

The achievement of justice through self-interested motivations fails just in case some people—potential parties to a contract that would secure principles of justice—do not see the fulfillment of their self-interests as dependent upon respect for the rights (and the welfare) of all others. Rawls does believe that everyone's self-interests are mutually dependent, even globally;[25] however, unless actual

24. This was exactly the response to Geras's account that I heard from the majority of students in an undergraduate seminar that I taught a few years ago on social contract theory.

25. See Rawls 1999.

privileged members of society come to hold this belief, no dents will be made in their indifference simply through appeals to self-interest. Self-interest within a liberal, capitalist society is much more immediately satisfied through private means.

Recognizing that the lack of equal positioning of the potential parties to a contract to secure principles aimed at enforcing mutual aid will undermine the possibility of that contract's being endorsed on the basis of self-interest, one may go searching for something other than self-interest to motivate concern for others, something that would not depend upon the prior equal positioning of those who will be moved to a commitment to mutual aid. One might, for instance, try to bypass Geras's use of the contract and move directly from pity or compassion to other-regarding actions. That is, one might milk the burdened disposition of sensitivity and attention to others' suffering for its political potential, hoping that it can answer those urgent political questions about what might serve as a motivation to attend to others who are in need.

Martha Nussbaum has attempted something along these lines, though she concludes, as I do, that compassion is unreliable and cannot replace the institutions that protect justice.[26] Borrowing and revising Aristotle's account of pity, Nussbaum argues that recognizing one's own vulnerabilities allows one to bring another person's suffering into one's own circle of concern:

> In order for compassion to be present, the person must consider the suffering of another as a significant part of his or her own scheme of goals and ends. She must take that person's ill as affecting her own flourishing. In effect, she must make herself vulnerable in the person of another. (2001, 319)

This judgment that another person's well-being is part of one's own scheme of ends is a eudaimonistic judgment, rather than strictly an egoistic judgment or a

26. Nussbaum formulates her position in Nussbaum 1996, where she does little to revise an Aristotelian account of pity, and adopts it as a model for the sort of compassion that can assist people in working for justice (though even here she considers it insufficient for justice). She maintains Aristotle's criteria for pity, including that pity involves a judgment of similar possibilities: one moves from seeing suffering to believing (and fearing) that one is vulnerable to such suffering oneself. Nussbaum subsequently revised her own position significantly, with the revised version appearing in Nussbaum 2001. Here she replaces the Aristotelian requirement for a judgment of similar possibilities with the more-nuanced claim that a judgment of similar possibilities epistemologically aids people in forming what she calls a *eudaimonistic judgment*, a judgment about what is included in or constitutes one's own scheme of ends (a judgment of what constitutes one's own *eudaimonia* or flourishing). Others' well-being—even distant others, if a judgment of similar possibilities leads one to see their vulnerabilities as like one's own—may be perceived as part of one's own scheme of ends. It seems that Nussbaum was trying, in her revisions, to avoid using compassion to link self-interest with altruism *directly*, perhaps recognizing that—as I argue here—this direct link is disrupted in a hierarchical society. For instance, she notes: "valuing another person as part of one's own circle of concern . . . may be done consistently or inconsistently, and it may embrace some people rather than others" (2001, 336), and "[t]he movement of imagination that might lead to compassion can be blocked in several ways. One impediment, Rousseau argues, is supplied by social distinctions of class and rank (and, we could easily add, distinctions of religion, race, ethnicity, and gender)" (2001, 342; see also 386–387). I find her revised version more convincing, since she has become much more attentive to the ways that oppressively structured societies block the judgment of

judgment about one's own self-interest. However, according to Nussbaum, the eudaimonistic judgment typically depends epistemologically on a (more clearly self-interested) judgment of similar possibilities, for "human beings have difficulty attaching others to themselves except through thoughts about what is already of concern to them. Imagining one's own similar possibilities aids the extension of one's own eudaimonistic imagination" (2001, 319). Nussbaum claims that the judgment of similar possibilities—central to Aristotle's own account of pity—serves to get someone to "the eudaimonistic judgment that others (even distant others) are an important part of one's own scheme of goals and projects, important as ends in their own right" (2001, 320).[27] She rightly notes that acknowledging one's own vulnerability—forming the judgment of similar possibilities—can be key in generating compassion.[28] However, she pictures a rather implausible scenario about where compassion tends to lead: she imagines that even a privileged member of society, recognizing the possibility of bad luck and of her/his own subsequent suffering, will counter that risk with social action rather than with increasing her/his private security. Nussbaum's story of compassion begins like this:

> Equipped with her general conception of human flourishing, the spectator looks at a world in which people suffer hunger, disability, disease, slavery, through no fault of their own. She believes that goods such as food, health, citizenship, freedom, do matter. And yet she acknowledges, as well, that it is uncertain whether she herself will remain among the safe and privileged ones to whom such goods are stably guaranteed. She acknowledges that the lot of the beggar might be (or become) her own. (2001, 320)

---

similar possibilities, which is important even if such a judgment has now been moved to the status of an "epistemological aid." Nussbaum's worries about the unevenness of compassion lead her to reject a reliance on compassion in place of justice, though she thinks of compassion as the best way of bringing others' well-being into one's own circle of concern. I believe she is, however, overly optimistic about the role of education in undoing the impediments to compassion for others, including those with less social, political, and economic status and power. Thanks to Chris Frakes for alerting me to the fact that Nussbaum 2001 contains a revised version of the argument given in Nussbaum 1996; I had written an earlier draft of this section of the present chapter based on Nussbaum 1996.

27. In the Nussbaum 1996 version, this appears quite a bit more bluntly as "the judgment of similar possibilities is part of a construct that bridges the gap between prudential concern and altruism" (1996, 36).

28. She illustrates this point by quoting from Rousseau's *Emile*:

> Why are kings without pity for their subjects? Because they count on never being human beings. Why are the rich so hard toward the poor? It is because they have no fear of being poor. Why does a noble have such contempt for a peasant? It is because he never will be a peasant. . . . Each may be tomorrow what the one whom he helps is today. . . . Do not, therefore, accustom your pupil to regard the sufferings of the unfortunate and the labors of the poor from the height of his glory; and do not hope to teach him to pity them if he considers them alien to him. . . . Show him all the vicissitudes of fortune. (Rousseau 1979, 224; quoted in Nussbaum 2001, 316; Nussbaum has altered the translation somewhat)

Even if one accepts this much of Nussbaum's description of compassion, the next move is problematic. Nussbaum claims that as a next step:

> This leads her to turn her thoughts outward, asking about society's general arrangement for the allocation of goods and resources. Given the uncertainty of life, she will be inclined, other things being equal, to want a society in which the lot of the worst off—of the poor, of people defeated in war, of women, of servants—is as good as it can be. Self-interest itself, via thought about shared vulnerabilities, promotes the selection of principles that raise society's floor. (2001, 320–321)

At this point Nussbaum, though she begins by describing compassion and emphasizing the role of the eudaimonistic judgment, ends up pointing to self-interest as operative in promoting a social good, just as it operates in Rawls's model.[29] Nussbaum's caution, though, about relying politically (or even morally) on compassion indicates an awareness of a fact that I think is central to the issue: self-interest, even via a eudaimonistic judgment in which others are a part of what one takes to be one's own ends, one's own flourishing life, does not lead to an egalitarian state of affairs.

Thus in place of Nussbaum's picture of compassion turning one to critically view unjust allocations of resources, one must consider an alternative, less-rosy scenario, in which the compassionate but (even if temporarily) privileged viewer of suffering is moved not to social action, but to a fearful, sometimes even panicked movement inward, a scurry to protect all that might be lost. In the present political and economic structures, the privileged do not protect against loss by investing in the good of the public. They protect themselves through such means as individual retirement accounts, private education for their children, security systems for their homes, and, often, through greater segregation from and discrimination against the disadvantaged, who are likely to be not only the targets of their pity or compassion but also the figures in their nightmares. When privileged people fear that loss will befall them, the threat takes a shape formed in, for instance, the racist and xenophobic imagination that anxiously and vividly conjures up images of (black) criminals and (Arab) terrorists. If pity or compassion functions by triggering a fear of loss, it is indeed a dangerous emotion in a context where fear itself is so undemocratic.

I am not suggesting that a painful sensitivity to others' suffering can never lead one to actions aimed at alleviating or eliminating the (unjust) sources of that suffering. But I do want to point to the unreliability of this disposition for the purpose of motivating its bearers to fight against injustice. First, as I have argued above, in a hierarchical society, self-interest does not lead privileged people to concern themselves with the disadvantaged even when they recognize

29. Nussbaum also makes the comparison between compassion-generated altruism and Rawls's constructed apparatus for concern for others. See Nussbaum 2001, 340–342; she faults Rawls's account for lacking the eudaimonistic judgment, implying that she believes this judgment (in her own account) can do quite a bit of work.

their own vulnerability in the context of perceiving the consequences of mutual indifference or in the context of witnessing suffering and imagining it befalling themselves. Second, I do not think that one can rely on there being any direct passage from sensitivity to others' suffering to actions aimed at ending it, precisely because the self-reflective moment that takes place in the apprehension of another's suffering—the moment in which one understands how another suffers because one might suffer similarly oneself—leads to a fear of loss that has variable and not necessarily commendable results.

I must return, then, to the problems with Aristotle's account of pity that I set aside earlier, for they have reemerged. There are two problems that are striking now. First, under Aristotle's account one can only have pity for sufferings that one can imagine befalling oneself. Because privilege insulates or at the very least gives a solid illusion of insulation against many sorts of sufferings, well-off members of well-off societies may fail to identify with victims of, say, starvation, or torture, or even prison abuse or homelessness. One may counter this by pointing to the ability to generalize about loss. Recall Aristotle's observation that pity comes easily to any who have loved ones of their own ("those who have parents living, or children, or wives; for these are our own" [*Rhet.* 1385b24–29]); even a person who cannot imagine losing her/his child to some specific evil (say, losing a child to death because of lack of access to safe drinking water or medication) can still imagine the loss of her/his child.

But there remains a second way in which Aristotelian pity is self-referential: when one feels pity one turns back to oneself, focusing on one's own fear of loss; the pitied other is just a vehicle for this attention to oneself. In fact, as Aristotle suggests in a discussion of courage, the more one has to lose, the harder it is to risk on behalf of others.[30] As I have pointed out critically, some contemporary theorists have tried to implant a motivation of self-interest to help the pitying or compassionate person to cross back over to a concern for others. But if, as I have suggested, this motivation fails too, then a sensitivity to others' suffering, as long as it at some point brings one back to a fear of loss for oneself, may never lead one to political action targeting the unjust causes of great suffering. In particular, turning back to oneself may not lead to one's helping others if one is situated in such a way that one can best protect oneself from loss through private means.

I can reflect back, now, on the story with which I opened this chapter, which happens to fit Aristotle's account of pity all too well. I described holding my newborn baby and watching on the news scenes of violent destruction and loss; the anguish that I felt on this occasion had such force precisely because it ricocheted back and forth between the pain depicted on the news and the terror

30. Aristotle makes this point when he entertains the idea that the best soldiers may be those who have not so much to lose, rather than those who are the most courageous. The courageous man has much to lose: his own life is quite valuable because it is the life of a noble man. A less-virtuous and therefore less-courageous man has, according to Aristotle, a less-valuable life and therefore less to fear in losing it (*NE* 1117b10–21). Without accepting his hierarchical valuing of lives, one can still borrow the insight: having much to lose (think here especially about those who have children) makes one less willing to take the sorts of risks that may be involved in struggling against injustice.

I felt imagining harm befalling that tiny precious one I held in my arms. What is there to be said about such an experience? Politically, I find it unreliable; when fear shifts its focus back and forth between oneself and others quite unlike oneself, one's impulses at ending the suffering may get redirected away from social or political action.

Nonetheless, the response is not without value. In part this is because care and love, even when directed at the very nearest of one's "own," is still morally valuable. Without the sort of awe, devotion, and utter appreciation of a life with intimate attachments that are contained in this care and love, our moral lives would be altered beyond recognition, if they could even be described as moral lives at all.

But even beyond the value of the response in terms of manifesting care for one's own, I would like to suggest an additional moral value to that pained sensitivity to the suffering of others that is independent of its usefulness as a motivation to action. To see the moral value of the pained sensitivity itself, imagine first its absence: an unnoticing, unmoved, indifferent carrying-on that gives no sign of recognition to a sufferer. The pain itself is morally required because its absence would constitute a terrible isolation or abandonment of the sufferers, a failure of human response.[31]

Geras has collected images of this indifference. Some portray an "unnoticing cosmos," providing metaphors for human indifference: "Why did the heavens not darken and the stars not withhold their radiance, why did not the sun and moon turn dark?"[32] and "So many children died of hunger, so many were gassed . . . so many, so many . . . Six million people died, and the sun didn't cease to shine."[33] Some remark directly on human indifference: "Mass destruction was accompanied not by the uproar of emotions, but [by] the dead silence of unconcern."[34] If a lack of pained sensitivity and attention to others' suffering is itself morally horrifying, its presence at least provides sufferers with recognition.

While the question about motivating struggles for social justice has not been answered by an analysis of the disposition of sensitivity and attention to

31. As Lawrence Blum points out about compassion, the painful emotion itself has moral value even when one is unable to take action to relieve suffering (say, if someone is terminally ill and nothing more can be done):

> That compassion is often appropriate when there is little or no scope for the subject's disposition to beneficence indicates that compassion's sole significance does not lie in its role as motive to beneficence. Even when nothing can be done by the compassionate person to improve the sufferer's condition, simply being aware that one is an object or recipient of compassion can be an important human good. The compassionate person's expression of concern and shared sorrow can be valuable to the sufferer for its own sake, independently of its instrumental value in improving his condition. (1980, 515)

32. Geras attributes this to Solomon bar Simson, but notes that the lines have been used by Arno Mayer in his book title (Geras 1998, 8). See Mayer 1988.

33. Szwajgier 1990, 136, ellipses in the original; quoted in Geras 1998, 9.

34. Bauman 1989, 74; quoted in Geras 1998, 18.

others' suffering because this disposition has turned out to be unreliable and therefore insufficient for motivating these struggles, I still believe this disposition is a morally worthy and necessary accompaniment to actions aimed at ending injustice. Because the absence of any pained response to another's suffering is so appalling, a program of engaging politically in social justice struggles without sensitivity and attention to the suffering one aims to end is unacceptable. This is unfortunate because political struggles not burdened with this disposition could perhaps proceed faster and more efficiently, free from the weight of anguish and less prone to consequent feelings of discouragement or hopelessness. If sensitivity and attention to others' suffering does not do the work—at least not reliably—of compelling people to undertake social justice struggles, something else must provide this motivation: it could be a principled commitment to justice, perhaps in combination with other political emotions such as anger. It seems as though much can be said against the disposition of sensitivity and attention to others' suffering: it is burdensome and questionable as a virtue, and it functions poorly to motivate the right sorts of actions. Yet muddy as it is, its absence is immeasurably worse.

5

The Burden of Political Resistance

I

Liberatory movements must offer praise for those whose political resistance gives life to the movement, and from the patterns of such praise arises a portrait—intended to be admired—of the politically resistant self. This chapter dwells on this portrait of political resisters. The moral praise heaped on politically resistant selves is striking against the Aristotelian background I have been drawing on, because in this framework one ordinarily (though, as I will point out, not always) expects traits that are morally praiseworthy—the virtues—to be conducive to and largely constitutive of flourishing. However, it may frequently be the case that the actual character traits of the resister are not connected to the resister's own flourishing, at least not given the understanding of flourishing contained in the resister's (often unrealized) political goals. For those influenced by more Kantian assumptions, this may seem unproblematic, for Kantians tend to associate moral praise with the fulfillment of those moral duties that are most difficult and taxing, and political resisters may score well in this regard: they sacrifice themselves or their own possibilities of flourishing.

Normally, Aristotelian virtues are not (self)-sacrificial: quite the opposite, they are sources of well-being for their bearer. An Aristotelian need not disqualify the traits of the politically resistant self from being virtues, however. Instead, it is possible to conceive of them as "burdened virtues" associated with resistance, namely, traits that while practically necessitated for surviving oppression or morally necessitated for opposing it, are also costly to the selves who bear them. Their claim to being virtues at all derives from their value as means to the envisioned goal of liberation (assuming—well beyond anything in Aristotle's own schema—that this is a "noble" end). While the traits can be labeled virtues, however, the fact that conditions of oppression disrupt the usual pattern of an Aristotelian virtue and lead some of these traits to be burdens on their bearer must be disturbing if one is committed to some form of eudaimonism.

I will be exploring, here, some of the particular vulnerabilities of political resisters to having their virtues burdened or, put differently, to needing virtues that are unlinked from their own flourishing. The political resister may certainly be deserving of moral praise, precisely because she/he displays the traits needed for pursuing an end to oppression, which is, one assumes, what someday could enable—for all—a version of flourishing endorsed by the resister: human lives that are free from domination, exploitation, abuse, war, great deprivation. But these goals are likely to remain unattained, and the resister will be in a position of perpetual struggle, with a constant demand for the virtues of resistance. The struggle itself requires character traits that may strain if not wreck psychological health, and presumably such health is part of the good life imagined to follow an end to oppression; after all, oppression itself has been portrayed as psychologically harmful. Thus evaluated from the perspective of the account of flourishing implicit in the goals of liberatory movements, the traits of the politically resistant self will appear "unhealthy," not the sort of traits that would be part of (or constitute) a flourishing life.

Exposing the politically resistant self as ailing would uncover a tension between feminist or other liberatory politics and a eudaimonistic ethics if one were to understand such an ethics crudely, as requiring praise only for those traits that help constitute their bearer's flourishing. However, eudaimonism can be understood as connecting virtue and flourishing less crudely; as I argued in the previous chapter, a revised eudaimonistic ethics could emphasize the contingency of the relationship between virtue and flourishing, taking account of the ways that traits may be understood as virtues despite the inability of the bearers of these traits to flourish. Aristotle himself—in his discussion of "mixed actions" (*NE* bk. III, chap. 1)—provides a way of understanding this troubling unlinking of virtue and flourishing. My suggestion is that resistance to oppression routinely involves a similar unlinking: when political resisters have virtuous characters, these characters are often, unfortunately, either unable to contribute to the resisters' flourishing or are themselves vulnerable to damage.

While the goal of liberatory struggle may be to make good lives possible, during the actual engagement in struggle one faces a steady stream of moral dilemmas in which there are no good choices. These dilemmas, including those resulting in "dirty hands," are similar to Aristotle's mixed actions and have implications for either the agent's possibilities for flourishing, or for her/his character, or both. I do not mean to suggest that one fares better, morally, by succumbing to oppression, but resistance, while politically necessary, does not automatically release the self from the burdens or the damages that oppressive conditions evoke. The moral praise due to the political resister must be accompanied by the recognition, and lament, that the virtues under oppression—even if they are associated with resistance—tend to be burdened virtues.

I pointed to the burdening of a virtue in the previous chapter when I described a disposition to be sensitive and attentive to others' suffering; the burden in that case comes from the need to center a trait whose exercise is commendable but inherently painful, thus creating for the agent something like the external conditions that Aristotle thought would interfere with flourishing. In this chapter, I will be describing political resistance as itself burdensome—at least in some cases—despite being in other ways potentially praiseworthy. Focusing on traits that have been recommended as especially appropriate for effective oppositional political struggle—and taking anger as my primary example—I will be asking what these traits meanwhile do to or for their bearers. If oppression is so pervasive that all the virtues become burdened ones, weighted down by the constant background of oppression and the constant demand for resistance, the possibility of flourishing disappears. The burdening of the virtues is one of the harms of oppression that one does not escape merely by engaging in resistance, for fashioning one's self into a political resister may alter one's character traits, but the new traits are burdened in new ways.

II

Victims of oppression face direct barriers to flourishing, no matter how successfully they are able to maintain the virtues. As Aristotle is careful to point out, deprivation of external goods can make it impossible to flourish (*NE* 1099a31–1099b8, 1101a14–16, 1153b14–21; *Rhet.* 1360b20–30) either because the lack of certain goods "takes the lustre from blessedness" (*NE* 1099b2), or because without "the proper equipment" (*NE* 1099a32) or in the face of great misfortunes one may be impeded in carrying out virtuous activity (*NE* 1153b17–21). When oppression results in the deprivation of the material conditions for living well or in devastating or traumatizing experiences, virtue will certainly be insufficient for securing the well-being of oppressed people. But apart from what arises from the deprivation of resources, there are additional, more-subtle ways in which virtue, under bad conditions, may be disjoined from flourishing. Considering how persistently some victims of oppression may have to struggle to develop or maintain virtue in the unconducive conditions presented by oppression, it may be especially depressing to acknowledge how impotent even hard-won virtue can be.

Luck—by which I mean anything outside of the control of an agent—may bring to anyone situations that make it impossible to act well. Aristotle touches on this point in his discussion of voluntary actions and in particular when he focuses on actions that are in some way mixed in being voluntary, as in the case of "things that are done from fear of greater evils or for some noble object" (*NE* 1110a4–5). He gives two examples of such cases: "if a tyrant were to order one to do something base, having one's parents and children in his power, and if one did the action they were to be saved, but otherwise would be put to death" and "with regard to the throwing of goods overboard in a storm; for in the abstract no one throws goods away voluntarily, but on condition of its securing the safety of himself and his crew any sensible man does so" (*NE* 1110a5–11).[1] In both cases

1. There are other cases where one should rather die than be "forced" to perform an act, such as the case of Euripides' Alcmaeon slaying his mother (*NE* 1110a25–28).

the actions are such that they are chosen *given the circumstances* (and in this way are voluntary) but would never be chosen (at least by a virtuous agent) otherwise. The case of doing something base in order to save one's family from being held hostage by a tyrant is, as Michael Stocker has argued, a "dirty hands" case, namely, a case of a moral dilemma from which one cannot emerge without committing an immoral act.[2] In cases like this, even if one acts in the best way possible given the choices, praise is not appropriate, according to Aristotle, but rather pardon is, "when one does what he ought not under pressure which overstrains human nature and which no one could withstand" (*NE* 1110a24–25). The case of jettisoning cargo to save a sinking ship is not a similarly tragic dilemma, for one does not commit what is base but only what hinders the immediate goal of delivering the ship's goods, a goal which becomes unattainable anyway as soon as the storm strikes.

Aristotle's mixed actions are important because they point to a way in which even a virtuous agent can be barred from flourishing, through the bad luck of encountering circumstances that force an action that otherwise would never have been chosen. Since flourishing is a certain sort of excellent activity (*NE* 1098a15–17), diverting the activity effectively disconnects a virtuous disposition from flourishing. Stocker, whose argument I will rely on below, puts it as follows: "what makes mixed acts mixed has to do with how they stand to *eudaimonia*. They tell against *eudaimonia*, even though morally they must be done" (1990, 64). The case of doing what is base to free one's family from the tyrant potentially tells against *eudaimonia* constitutively, Stocker argues, because noble rather than base activity is constitutive of *eudaimonia*, and while one might be able to recover from having performed a single base act, "many great misadventures" such as the performance of serious or numerous base acts will destroy what is constitutive of *eudaimonia* (*NE* 1101a7–13). Stocker contends that "base deeds are among those severe disasters that can make *eudaimonia* difficult if not impossible," not only when the base deeds are fully voluntary but also when they are voluntary in a mixed way, that is, "where a good person is morally compelled to do what is base" (1990, 65). The case of jettisoning cargo is simpler: it does not tell against *eudaimonia* constitutively, Stocker reasons, but only externally, since if the loss of the cargo (or the deprivation of any material goods) does indeed interfere with *eudaimonia*, it does so only through an external means.

In addition to drawing the distinction between the two mixed acts (the tyrant with hostages and the ship in the storm), Stocker also emphasizes a different distinction between both of the mixed acts (on the one hand) and cases of using mere means to the end of *eudaimonia* (on the other hand). While using mere means to *eudaimonia* (a necessary part of any human, rather than divine, life) is necessitated only by circumstances, it does not tell against *eudaimonia*. The mixed acts, like mere means, are necessitated only by circumstances, but they *do* tell against *eudaimonia*. Stocker states the distinction nicely: "Mere means are such that, apart from the circumstances, one could not infer that they

2. See Stocker 1990 (chap. 3: "Dirty Hands and Conflicts in Aristotle").

would be in a *eudaimon* life. But what makes mixed acts mixed are such that, apart from the circumstances, one could infer that they would not be in a *eudaimon* life" (1990, 66).

Committing a base act when circumstances morally necessitate it is not the same as having a base character, and I do not mean to imply that what interferes with flourishing even in dirty hands cases is (necessarily) the depreciation of the character of the agent who commits the act. Indeed if every engagement with evil forced by circumstances destroyed the virtues, then these cases would not reveal a disconnection between virtue and flourishing; they would be cases where both virtue and flourishing were destroyed. My point is precisely that these cases, in disuniting virtue and flourishing, display what I have been calling the burdened virtues; they show that there are virtues whose exercise is, due to bad (including unjust or oppressive) conditions, not conducive to or constitutive of their bearer's flourishing

While bad conditions, including encounters with tragic dilemmas, sometimes interfere with flourishing without destroying the virtues, it is true that they may also or eventually have the effect of eroding good character. Martha Nussbaum considers this possibility (and the extent of Aristotle's agreement with it) by pointing to a passage from the *Rhetoric* in which Aristotle details ways in which excellence of character may diminish with age as people accumulate bad experiences:

> They [the elderly] have lived many years; they have often been taken in, and often made mistakes; and life on the whole is a bad business. . . . They are cynical. . . . their experience makes them distrustful and therefore suspicious of evil. . . . they are small-minded, because they have been humbled by life: their desires are set upon nothing more exalted or unusual than what will help them to keep alive. . . . They are cowardly, and are always anticipating danger. . . . They are too fond of themselves. (*Rhet.* 1389b13–1390a23)

Nussbaum's comment on this passage is that it demonstrates "to what extent Aristotle is willing to acknowledge that circumstances in life can impede character itself, making even acquired virtues difficult to retain" (1986, 338).

Thus the virtuous are vulnerable in several ways. They may encounter moral dilemmas that lead them to perform base actions or in any case actions that "tell against *eudaimonia*" (Stocker 1990, 64); they may have virtuous dispositions that, because of adverse circumstances, they are unable to express through activity. In either of these cases their virtues endure, but these virtues are unable to help their bearers to flourish. The virtuous may respond to these experiences with regret, sorrow, shame, guilt, remorse, or a loss of a sense of themselves as honorable.[3] If these responses or other effects of bad experiences

3. In the previous chapter I discussed these "negative emotions" as appropriate responses that the virtuous agent has to dirtying his/her hands. See Williams 1973, 1981a, 1981b; Stocker 1990, chap. 1, sec. 8; Walzer 1973; Hursthouse 1999, chaps. 2–3; and Bishop 1987.

are serious enough, they will be incorporated into character, in which case one will want to say that not just the possibility of flourishing, but also excellent character itself has been diminished. Nussbaum summarizes the situation similarly, claiming that the excellence of the virtuous person must

> find its completion or full expression in activity; and this activity takes the agent to the world, in such a way that he or she becomes vulnerable to reversals. . . . The vulnerability of the good person is not unlimited . . . but the vulnerability is real: and if deprivation and diminution are severe or prolonged enough, this person can be "dislodged" from *eudaimonia* itself. . . . Aristotle's final point . . . is that even then virtuous condition is not, itself, something hard and invulnerable. Its yielding and open posture towards the world gives it the fragility, as well as the beauty, of a plant. (1986, 340)

Nussbaum emphasizes the vulnerability of virtue and of *eudaimonia* due to the risks incurred by virtue itself: virtue requires activity to be fulfilled and is dependent upon luck to make this activity possible and to also make possible various goods, including the relational goods (such as friendship) that rely quite heavily on what is outside of the agent's own control.[4] This vulnerability of virtue can be analyzed, as Nussbaum does, by looking for the sources of vulnerability in the nature of virtue (given the background assumptions that luck will not always be good and that virtue and flourishing are partially dependent on luck); however, I am more interested in looking for sources of vulnerability in the very conditions that luck presents, remembering that luck is not always accidental and is often based on what is systemic.[5] That is, while everyone is subject to luck (a point that is important to Nussbaum), only some bad luck is also a result of injustice or of one's engagement with injustice in the form of resistance to it. My question, then, is: what are the particular vulnerabilities to the unlinking of virtue and flourishing that are faced by those who devote themselves to resistance to oppression?

The vulnerability of political resisters takes many forms. One that I will point to only briefly is due to the probability of encountering dirty hands cases rather regularly while doing the work of resistance. The role of dirty hands in a revolutionary movement is treated in Jean-Paul Sartre's 1948 play *Dirty Hands*, and a similar theme is taken up by Michael Walzer (1973), who shifts the focus from revolutionaries to ordinary (but "good") politicians, who are also led into dirty hands dilemmas and whose goodness as politicians depends on both their willingness to dirty their hands (when it is necessary, as it frequently is, to achieve their praiseworthy goals) and their feelings of guilt at doing so. Knowing that they have committed base acts, even if they have done so only because they were caught in a dirty hands dilemma, resisters may be forever weighted down by their sense of responsibility for this. Their very goodness in part is revealed

4. On the relational goods, see Nussbaum 1986, chap. 12.
5. Thus Claudia Card's notion of the "unnatural lottery"; see Card 1996.

through their discomfort, sorrow, and remorse. Their virtues are then, to use my language, burdened.

Political resisters thus face one vulnerability when they are led to commit certain *acts* because of unjust circumstances, just like in Aristotle's case of doing what the tyrant orders to save one's family. But another vulnerability arises from the pressure to develop certain *traits* that are called for only because they are the traits needed for facing—and fighting—injustice. The politics of resistance is not just a politics of action; some resistance movements have also developed prescriptions for what kind of a self a good comrade should be.

Certain movements—such as the Civil Rights movement—have done so self-consciously and have based these prescriptions on two factors that were thought to coincide: first, what kind of selves are best suited to achieve the aims of the movement? and second, what kind of selves are morally commendable even apart from circumstances calling for resistance? Training political resisters through the discipline of nonviolence, which was a cornerstone of the Civil Rights movement, was believed by, for instance, Martin Luther King, Jr., both to be the most effective means to the ends sought by the movement and to be the only morally praiseworthy approach to life. These two considerations were connected: King argued that effectiveness in achieving liberatory ends was dependent on bringing the oppressor to be ashamed of his injustices, and he maintained that through the resisters' displaying great moral integrity, white supremacists could be shamed into developing a moral conscience and consequently accepting the demands of the movement.[6]

Thus some resistance movements have refused in a principled way to embrace acts or traits that create an inconsistency between their means and their ends: they reject those traits that, apart from the circumstances, would have no place in a flourishing life. Other movements have disagreed with the premise that the oppressor may be brought to moral conscience peacefully and have advocated a range of other tactics, including separation from the dominant group and armed resistance.

It is not my intent here to enter into—and certainly not to settle—the question of whether liberatory goals are best achieved through a commitment to nonviolence and related virtues, or through a readiness for violence. Nor will I try to determine the relative efficacy of ending oppression through negotiation and communication with dominators—requiring virtues like compassionate understanding—or through separation and a refusal to cooperate within existing structures—requiring a stance of oppositional anger or at least indifference toward the dominant group. Not settling these questions, I leave open the

6. This sort of argument permeates many of Martin Luther King, Jr.'s speeches and writings. See, for instance, *Why We Can't Wait* (1963; especially chap. 2, "The Sword That Heals"); many of the pieces collected in King 1986, such as "The Time for Freedom Has Come" [1961] (where he claims that nonviolence "offers a unique weapon which, without firing a single bullet, disarms the adversary. It exposes his moral defenses, weakens his morale, and at the same time works on his conscience" [79]) and "I Have a Dream" [1963]; and "A Long, Long Way to Go" [1965] in King 2003; see also "Black Power Defined" [1967] in King 1986.

possibility that the more-militant or more-radical approaches are the most effective. I find this possibility to be plausible enough that it is worth analyzing the *moral* questions that arise in the face of radical resistance, questions that are separable from the now bracketed question of what may most effectively promote liberatory goals. These moral questions could arise out of various concerns: traits associated with an oppositional stance could, for instance, be morally condemned for failing to be sufficiently other-regarding and for supporting injustices against members of dominant groups that are the targets of militant opposition. But it is not concern for members of dominant groups that motivates or occupies me here. I am concerned instead with the resisters themselves and am interested in revealing how some of the traits promoted by radical resistance movements may burden the bearers of these traits.

I will thus focus now on traits that have been chosen and promoted by some resistance movements on the basis of their presumed effectiveness in achieving certain ends, but that I find morally problematic in this specific respect: they are burdens to their bearer because they are disconnected from her/his own flourishing. My claim is that these traits—while prescribed because they are taken to be the traits that enable resisters to achieve the liberatory goals of the movement—may be "mixed traits" parallel to Aristotle's "mixed actions." That is, they may be traits that, apart from the terrible circumstances, would never be endorsed. And, apart from the circumstances, they would be thought to have no place in a flourishing life; in particular, they would be excluded from the account of flourishing implicit in the goals of a liberatory movement. For instance, if oppression is psychologically damaging and one of the aims of eradicating oppression is to relieve victims of this damage, then some conception of psychological health must be a part of the good life that resisters are struggling to enable. Thus a trait that is psychologically harmful—though commendable because it enables successful resistance and thereby serves a noble end—must be seen as a mixed trait.

III

There is a certain sort of a self that one must try to fashion oneself into in order to be a radical or militant resister. The image of such a resister can be invigorating or thrilling if one envisions the bold and determined fighter striving tirelessly for fundamental change, never giving in to the lure of compromising reforms but maintaining instead a clear knowledge of who the enemy is and a driving anger against this enemy, never bowing down under threats or rejections from the mainstream but enduring instead the risk and the loneliness of going against the grain. But this is a romanticization of the resister, and below the surface of this image there is something sad having to do with what the resister sacrifices or loses. The traits that enable resistance and the traits that enable human flourishing often fail to coincide. This does not suggest abandoning radical resistance for, in a context of great injustice and widespread oppression, if this sort of resistance is what can overcome oppression (a possibility that I am taking seriously), then it may be morally required, though since it is not all that may be morally required, other values may take precedence.

I spent about a decade of my life trying to cultivate the politically resistant self—letting the idea of political resistance inform my every move—in the context of various communities that were self-consciously radical.[7] While I do not regret this political engagement and remain committed to it in a modified way, it is worthwhile to reflect not only on what the value of it is but also on its costs. I am concerned about the well-being of the politically resistant self, a self that is meant either to emerge purposefully through the transformation of a prior self that has been constructed under dominant values, or to arise more spontaneously without a conscious apprehension of conditions of oppression. While I considered in chapter 1 how the transformation of character—and the repair of moral damage—that is meant to accompany feminist or other radical politics may fail in a way that is tied to moral luck, here I want to look not at the possibility of the self's failure to be critically transformed, but at the dangers for those selves that succeed.

Certainly not all of the traits that are valuable for resistance are suspect ones. For instance, becoming habituated not to feel socially sanctioned revulsion at despised groups (disabled people; gays, lesbians, transsexuals, and other "deviants"; people of color; etc.)—but to instead feel proud (especially if the pride is self-referential) or celebratory or open—can be described as a character trait that enables resistance to social exclusion and that does not meanwhile seem to undermine the possibility of one's own or others' flourishing. The cultivated disposition to not only refrain from but also to have no desire for the type of overconsumption promoted under capitalism is a form of resistance and meanwhile is probably (as long as it does not become a sort of extreme asceticism or self-denial) a mark of health and part of a capacity to live well. Integrity, sociality, sustained focus, creativity, visionary imagination, and perseverance may all be suggestive of dispositions that make resistance possible and that are also directly tied to flourishing; this list could continue, but my focus is elsewhere, on the traits that create a tension because while they enable resistance (and thus may further an eventual goal of flourishing for all), they disable a good life for their bearers.

The worrisome traits marking the radical, politically resistant self fall loosely into three sets. The first set is composed of traits that contribute to developing and maintaining a hard resolve against the oppressors, which often entails encouraging or cultivating anger or rage in addition to withholding more sympathetic forms of attention. From this set, I will examine anger in detail below. The second set includes those traits that lead some resisters to take risks bravely and/or to accept or even welcome personal loss and sacrifice as a part of

7. These included different feminist and lesbian (some separatist) communities, a popular education project focused primarily on creating radical political movement among U.S. Latino/as and Chicano/as, a (communalist)-anarchist direct-action group, and many informal networks and ad hoc groups active on the Left.

their political work. The third set encompasses the character traits that resisters are expected to display in their relationships with one another: loyalty coupled with an openness to intense, politically motivated criticism and self-criticism. I will comment briefly on the second set—focusing on courage (and adding a bit to the analysis of courage begun in the previous chapter)—and on the third set at the end of this chapter. While, as I will explore further, all of these traits are burdened virtues if they are virtues at all, each of these sets of traits is generally admired in at least some resistance movements.

IV

I will now discuss anger, a central trait in the first of the three sets named above. Anger at injustice or at the agents of injustice may come easily: psychiatrists William Grier and Price Cobbs in their influential *Black Rage* asserted that "of all the things that need knowing, none is more important than that all blacks are angry" (1968, 4); Audre Lorde conjectured that "every woman has a well-stocked arsenal of anger potentially useful, against those oppressions, personal and institutional, which brought that anger into being" (1984, 127). However, in many cases, anger is hard to call up or even recognize, and an angry disposition is challenging to maintain. This is so not just because anger can be repressed, but also because compassion—even for those who commit terrible abuses or injustices—may spring forth. I remember discovering how difficult it can be to harden oneself against sympathetic responses to an oppressor, a discovery that was tied to my reading for the first time Alexander Berkman's account of his attempt to assassinate Henry Frick during the Homestead strike against Carnegie Steel in 1892. Upon reading the details of the attempted assassination, I chastised myself for involuntarily cringing in pain—as a sympathetic response on behalf of Frick, who was injured but not killed and whose fear, as described by Berkman, made me want to comfort rather than attack him—a response that, at the time, I believed diminished my capacity to act as a true resister, for Frick was clearly one of the "bad guys."[8] Apparently, Berkman himself had to work rather hard to maintain the character traits that led him to experience righteous anger rather than pain and shame at the thought of shooting Frick. He writes of facing the bleeding Frick: "For an instant a strange feeling, as of shame, comes over me; but the next moment I am filled with

8. See Berkman 1970:

> I step into the office on the left, and find myself facing Frick. . . . "Fr—," I begin. The look of terror on his face strikes me speechless. It is the dread of the conscious presence of death. "He understands," it flashes through my mind. With a quick motion I draw the revolver. As I raise the weapon, I see Frick clutch with both hands the arm of the chair, and attempt to rise. . . . With a look of horror he quickly averts his face, as I pull the trigger. . . . I hear a sharp, piercing cry, and see Frick on his knees, his head against the arm of the chair. (1970, 37)

anger at the sentiment, so unworthy of a revolutionist. With defiant hatred I look him full in the face" (1970, 38–39). I now think that Berkman's moment of shame—and my moment of sympathy for Frick—were actually quite interesting and worthy moments in which we revealed that despite the pressures to conform to the ideal of a political resister, something survived of the character traits that enable not resistance but what would be the flourishing of interdependent human lives if one could imagine this taking place in the absence of great oppression. My own self-critical reflections on my sympathetic response to Frick's fear and pain came not because I supported political assassinations or any variety of political violence—I never did—but because my sense of even milder (but still radical) strategies of resistance was that they required anger, hatred, or at least a withholding of attention toward the oppressors;[9] certainly, compassion for one's oppressors seemed inappropriate. I may have been right about this: resistance may be enabled or at least facilitated by a resolutely unsympathetic attitude toward the oppressors; this has been the consensus of some radical liberatory struggles, including the Black Power movement and the more radical and separatist branches of second wave feminism (while precisely the opposite approach animated the Civil Rights movement), and I am not convinced that these movements have been mistaken about this.

It is worth looking at the accounts of these traits—I will focus here specifically on anger—offered by its (theoretical) proponents. There is a thread of feminist writing on the topic.[10] Audre Lorde spoke in 1981 of the importance of anger to feminist struggle for responding to racism, including importantly the racism poisoning the interactions between women.[11] She takes the presence of anger as a fact: "My response to racism is anger" (1984, 124), leaving only the questions of whether one silences or expresses one's own anger (she points out the deep harm that comes from silence) and how one responds to the justified anger of others (she cautions against defensiveness and guilt). Her claim that anger is a source of strength and a positive motivating and clarifying force in struggles against oppression serves to counter the charge that anger is either useless or destructive: "Focused with precision it [anger] can become a powerful source of energy serving progress and change" (1984, 127).

Some feminists have embraced women's anger as a way of reclaiming what has been off-limits according to the norms of (especially white) femininity and as a way of refusing the subordinate status of women assumed by these norms.

9. Marilyn Frye argues that reorienting one's attention away from "phallocratic reality" and toward women is an important form of resistance that lesbians engage in: "the maintenance of phallocratic reality requires that the attention of women be focused on men and men's projects . . . and that attention not be focused on women. . . . Woman-loving, as a spontaneous and habitual orientation of attention is then, both directly and indirectly, inimical to the maintenance of that reality" (1983, 172).

10. In addition to the sources discussed here, see Donner 2002, who borrows from feminist Buddhist writers to develop an analysis of anger as a virtue.

11. The talk, "The Uses of Anger: Women Responding to Racism," given in 1981 at the National Women's Studies Association Conference, was published in Lorde 1984.

Consider, for instance, Marilyn Frye's 1983 "Note on Anger," included in a book in which she argues for a feminist/lesbian separatism. She points out that when one is angry, one

> claims that one is in certain ways and dimensions *respectable*. One makes claims upon respect. For any woman to presuppose any such thing of herself is at best potentially problematic and at worst incomprehensible in the world of male supremacy where women are Women and men are Men. A man's concept of Woman and of Man, and his understanding of what sorts of relations and connections are possible between beings of these sorts, to a great extent determine the range of his capacity to comprehend these claims, and hence of his capacity to give uptake to women's anger. (1983, 90)

Given sexist understandings of women's place, Frye argues, men give women's anger the right sort of uptake—that is, they respond to it with respect—only when it is anger in defense of a justified aspect of womanhood (as mother, nurturer, helpmate, even as a public champion of moral causes connected to caretaking). But a woman's anger on her own behalf—about her own competence, rights, autonomy, interests—is seen as crazy precisely because the woman is seen as insanely outside of the bounds of her own proper, subordinate place. Thus, "others' concepts of us are revealed by the limits of the intelligibility of our anger" (1983, 93); women become unintelligible when they fail to perform without anger in a subordinate manner.

A similar theme is echoed by Elizabeth Spelman in her 1989 "Anger and Insubordination":

> To be angry at [someone who can be blamed for doing something he should not have] is to make myself... his judge—to have, and to express, a standard against which I assess his conduct. If he is in other ways regarded as my superior, when I get angry at him I at least on that occasion am regarding him as no more and no less than my equal. So my anger is in such a case an act of insubordination: I am acting as if I have as much right to judge him as he assumes he has to judge me. (1989, 266)

Anger on the part of those who are in subordinate positions, then, signals a recognition of the wrongness of the subordination and a refusal to accept it: "the systematic denial of anger can be seen as a mechanism of subordination, and the existence and expression of anger as an act of insubordination" (1989, 270). Assuming the Aristotelian understanding that emotions such as anger can be informed and guided by beliefs and are potentially trainable, Spelman considers whether anger should be purposefully cultivated as a response to oppression: perhaps there is a moral ought to anger and the oppressed *should* be angry. Her qualifications, here, have to do with weighing this imperative for anger against its possible risks. For instance, one might be punished for it, or one might find it unbearable to engage in the mere act of noticing how much injustice there is at which to be angry (1989, 271–272); additionally—and drawing again on Aristotle—Spelman worries that anger may not be carried out properly, since it can occur to the wrong degree, be directed at the wrong target, stem from the wrong motive, and so on (I will return to this worry below).[12]

In accord with these sorts of feminist insights on anger, women's consciousness-raising groups regularly helped women to identify and then become angry about the systemic nature of their mistreatment.[13] Even outside of the context of consciousness-raising groups (which have become quite rare), feminist anger can become a motivation for activism or for more spontaneous acts of defense against one's own or others' subordination. For example, women learning self-defense techniques and strategies are often still taught—by feminist martial arts and self-defense practitioners who raise consciousness about male violence against women—to draw on their anger to fuel their physical fighting.

Additionally, feminists have seen positive epistemic value in anger. Lorde writes that "anger is loaded with information and energy" (1984, 127); Diana Tietjens Meyers (1997) unpacks this sort of claim by arguing that what she calls "heterodox moral perception" can be aided by a chronically angry (or otherwise "rancorous") emotional attitude. According to Meyers, approaching the world with a rancorous emotional attitude as opposed to a more genial or "nice" one enables one to feel what one is not expected or permitted to under dominant values, what Alison Jaggar has called "outlaw emotions" (Jaggar 1989b); Meyers writes, "when people have become hypersensitive, paranoid, angry or bitter as a result of being subjected to a devastating injustice (or series of injustices) or to disabling systemic oppression, they become preternaturally sensitive to unjust practices and oppressive conditions" (1997, 209). While not arguing that people ought to *become* chronically angry or otherwise rancorous in order to enhance their ability to discover injustice, Meyers points out that since "it is a fact that rancorous individuals already exist," oppositional groups should pay attention to them: "If social groups were organized to seize upon claims kindled by hypersensitivity, paranoia, anger, and bitterness and to give them a good airing and a fair hearing, insightful moral perception might be greatly increased, and emancipation might be hastened" (1997, 213).

I want to complicate this generally positive appraisal of oppositional anger by adopting some Aristotelian analysis of it and by juxtaposing the Aristotelian (descriptive and prescriptive) account of anger with the conditions presented by oppression. In chapter 1, I myself implied an endorsement of anger by suggesting that anger could accompany agent-regret as part of a response to the bad moral luck of oppression; while not withdrawing that endorsement here, I do want to highlight the burdens that come with oppositional anger.

Aristotle's descriptive account of anger as the response to being wronged is compatible with feminist assumptions about anger (though of course Aristotle

12. Spelman further theorizes about anger in Spelman 1999.

13. Naomi Scheman (1993 [1980]) argues that the political insights and analyses offered in the context of consciousness-raising groups actually enable an expansion or change in what counts as anger; they do not just enable the woman to *identify* what was previously unidentified, but still existing, anger.

would disagree with feminists about what constitutes a wrong and about who can wrong whom). Anger, for Aristotle, is a feeling of pain at being unjustifiably harmed by another, especially if one is harmed by being slighted, that is, denied the respect that one deserves, and this pain is mixed with pleasure at the thought of revenge (*Rhet.* bk. II, chaps. 2–3).[14] One can only be slighted by—and therefore one only becomes angry at—someone from whom one expects respect, and "a man expects to be specially respected by his inferiors in birth, in capacity, in goodness, and generally in anything in which he is much their superior" (*Rhet.* 1378b35–1379a2). While rejecting this last remark, feminists would nevertheless agree (as both Frye and Spelman have emphasized) that becoming angry with someone marks oneself as the person's equal, as someone to be respected as a moral agent.

Aristotle's prescriptive account of anger, however, presents difficulties for those trying to cultivate proper anger in the context of oppression. The prescription follows the same pattern as most other virtues: to be morally praised, a man must be angry "at the right things and with the right people, and further, as he ought, when he ought, and as long as he ought" (*NE* 1125b32–33). Only the moderate state of good-temperedness is praised: through an excess of anger, designated as irascibility, one could reveal more specifically a character flaw of being "hot-tempered," "choleric," "sulky," or "bad-tempered" (*NE* 1126a9–27); the deficiency (inirascibility) is also morally troubling:

> Those who are not angry at the things they should be are thought to be fools, and so are those who are not angry in the right way, at the right time, or with the right persons; for such a man is thought not to feel things nor to be pained by them, and, since he does not get angry, he is thought unlikely to defend himself; and to endure being insulted and put up with insult to one's friends is slavish. (*NE* 1126a3–8)

I am especially concerned with two ways in which—under an Aristotelian account—the angers of political resistance may go wrong: such anger might be mistargeted or it might be excessive in degree. The first error—hitting the wrong target—I think must be cautioned against, and I believe that political resisters must indeed train their angers carefully so that this failure is minimized. But the second of these potential failures of anger—that anger might be felt too much or too strongly by political resisters—is quite complicated under conditions of great systemic injustice. It can be confusing to evaluate anger of enormous proportions, for under conditions of unrelenting injustice, such anger can be characterized (surprisingly) as a deficiency even as it appears as an excess; there may be no

14. Or as Aristotle offers in an offhand definition, anger is "pain with a consciousness of being slighted" (*Top.* 151a15). See also the definitions of anger that Aristotle thinks would be produced by, on the one hand, a physicist (who emphasizes the material manifestations of it: "a boiling of the blood or warm substance surrounding the heart") and, on the other hand, a dialectician (who refers to its form—"the appetite for returning pain for pain"—while ignoring the embodiment required for actual anger to exist) (*DA* 403a26–403b4).

moderate state that allows one to be angry all the times one ought to be. This suggests not a warning to resisters to train their anger into a moderate level, but rather a critique of the call for moderation. At the same time, however, ignoring the desirability of moderation in anger allows one to also ignore how the resister is burdened by the imperative to carry an awesome level of anger.

The problem of anger hitting the wrong target is described in detail by Lorde in the second of her essays on anger, "Eye to Eye: Black Women, Hatred, and Anger" (1984).[15] In contrast with "The Uses of Anger: Women Responding to Racism," which concerns the anger that women of color feel toward white women and in which Lorde characterizes the anger as correctly targeted, cleanly distinguishable from hatred, and constructive in instigating change, Lorde's examination of anger in the second essay focuses on the anger—and hate—that black women misdirect at one another. Lorde reports both that her anger is constant and potent ("My Black woman's anger is a molten pond at the core of me. . . . my life as a powerful feeling woman is laced through with this net of rage") and that "how to train that anger with accuracy rather than deny it" is a pressing question because despite her knowledge that "other Black women are not the root cause nor the source of that pool of anger," the anger does "unleash itself most tellingly against another Black woman at the least excuse" (1984, 145). Analyzing her own tendency to misdirect her anger, Lorde points to the internalization of oppression, the development of self-hate that comes from growing up as a member of socially despised groups. Lorde describes the childhood experience of finding herself inexplicably but repeatedly treated as an object of hate and concluding that there must be something wrong with herself, then expanding the target of this hatred beyond herself to include other black women, "for each of us bears the face that hatred seeks" (1984, 146). This hate-infused anger causes significant harm in a way that the clean anger directed at a proper target does not.[16] Psychologically complicating the misdirected anger even further, Lorde explores the fact that it is easier to be angry than to be hurt, so her anger at other black women covers up the pain of unfulfilled desire for another black woman's unconditional love, a yearning to replace the loving black mother whose image is tied to a (mythologized) black or African sisterhood. This unconditionally loving mother—while perhaps an object of desire generally—is according to Lorde especially crucial for black women, who have depended on and trusted only their own mothers in the face of a hostile world.[17] Thus under these particular conditions of

15. A version of this essay first appeared in *Essence* (vol. 14, no. 6) in 1983.

16. Lorde distinguishes anger and hatred: "Anger—a passion of displeasure that may be excessive or misplaced but not necessarily harmful. Hatred—an emotional habit or attitude of mind in which aversion is coupled with ill will. Anger, used, does not destroy. Hatred does" (1984, 152). Aristotle's distinction between anger and hatred differs quite a bit from Lorde's; see *Pol.* 1312b19–34 and *Rhet.* 1382a1–16.

17. Lorde writes: "All mothers see their daughters leaving. Black mothers see it happening as a sacrifice through the veil of hatred hung like sheets of lava in the pathway before their daughters. All daughters see their mothers leaving. Black girls see it happening through a veil of threatened isolation no fire of trusting pierces" (1984, 158).

oppression—where one internalizes a hatefulness toward oneself and others like one, and where one desperately needs unconditional love as protection from a cruel and unjust society—it is all too easy to aim one's anger at others subject to the same mistreatments as oneself is and for this anger to be a messy, hateful one.

Consider, also, that anger at those who are more powerful may be quite dangerous, and as a result, others who are as vulnerable or more vulnerable than oneself may be the only available targets for anger. As bell hooks explains: "We learned when we were very little that black people could die from feeling rage and expressing it to the wrong white folks. We learned to choke down our rage. . . . Rage was reserved for life at home—for one another" (1995, 13–14).

Not only are there multiple reasons for anger to be misdirected under oppression, but furthermore, the fact that oppressions interlock makes it difficult to even identify and isolate a proper target for politically resistant anger; many people are both the agents and the victims of oppression. Lorde's portrait of the anger that women of color direct toward white women represents that anger as unbelievably clean, as if it could escape being tainted with the contempt for (white) women that women of color, along with everyone else, absorb from society. More drastically, the anger of some male Black nationalists against whites has manifested itself as a misogynist and often sadistic targeting of white women.[18]

Learning not to misdirect anger under oppression is a daunting task, since it requires a high degree of recovery from the effects of internalized oppression, the courage to be angry at those whose retaliation may be backed by great force, and an ability to separate out the ways someone may be implicated as an agent or beneficiary of one form of oppression even while subject to another. Politically resistant anger, then, will have trouble hitting the right target: those responsible for perpetrating injustice. Nevertheless, as hard as it may be to target anger well, anger that fails in its targeting is not to be praised; there is no temptation to praise it, though, because it is not even helpful as an oppositional force in the service of liberatory politics.

While training one's anger to hit the right target is imperative for political resistance, another Aristotelian requirement for proper anger—that it occur in a moderate proportion—cannot necessarily be recommended for resisting oppression. Resistance may be radicalized—particularly by taking a separatist dimension—when anger is permitted to take on huge proportions; this is what is suggested by María Lugones in "Hard-to-Handle Anger."[19] Lugones compares what she calls first-level and second-level anger. *First-level anger* is the sort

18. For an extreme example, see Cleaver 1968.

19. See also Bernadette Hartfield's 1995 response to Lugones's article, which adds a compelling (childhood) example of "anger compounded." Angela Bolte distinguishes between anger and rage (differently than Lugones does) and defends the role that rage can play for those facing great injustice: "Where anger can point toward an injustice, rage can point toward an injustice of much greater magnitude" (1998, 48).

of anger that Frye and Spelman captured in their accounts of anger used by subordinated peoples to communicate their refusal to accept subordination and their demand of respect for themselves as moral agents. But because it has "communicative intent," Lugones argues, such anger must try for respectability within the "world of sense" belonging to the dominator, because it is, in part, an attempt to get uptake from those who have denied one respect. Since "rage is equated by dominators with hysteria or insanity" and would therefore have no possibility of getting the desired uptake, first-level anger must, in order to be communicative, be measured or moderate as opposed to excessive and raging; thus Lugones interprets Spelman's acceptance of Aristotle's endorsement of the mean regarding anger to stem from the fact that "rage cannot express, in a justifiable manner, a judgment addressed to those who have wronged one" (1995, 210). But instead of rejecting rage as Spelman does, Lugones rejects the assumption that resistant anger ought to aim at being communicative with the dominator. She proposes instead *second-level anger*, anger that becomes fury or rage and is hard to handle or control, that "places one beyond the pale"; in such anger, "the gestures are wild or extremely hieratic, contained; the voice loud; the use of space extensive; the body flushed" (1995, 206). These awesome, second-level angers

> [p]resuppose worlds of sense against which the anger constitutes an indictment or a rebellion, worlds of sense from which one needs to separate. These angers also presuppose or establish a need for or begin to speak from within separate worlds of sense. Separate, that is, from worlds of sense that deny intelligibility to the anger. (1995, 204)

This is separatist anger whose very refusal to be toned down or moderated is key to its radical potential and its capacity to generate change. In part, its potential is in the possibilities of opening up new worlds of sense in which to be creative, instead of being limited to making only backward-looking claims focused on redressing wrongs already committed.

Even from within Aristotle's own account of anger one could infer that resisting oppression requires enormous anger. Aristotle asserts that one displays a moral defect if one becomes angry so little that one "endure[s] being insulted and . . . put[s] up with insults to one's friends" (*NE* 1126a7–8). But, for instance, people of color may be subjected to racist insults and degradation daily, and under such conditions, the "proper" level of anger for people of color (or their friends/political allies) becomes, relative to the anger appropriate to those who do not regularly encounter such insults, extreme. If one believes (correctly) in one's own moral worth while others in the society—in dominant positions—do not believe in it, one will constantly find oneself "slighted" (to use Aristotle's term); the frequent or unabating nature of this slighting—or as Lugones points out, the fact that it may be unacceptable to conform to the dominators' requirements for gaining respectability—are conditions that make the right level of anger a tremendous level, the level of fury or rage.

According to Aristotle, a mean is always to be calculated relative to particular circumstances. Constructing an analogy to the procedure for calculating how much food one should consume, Aristotle says:

> If ten pounds are too much for a particular person to eat and two too little, it does not follow that the trainer will order six pounds; for this also is perhaps too much for the person who is to take it, or too little—too little for Milo [a wrestler], too much for the beginner in athletic exercises. (*NE* 1106a36–1106b3)

Thus, just as it is appropriate for Milo (or, as Aristotle did not think to say, any pregnant or lactating woman) to eat huge quantities of food, so it is appropriate and praiseworthy for those who are constantly subjected to "slights" (to understate it) stemming from systemic mistreatments to become hugely, furiously angry. Since this impressive level of anger is actually the mean relative to the circumstances, it is the virtuous, morally praiseworthy level of anger.

However, there is something like a "moral remainder" (Williams 1973) to solving the problem this way: while being intensely or chronically angry may be morally right or the best option in the circumstances, there is something that is to be regretted about it. While Milo presumably is able to metabolize his supersized meals—so that the food is actually *good* for his health—it is far from likely that raging political resisters can metabolize their anger; instead, I contend, they themselves suffer from the level of anger prescribed for them, even if such a high level best serves their oppositional struggles. When anger at oppression is defended, it is applauded in comparison to a worse state: for instance, the acceptance of subservience or perhaps depression that follows from unrecognized anger.[20] But being the best state that is possible in the circumstances does not make an angry disposition ultimately praiseworthy; it would unlikely be a part of the good life that liberatory movements are trying to enable.

If tremendous anger is ultimately unhealthy or corrosive for its bearer, then the political resister with an angry disposition displays an example of what I have been calling a burdened virtue: a morally praiseworthy trait that is at the same time bad for its bearer, disconnected from its bearer's well-being. The resister to oppression faces a dilemma that challenges or burdens the virtues like the dilemmas resulting in Aristotle's mixed actions: if one chooses to be angered only in a measured way, then one must endure the degradation of oneself or of others on whose behalf one acts, but if one chooses to develop a fully angered/enraged

20. While seeing anger or rage as connected to pathologies in black people, Grier and Cobbs also describe black rage as a sign of health in comparison to the widespread and profound depression that is caused by oppression:

> As grief lifts and the sufferer moves toward health, the hatred he had turned on himself is redirected toward his tormentors, and the fury of his attack on the one who caused him pain is in direct proportion to the depth of his grief. When the mourner lashes out in anger, it is a relief to those who love him, for they know he has now returned to health. (1968, 209–210)

disposition in response to the vast injustice one is fighting, then the anger can become consuming. This dilemma did not occur to Aristotle presumably because he did not consider the possibility that someone who actually deserves respect would be a regular victim of systemic harm; he assumed the opportunities for appropriate anger would be infrequent and unpatterned.

V

Courage—the central trait in the second set of characteristics particularly valued by some resistance movements—follows a pattern similar to anger, in that a burden is produced by the excessive demand for courage that occurs in the context of oppression; as in the case of anger, Aristotle did not anticipate the burden of courage because he did not expect the demand for courage to be so constant.[21] While I will not develop in full detail here the analysis of courage that would parallel my analysis of anger above, I believe one could argue that courage, like anger, is a virtue that takes a toll on its bearer despite being valuable for pursuing the liberatory goals of an oppositional movement. While a certain level of courage may not be damaging to its bearer—and I would not deny that the challenges of any human life make the necessity for some courage simply part of the human condition—the courageous disposition that the political resister is encouraged to cultivate and to foreground in her/his character may crowd out other virtues in a deleterious way,[22] so that at least some of those who are highly and admirably courageous have reason to envy the frightened.[23] Courage can go awry for political resisters in ways that Aristotle would recognize:[24] for instance,

21. The truest example of courage, for Aristotle, is that of those who are "fearless in face of a noble death" especially in war (*NE* 1115a32–34). He does not expect the opportunities for such courage to be constant or even necessarily frequent, nor does he consider that even a short burst of such a demand for courage in the context of war could be traumatizing.

22. This worry about courage coming to dominate over other virtues is also expressed by Amélie Rorty. She proposes a revision of courage because traditional courage—"a set of dispositions to overcome fear, to oppose obstacles, to perform difficult or dangerous actions" (1986, 151)—tends to overstep its bounds, introducing an oppositional stance where it does not belong: "The exciting attractions of risk and danger that require courage are introduced into activities which do not—or did not originally—require it: romantic love, professional work. But the dispositions that constitute courage are rarely strongly correlated with the happy outcome of such activities" (1986, 155). Her alternative involves "checks and balances" for the virtues.

23. *Envy the Frightened* is the title of a novel by Yaël Dayan (1960). The book's protagonist, Nimrod—a child born in 1933 to Jewish pioneers in Palestine—is molded from birth by his father and more generally by the emerging Israeli national agenda to be, above all else, strong and fearless, courageous. The project "succeeds," and Nimrod grows to be called "the Rock." The tragedy is that he cannot really feel at all. When he becomes a father, he sets out to mold his own son into a similarly tough character, until one day when observing his son intent upon proving his fearlessness to other little boys by swimming in a life-threatening river current, an unfamiliar feeling of terror overcomes Nimrod, an event that Dayan portrays as ultimately healing Nimrod from the damages of having borne extraordinary courage.

24. See *NE* bk. III, chap. 7, and *EE* bk. III, chap. 1; I will avoid, here, a discussion of the inconsistencies between these two accounts.

while aiming at the mean of courage, they might instead develop a deficiency of fear regarding things that are truly fearful; or, the attempt to become courageous may give rise to an insensibility toward pain and (to go beyond what Aristotle suggests) an inability to feel any emotions, or a reluctance to form attachments because doing so is at odds with a commitment to a risk-filled life. Anyone could fail to hit the mean when aiming for courage; however, the conditions faced by the political resister demand courage constantly, urgently, and intensely, and it is especially hard to face this demand without falling into one of these perversions of courage. Additionally and more important, if the resister *does* manage to display the appropriate level of fear and confidence that together constitute the virtue of courage and to be motivated in the proper way, namely, by the pursuit of the noble, even this true courage becomes problematic. Courage is a virtue that—especially if not balanced with other virtues that have a better connection to their bearer's well-being—is burdensome: the courageous actually risk sacrificing themselves.

Just as in the case of anger where the conditions of oppression make the prescribed level of anger extreme, so in this case, oppression and resistance to it call for extraordinary courage. When resistance movements make heroes of the courageous, they add to the pressure to prioritize courage as a/the praiseworthy character trait of the politically resistant self. In part this is troublesome because the image of courage tends to be based on a masculinist, military model (sometimes even within feminist organizing), which avoids rather than works through a question about what is really more noble: risking oneself in order to achieve victory in a battle against injustice or seeing to it that one returns home consistently, attentively, and safely enough to be able to love and care and be loved and cared for well. With this question obscured, the resistant self is urged to fight and to face the consequences of it: anything from being socially ostracized and harassed and having one's children taunted, to losing one's job or being jailed, or more drastically, to being tortured or killed. As Aristotle claims (in what I would argue is an overstatement due to his limited sense of what counts as courage), if there were no injustice, there would be no need for courage;[25] it is precisely because political resisters are facing and fighting injustice that they press one another to prioritize courage.

One might think, here, of something like the "circumstances of courage" parallel to the "circumstances of justice": as John Rawls has declared, "unless [the circumstances of justice][26] existed there would be no occasion for the virtue of justice, just as in the absence of threats of injury to life and limb there would be no occasion for physical courage" (1971, 128). Of course, there

25. See *Top.* 117a38–117b2. He makes this claim in order to illustrate the point that justice is more useful than courage, for one always needs justice but only on some occasions does one need courage. I think he overstates the case, since in fact one needs courage for some things other than fighting injustice.

26. "The circumstances of justice obtain whenever mutually disinterested persons put forward conflicting claims to the division of social advantages under conditions of moderate scarcity" (Rawls 1971, 128).

are kinds of courage other than physical courage,[27] and to the extent that courage is needed for facing the challenges that are to be expected as part of any human life, everyone will face some circumstances of courage, and courage will remain a virtue. But there is a level of courage that is needed only for facing what no one should have to face.

I argued above that conditions of oppression put resisters in a dilemmatic position regarding anger: to fail to be angry enough about the constant lack of respect shown to themselves or their "friends" (or any subordinated person) is a moral failure (and perhaps psychologically debilitating), and yet to be angry at the extreme level called for may (also) be detrimental to the self. In the case of courage, Aristotle again would have to acknowledge the same sort of dilemma: to see injustice and to run away from the battle against it is morally condemnable, for the courageous confidently face their fears for the sake of the noble. But the alternative, courageously accepting the many possible risks and sacrifices in the life of a committed political resister, puts a burden on the self. The burden—even a sacrifice of one's own life—must be accepted, according to Aristotle, for a life marked by moral failure may not be worth preserving anyway (*NE* 1124b8–9).[28] Courage, then, can easily be seen as a virtue that is unlinked from (its bearer's) flourishing, not because a failure of courage *could* enable flourishing, but rather because courage is called for in circumstances that may block any route to a flourishing life.

Aristotle thus acknowledges that courage, when it is demanded at all, differs in some ways from other virtues: besides being inherently painful (as I discussed

27. Moral courage could be thought of as the courage to maintain one's integrity when there is a significant risk involved in doing so. For a feminist discussion of such courage, see Ginzberg 1991, who emphasizes the courage to dissent from one's moral community and to risk expulsion from it. Holloway Sparks (1997) gives a feminist argument for political courage and in particular for the courage that women activists have displayed when engaging in democratic dissent; she develops a "conception of citizenship that recognizes both dissent and an ethic of political courage as vital elements of democratic participation" (1997, 76). Daniel Putnam suggests "psychological courage," namely, the "type of courage involved in facing the fears generated by our habits and emotions"; in particular, what he has in mind is the type of courage needed for facing psychological problems such as "destructive habits, irrational anxieties, and psychological servitude in which one individual emotionally controls another"; the fear faced by one who is courageous enough to work through these kinds of psychological problems is a "deep-seated fear of psychological instability" (1997, 1; see also Putnam 2001). The necessity for moral courage, political courage, and psychological courage may be permanent features of human life. Psychological courage, especially, may not be unlinked from its bearer's own flourishing in the way that the courage needed for fighting injustice may be, a courage which is itself more often moral and political than physical courage. Aristotle does not bother to distinguish between fighting injustice and fighting in wars, on the assumption that the wars are just ones. Rejecting that assumption, one could think about the burden that the demand for courage produces for soldiers in unjust, as well as just, wars.

28. Kelly Rogers makes this point in her examination of Aristotelian courage, wondering whether Aristotle could "really maintain the possibility of happily going to one's death" (1994, 309), a concern that arises because courage has (at least) two apparently conflicting motives: happiness and nobility. The conflict dissolves when one accepts that happiness is unattainable if one is faced with a choice between a shameful course of action and death.

in chapter 4), it may lead the courageous to sacrifice their own (virtuous and thus especially valuable) lives (*NE* bk. III, chap. 9).[29] His virtue ethics can withstand having a virtue with these features only because on the whole, the life of the virtuous is not a painful, self-sacrificial life. Aristotle's assumption that courage is not called for all the time, and that it will be integrated with other virtues, allows him to not worry about the overburden that courage produces. What I am suggesting is that great oppression and the necessity of resistance to it create circumstances of courage that are extreme and that therefore imbalance the virtues, calling for a prioritizing of a virtue that is unlinked from its bearer's well-being.

The third worrisome set of character traits associated with resistance encompasses those traits that have to do with the relationship to one's comrades in struggle, and while these traits can also be burdened ones, they follow a somewhat different pattern from those of the first two sets. The expected relationship between political comrades is one of deep loyalty, a requirement that I will only remark on briefly here and that I will explore thoroughly in the next chapter. Additionally or as a part of loyalty, feminist and other radical communities have demanded of their members an openness to being critically scrutinized by the other members of the community, as an aid in achieving the personal transformation necessary for embodying a self free from dominant values. This inspection—justified by a certain interpretation of a phrase embraced by second wave feminism, "the personal is political"—is often not accompanied by an assessment of how much change is possible (given the likely depth of socialization into dominant values, including an internalization of an inferiorized sense of self) or of whether the pressure to change will create painful and unresolvable conflicts of values and desires.[30] The changes that can result from feminist or other progressive revaluations are often liberatory, but they are at the same time quite demanding, and the cost of failing to change can be either shame (if the emotional responses associated with dominant values are kept hidden) or a charge of disloyalty and the consequent exclusion from an

29. Some critics have worried that courage blurs the line between the virtuous and the continent, because it seems to require controlling or acting in spite of some of one's emotions, specifically, one's fears. If courage were really a case of continence rather than virtue, it would indeed be burdensome, for the continent act against their own desires and are psychically pained by doing so. However, then it would not be particularly interesting since it would not be a case of a burdened *virtue*, and it is the odd fact that an Aristotelian virtue—usually tied to flourishing—can be burdensome that is interesting to me. Fortunately, there are ways of saving Aristotle from the blurring of the virtue/continence distinction in the case of courage; see, for instance, Pears 1980 and Leighton 1988.

30. Alison Jaggar, in theorizing the right approach to those emotions that remain in feminists but that are unwelcome because they seem to reflect dominant values, advocates critical scrutiny but also notes that while "the persistence of such recalcitrant emotions probably demonstrates how fundamentally we have been constituted by the dominant world view," there is also another possibility, namely, that the difficulty in changing these emotions "indicate[s] superficiality or other inadequacy in our emerging theory and politics" (Jaggar 1989b, 164). For a story about failure to change in accordance with feminist values—a failure accompanied by shame—see Sandra Bartky's "Feminine Masochism and the Politics of Personal Transformation" in Bartky 1990.

oppositional community (if the failure to change is exposed). What might have provided refuge from the pressures of collective judgment—namely, a retreat into some protected private realm—is itself forbidden according to a politics that has rejected a public/private split.

Thus like the self manifesting the other sets of suspect character traits, the self who is expected to be both loyal to and open to criticism from a community of resistance is burdened. Being properly loyal and sufficiently malleable so that one can come to embody the values of the community, one becomes also quite vulnerable, for instance, to the possibility that one's community is misguided or myopic or too filled with fervor to be thoughtful and critical and compassionate. Risking such vulnerability may be a necessary step in making political resistance possible, for without it, one might be unable to move away from dominant values. Nevertheless, the demand to make this dangerous commitment to the collective refashioning of the self must be considered another burden created by oppression and the need for resistance.

VI

Acknowledging the three clusters of problematic character traits promoted in communities of resistance is discouraging, because it reveals the distance between what is possible under oppression and what one would hope to be possible in a different world. Under conditions of oppression, the politically resistant self may be the healthiest self possible—compare it, for example, to a fully victimized self, burdened with something completely different, such as an internalized sense of inferiority—but this comparison demonstrates only that the resistant self is not the *worst* possibility. The resistant self, I contend, is still in some trouble.

A more optimistic line of reasoning—one that depicts the resistant self as escaping the burdens of oppression—is employed in many liberatory struggles. The reasoning seems to go something like this: acceptance of one's own unjust subordination is psychologically unhealthy and undermines the possibility of flourishing, and resistance to oppression is the opposite of its acceptance; thus it must be the case that resistance to oppression is psychologically healthy and promotes flourishing. What is missed by this (fallacious) line of reasoning is any basis for thinking about the character traits associated with resistance as burdens. For instance, bell hooks (1995) employs reasoning of this sort when she argues for the value of black rage, including an extreme version that she identifies as "killing rage." Rightly noting that rage can be tapped to motivate courageous, militant resistance to racism, and also accurately pointing to the suppression of anger as an unhealthy response—though sometimes a practical survival tactic—under white supremacy, she concludes that rage must be not only useful for resistance but also a sign of psychological health and healing. Hooks insists upon portraying rage as healthy because she wants her writing to counteract a dominant understanding in which the image of black people (especially males) as angry and violent has been distorted, pathologized, and demonized by whites. However, hooks conflates the diagnosis of rage as pathological—or any critical view of rage—with a prescription against rage.[31] They need not be conflated; in my analysis of anger above, for instance, while I described rage as potentially psychologically harmful, I argued that rage could still be considered a virtue (just a burdened one), and I did not prescribe against rage.[32] In fact, I am willing to endorse it in cases where it truly has radical potential. But the endorsement must be accompanied by regrets, primarily regrets about what the anger does to its bearer (but also worries about what the angry self may do to others). Labeling someone in a constant or frequently recurring state of anger as flourishing would be a mistake; I have suggested that such a person should be seen instead as burdened with the necessity of such a high level of anger. Thus I caution against the tendency—that some communities of resistance seem tempted by—to imagine an escape into psychological health (if not full flourishing) by way of a commitment to being thoroughly formed by a politics of resistance.

On the one hand, resistance to oppression is clearly morally praiseworthy: it is evidence of a commitment to justice and a willingness to act on that commitment. But while a resister may be guided by this commitment to choose as well as possible when facing the moral dilemmas presented by oppressive conditions, even the best choices under terrible circumstances are morally problematic. I am

31. In some ways, hooks's position is surprising since she has emphasized the importance of acknowledging and attending to the psychological woundedness of black people under oppression (see hooks 1993 and "Healing Our Wounds" in hooks 1995). However, it seems that she sees only the repression of anger and not the experience of anger or rage (even if it is intense or constant) as psychologically debilitating.

32. The fact that one ought not conflate "action guidance" and "action assessment" has been emphasized by Rosalind Hursthouse, who points out that the two may "come apart" in the case of dilemmas that are resolvable only with a remainder (1999, 50). Action guidance is what one provides when, in the face of a dilemma, one decides "one should do *x*" or declares "do *x*"; engaging in action assessment allows one, alongside the decision to "do *x*," to assess the action *x* to be a bad action. While action guidance is concerned only with right decision, action assessment is also connected to the concept of a good or flourishing life (Hursthouse 1999, 74). Thus it is sometimes appropriate for action guidance and action assessment to come apart from each other, leading one in certain dilemmatic situations both to correctly choose an action and to assess it as bad. Drawing on Hursthouse's account, I would like to distinguish between what one might call "trait guidance" and "trait assessment," where in dilemmatic situations such as those presented by conditions of oppression, these two will not always line up with one another. That is, one may provide trait guidance in deciding that trait *y* should be developed or maintained (thus one might say, "be *y*" or "be a *y* person": for instance, "be enraged" or "be a chronically furious person" in the face of unrelenting injustice), but at the same time evaluate or assess *y* as a burdened virtue rather than as an unqualified virtue, since it interferes with one's own flourishing. This is what I have done with respect to anger, a trait that under conditions of oppression may generate this incongruity between trait guidance and trait assessment. Thus I have argued both that one may correctly decide to maintain a chronically angry disposition and that anger may not be a trait that it is (unproblematically) good to have. However, instead of simply designating the trait as "bad" and disqualifying it from being a virtue at all, I have pointed out that it may still be considered a virtue (because of its connection to a struggle to create conditions under which all may eventually flourish and thus to a noble end), but a burdened one. In the conclusion of this book, I will elaborate on the trait guidance/trait assessment distinction.

suggesting that some of the problems are manifested on the self of the resister and that a liberatory politics needs to be accompanied by a critical examination of what happens to the self that resists. One should worry about who one becomes as one carries out what began as a noble commitment to justice, for the traits that are needed to actualize that commitment may be ugly ones, arising as they do out of such troubled conditions. I am reframing the old question about the necessity of consistency between means and ends; this version of the question asks whether one employs acceptable means if the character of the resister is damaged badly as it is fashioned for struggle, developing mixed traits that are unlinked from flourishing. I take it that since the alternatives to resisting oppression are unacceptable, the real issue here is not whether to resist but how to resist, and I am suggesting that the how should take into consideration the way the character of the resister is affected. There should be no glory in resistance to injustice, just a sad and regretful recognition of its necessity.

6

Dangerous Loyalties

I

For the virtue of loyalty—if indeed it is a virtue—to be exercised, there must exist an appropriate object of loyalty; it is in this way a "relational good,"[1] and one may say about it something similar to what Aristotle says about justice when he notes that "the just man needs people towards whom and with whom he shall act justly" (*NE* 1177a30–31). In order to exhibit loyalty as a virtue, the oppressed and/or resisting agent needs an object of loyalty. While loyalty to individual friends or relations may be possible in a wide range of circumstances, there is in addition a type of *group* loyalty that seems to be expected of oppressed people, especially in the context of resistance movements. Identifying the proper object of group loyalty will be key to exercising loyalty as a virtue. However, loyalty to an oppressed group conceived *as* a group or to an oppositional community that forms in resistance to oppression—which are the sorts of group loyalty typically exalted in the context of liberatory struggle—is advisable only when a group deserving of one's loyalty can be sustained. Loyalty to some communities of oppressed people may be possible, but such loyalty presents hardships for those whose place even relative to others in the community is as a subordinate. Oppositional communities that reject hierarchies—and that thus aim to be free of internal dynamics of subordination—appear promising as good objects of loyalty, but if the maintenance of such a community actually undermines liberatory goals in some way, loyalty (of this sort) will also be morally problematic or, put differently, will be unavailable as a virtue.

Robert Paul Wolff offers a description of what it is to have the character trait of loyalty; it will be useful to have this account as a starting point before

1. See Martha Nussbaum, "The Vulnerability of the Good Human Life: Relational Goods" (1986, chap. 12).

trying to determine whether loyalty understood as a virtue will be possible under oppression:[2]

> A loyal person is loyal to something. The proper object of loyalty is either another person, a group of persons, or an institution. The loyal man [*sic*] comes to the aid of the object of his loyalty when its interests are threatened; he identifies himself with its career, making its successes his successes and its enemies his enemies. He is prepared to sacrifice for it, even to the extent of giving his life in order that it may be safeguarded. The loyal man takes pride in his loyalty object and expresses solidarity with it through ritual acts which evoke and reinforce his emotional identification with it. . . . Strictly speaking, loyalty conceived as a personality trait is the disposition or tendency to exhibit a pattern of action which includes many of these particular acts. (1968, 55)

While others have considered the question of whether loyalty is a virtue in a general way,[3] my interest in the question is motivated by the concern that, within the discourses of both feminist movements and liberatory racial movements, loyalty is treated as an excellence of character when perhaps it should be viewed as morally suspect. Like the other character traits extolled as virtues for political resisters that I discussed in the previous chapter, loyalty seems to be a burdened virtue. Here I extend the critical examination of loyalty as a virtue for political resisters, not only by uncovering further senses in which it may be burdened, but also by questioning whether it is really a virtue at all in many of the contexts in which it is portrayed as one. It may be that loyalty actually functions as an obstacle to liberatory aims. In that case, not only could it present an impediment to a political resister's own flourishing as the other burdened virtues often do, but it may actually not serve at all even as a means toward

2. Wolff first makes distinctions among four different ways in which the term *loyalty* could be used, namely: (1) as a disposition of character, (2) as an ascribed legal status, (3) as an orthodoxy, and (4) as "remaining true, being faithful, honoring a moral commitment" (1968, 59). To distinguish between the first and fourth senses of *loyalty*, Wolff notes:

> To have a character trait is to be disposed to respond in certain ways to situations of a specific type. These responses are spontaneous and issue from inclination, not an awareness of duty. A man may be of a faithful disposition without having contracted a moral commitment to the object of his loyalty; conversely, he may loyally fulfill his obligation without feeling an unforced inclination to do so. (1968, 59)

Given Wolff's distinctions, it is the first sense of loyalty—as a disposition of character—that I am considering.

3. The philosophical work on loyalty has focused on many different species of loyalty, including loyalty to one's friends, to one's lover, to one's family, to one's country, to a god or gods, to one's political comrades, to one's heritage, to a way of thinking, and to a teacher or mentor; Josiah Royce (1908) even suggests "loyalty to loyalty." George Fletcher's *Loyalty* (1993) centers the question of whether and when loyalty is a *duty* instead of thinking about it strictly as a virtue, although he does begin with an Aristotelian/communitarian framework that could lend itself to thinking about loyalty as a virtue. Also see Pettit 1988.

actualizing the version of flourishing implicit in the goals of the very community that serves as an object of loyalty for the politically resistant self.

II

The *American Heritage Dictionary* chooses as its sample sentence to illustrate the definition of *loyalty* a quotation from J. P. Donleavy: "Loyalties flow deep between girl friends until they want the same man." Against such a background, where women cannot be imagined to have primary loyalties to one another, the concept of "loyalty" and its companion concept, "betrayal," have been potent ones in feminist thought. Failures of loyalty between women have been seen as terrible transgressions of a feminist ethics, transgressions springing either from false consciousness (causing one to be loyal, but to the wrong people) or from a dreaded weakness of the will (in which case, one knows whom one should be loyal to, but "sells out" to satisfy one's own individual self interest or desires). Within this discourse the charge of betrayal holds extraordinary power, because calling someone a traitor names her as bad to the core; she has not just committed a wrong action, but rather she suffers from a deficiency of character. In racialized communities of color—particularly in politicized contexts—the charge of betrayal functions perhaps even more powerfully, for there is generally a stronger sense of peoplehood based on ethnicity or racial membership than on gender and, correspondingly, a stronger expectation for loyalty. For instance, those who are traitors to their race are invoked as vilified figures in discussions about passing, assimilating, dating or partnering interracially, and "climbing" economically; those passing for white (intentionally or unintentionally), choosing or succumbing to assimilation, professionalizing, or escaping the ghetto in any other manner are taken either to be misguided about who their people truly are or, more likely, to suffer from a weakness of character whereby they do not have what it takes to stand honorably by their people and are tempted instead into the benefits procured by abandoning their people and individually escaping racial oppression.

However, some of what are taken to be acts of betrayal may not in fact arise either from false consciousness or from weakness of the will; they may be critically chosen departures from the hegemonic beliefs or practices of a community, departures that require other strengths of character.[4] Such critical acts may actually serve liberatory purposes—and thus, I shall assume, the ultimate purpose of enabling human flourishing—better than loyalty does. Perhaps the oppositional

4. See, for instance, Ruth Ginzberg's characterization of "the courage to dissent" from one's moral community as a type of "moral courage" (1991, 136). Such dissenting requires courage precisely because one risks losing one's moral community. Ginzberg points out that under the assumption that the personal is political, "any decision, by virtue of being political, is fair game for being held accountable by and to my moral community. It is also fair game for becoming grounds for my exclusion from a moral community" (1991, 137).

discourses that represent loyalty as a virtue are confused. To determine this, one would do well to inquire whether, for instance, fostering loyalty could stand in the way of the development of a habit of unrestrained critical thinking and acting, and thus prevent people from thinking and acting outside of what can be experienced as the confining, homogenizing unity of a political group or an identity-based community, such as a racialized community or a feminist community. One will have to consider whether it could be that no form of loyalty is a virtue in an oppositional political context in which critical thinking and acting must be fostered. Dispensing with loyalty, however, should not be done too easily, for can one imagine engaging in committed, oppositional politics without the loyalty of one's comrades? Can one imagine the possibility of surviving, let alone flourishing, as a member of a persecuted or marginalized group without depending on the loyalty of one's people?

Before beginning to answer these questions, I will turn to surveying how the ideas of loyalty and betrayal have been used within communities of resistance, particularly communities engaged in some form of "identity politics," namely, a politics where the identities of members of a subordinated group are understood as providing a basis for organizing against injustice. In these communities, loyalty to other members of the subordinated group are expected, and departures from the assumed identity or rejections of what are taken to be the defining features of the identity or of the political agenda of the group are considered to be acts of treason. In discourses where identity and politics are seen as closely tied, the contours of the proper object of loyalty appear ambiguous, for they are at the same time conceived as based on the identity group (for instance, women, gays and lesbians, Latinos, etc.) and on the oppositional political group, namely, those specifically committed to eradicating injustices against members of their identity group.[5]

Many women of color who are engaged in both feminist and racially based liberation movements—and who thus stand at the intersection of apparently competing identities—find themselves frequently accused of treason. A recurrent

5. Assumptions about the linking of identity and politics that characterizes "identity politics" were articulated by the Combahee River Collective in 1977 (published in Combahee River Collective 1981):

> We realize that the only people who care enough about us to work consistently for our liberation is us. . . . This focusing upon our own oppression is embodied in the concept of identity politics. We believe that the most profound and potentially the most radical politics come directly out of our own identity, as opposed to working to end somebody else's oppression. (1981, 212)

The collective (which was a collective of black women) explains its commitment to the liberation of black women as springing partly from the belief that "Black women are inherently valuable [and] that our liberation is a necessity not as an adjunct to somebody else's but because of our need as human persons for autonomy" (1981, 212), and partly from the claim that "if Black women were free, it would mean that everyone else would have to be free since our freedom would necessitate the destruction of all the systems of oppression" (1981, 215).

theme in the writings of feminists of color is of being pulled between the demands of racial loyalty and the desire for sexual autonomy or at least for room to become a feminist critic of one's home culture. Several writings by Chicana feminists refer to issues of loyalty by focusing on the legacy of Malintzin (also known as La Malinche), the Chicano symbol of the (female) traitor.[6] Cherríe Moraga writes in "A Long Line of Vendidas":

> The sexual legacy passed down to the Mexicana/Chicana is the legacy of betrayal, pivoting around the historical/mythical female figure of Malintzin Tenepal. As translator and strategic advisor and mistress to the Spanish conqueror of México, Hernan Cortez, Malintzin is considered the mother of the mestizo people. But unlike La Virgen de Gaudelupe, she is not revered as the Virgin Mother, but rather slandered as La Chingada, meaning the "fucked one," or La Vendida, sell-out to the white race. (1983, 99)

Because La Malinche is said to have betrayed sexually, the legacy of La Malinche functions to place suspicion on Chicanas' sexuality as a potential area of betrayal.[7] Chicanas can only prove loyalty to the race through sexual loyalty to men of their race. As Moraga writes, "[E]ven if she's politically radical, sex remains the bottom line on which she [the Chicana] proves her commitment to her race" (1983, 105). And yet this sexual loyalty—and thus loyalty to the race—is premised upon Chicanas' betrayal of each other; because racial loyalty requires putting the men first, it demands of women that they betray one another in favor of their men:

> You are a traitor to your race if you do not put the man first. The potential accusation of "traitor" or "vendida" is what hangs above the heads and beats in the hearts of most Chicanas seeking to develop our own autonomous sense of ourselves, particularly through sexuality. Even if a Chicana knew no Mexican history, the concept of betraying one's race through sex and sexual politics is as common as corn. As cultural myths reflect the economics, mores, and social structures of a society, every Chicana suffers from their effects. And we project the fear onto each other. We suspect betrayal in one another—first to other men, but ultimately and more insidiously, to the white man. (1983, 103)

Some feminist discussions of La Malinche and her legacy focus on refuting the accusation of betrayal, emphasizing, for instance, that in fact La Malinche was not a traitor because she did not act under her own agency; rather, she was sold into sexual slavery and raped. Furthermore, the myth counts as racial loyalty only acts of loyalty toward men, thus precluding the possibility that loyalty between Chicanas—as lesbians, for instance—would count as racial loyalty. In

6. See Alarcón 1994 for a commentary on some of the feminist, as well as nonfeminist, literature on Malintzin.

7. Alarcón 1994 emphasizes that Malintzin was a traitor not only because of her sexuality (and the fact that she bore Cortés's children) but also because she translated for him.

such a context, any feminist critique on the part of Chicanas becomes a betrayal of the Chicano male and as such a betrayal of the race. As Norma Alarcón states simply, "as Chicanas embrace feminism they are charged with betrayal *a la* Malinche" (1981, 188). For Chicana feminists, betrayal, understood as any critical stance toward the men of their race, becomes inevitable. Moraga, perhaps acting out of a conviction that loyalty must be a virtue, thus refuses this understanding of betrayal, insisting that "to be critical of one's culture is not to betray that culture" (1983, 108).

Despite her recognition of how accusations of betrayal are, for Chicanos, intertwined with sexist and heterosexist assumptions, Moraga uses the history of La Malinche as a springboard to discuss her real acts of betrayal, admitting, "I *have* betrayed my people" and telling a childhood story of ending a friendship with a darker-skinned girl after her mother had warned her against this girl (1983, 97). Betrayal pains Moraga, for true loyalty to her race is in her eyes undoubtedly a virtue. She writes proudly of her own loyalty and admiringly of the "breed-boys ever loyal to the dark side of their mestizaje," noting that the "blondest of the bunch writes it blue-veined into his skin: *Viva la Raza!* A life-long mark of identity, of loyalty to his mother's and to his own people" (1993, 126). But her own loyalty to *la raza*, a culturally nationalistic loyalty symbolized in the Chicano movement by allegiance to Aztlán, becomes possible for Moraga only when she critically revises the conception of the nation to which she will be loyal, reconceiving it as "Queer Aztlán," "a Chicano homeland that could embrace *all* its people, including its jotería" (1993, 147). This critical revision is, according to Moraga, still an act of loyalty, and she still considers loyalty to be a virtue.

Gloria Anzaldúa also insists on being profoundly critical of her culture and does not accept that such a stance justifies her being called a traitor. Instead of embracing the term *traitor* or *vendida* to underscore her critical stance, she, like Moraga, refuses the description of her actions as traitorous. For her, too, loyalty is still a virtue, as long as what counts as loyalty can be revised. In fact, she feels her community has betrayed her because she is made unwelcome—as a feminist and especially as a lesbian—in her own home, to the point where she reports being afraid of going home. So, she turns the accusation of betrayal around and claims that she is not the traitor but rather the betrayed, insisting, "not me sold out my people but they me" (1987, 21).

Feminists of color have been quick to complicate the concept of loyalty, because the fact that accusations of racial betrayal are often based on misogynist assumptions of a loyal woman as the woman who supports her man have led feminists of color to insist that loyalty may be manifested by criticism of one's own culture. Other discussions of racial betrayal have not uncovered so readily the critical edge of loyalty. These discussions typically focus on phenomena such as passing for white or, by some other means, abandoning or selling out one's own racialized community or people for the sake of private gain. Blacks who marry or have relationships interracially may get characterized as traitors; people of color who do not support the liberatory struggles of their people may be seen as betraying their race, being "Uncle Tom"; mixed-race people may be thought of as traitors if they do not identify with a racialized of-color group (Funderburg 1994).

As Naomi Zack writes: "Black people are likely to perceive the person who is culturally or ethnically white, but racially black, as an inauthentic black person, someone who is disloyal to other black people or who evades or denies racial discrimination by attempting to pass (for white)" (1992, 8). Similarly, blacks who assimilate, make it into the middle class, or become highly educated are often considered to be traitors. Bell hooks points to the charge that black intellectuals are traitors, and notes in response simply that they sometimes are and they sometimes are not—it depends on the work that they do. She writes:

> Black intellectuals who choose to do work that addresses the needs and concerns of black liberation struggle, of black folks seeking to decolonize their minds and imaginations, will find no separation has to exist between themselves and other black people from various class backgrounds. This does not mean that our work will be embraced without critique, or that we will not be seen as suspect, only that we can counter the negative representations of black intellectuals as uppity assimilated traitors by the work we do. (1995, 234–235)

Feminist communities have also generated a discourse about loyalty that focuses on a gender-based commitment of women to one another and that, like the racial discourses described directly above, have not recognized or at least not emphasized that loyalty may be demonstrated through critique of one's object of loyalty. In lesbian communities that tend(ed) toward separatism, "traitor" has been applied with quite a bit of vehemence to those who "sleep with the enemy"—even though that phrase is seldom said out loud any more.[8] Lesbians frequently question bisexuals' loyalty to women. Paula Rust's sociological study of lesbians' and bisexual women's attitudes about bisexuality reveals the prevalence of lesbians' belief that bisexuals are not loyal:

> When asked directly to agree or disagree with the statement "Bisexuals are not as committed to other women as lesbians are; they are more likely to desert their female friends," 61% of lesbian respondents agreed. When asked to agree or disagree with the statement "It can be dangerous for lesbians to trust bisexuals too much, because when the going really gets rough, they are not as likely to stick around and fight it out," 53% agreed.[9] (Rust 1995, 77–78)

8. See, for instance, *For Lesbians Only* (Hoagland and Penelope 1988), which contains selections—primarily from the 1970s—that use this language. Thus, the Gutter Dyke Collective writes in 1973: "Separatism, as a position, is the way in which we relate to other lesbians, women and the enemy. . . . Straight/heterosexual women can't be trusted in any real situation because they will sell you out if it gets too heavy for them—men are the focal point of their lives" (Hoagland and Penelope 1988, 27); "Alice, Gordon, Debbie, & Mary" write in 1973: "We see 'straight' feminists, or non-lesbian feminists, to . . . be a contradiction in terms: You cannot be dedicated to eliminating male-supremacy (sexism) and, at the same time, be relating to men, who are the enemy" (Hoagland and Penelope 1988, 35).

9. It is interesting to note that some bisexuals also agreed with these two statements. Rust writes that "a sizable minority of bisexuals actually *agreed* with each statement; one out of nine agreed that bisexuals are less committed than lesbians, and one out of four agreed that lesbians can't trust bisexuals to stick around when the going gets rough" (1995, 216).

Rust comments on the lesbians in her study who spontaneously expressed "the most bitter feelings toward bisexual women": "[a]t best, they see bisexual women as weak-willed and, at worst, as traitors to the lesbian community because they are unwilling to own their lesbianism" (1995, 85). Bisexual writers frequently focus on the experience of being called a traitor;[10] lesbians who get involved with men or "go back to men" are characterized as treasonous.[11] For instance, Ruth Gibian describes having "internalized the politics of a community that said by loving a man I was a traitor taking the easy—that is, straight—way out" and having to struggle against this image of herself (1992, 4); one of her fears about falling in love with a man is that "*the lesbian community will think I've defected*" (1992, 12). Amanda Yoshizaki reports the same experience: "when I come out in the lesbian community as having married a man, I am often viewed as a traitor at best and leper at worst" (1992, 156).

The idea of betrayal may be used even more widely than this in feminist communities. It may be used to speak of separatists who become nonseparatist, radical feminists who change their views (or their practices) of sex to include expressions of sexuality that were forbidden by their former political convictions, and, more broadly, anyone who shifts the primary focus of their political work—whether that work had been antipornography work, antiracist work, the work of building vibrant lesbian community, and so on. When one's political work defines one's community, one may be called a traitor for moving away from whatever that work is, for by doing so, one breaks with the community.

III

Loyalty has not been conceived as praiseworthy under all conditions, for not just any object of loyalty will do. Loyalty has been cast simultaneously as a virtue—when it is loyalty to a struggling, oppressed group that one is a member of, such as loyalty to women qua women or loyalty to blacks qua blacks—and as a vice—when it is loyalty to an oppressor group that one is a member of, such as white women's loyalty to the white race or, in Marilyn Frye's (1992) terminology, to "whiteliness," a racial term that she uses as analogous to the gender term "masculinity." In any discourse that advocates disloyalty to an oppressor group—with this disloyalty construed as an act of resistance—the possibility of being loyal and yet profoundly critical is ruled out; according to these stories of commendable betrayal, one expresses opposition to, say, racism, not by being a loyal critic of racist, white communities, but by refusing any allegiance to the (white) community.

There is a body of feminist literature that valorizes white women's refusal to be loyal to a world order that is at once patriarchal and racist; women are

10. See, for instance, Armstrong 1995; Ault 1996; Gamson 1996.

11. Examples of this abound in lesbian publications; Rust 1995 includes a survey of these publications in her study. Stacey Young (1992) reports on similar portrayals of bisexuals in lesbian publications and analyzes the implications of the term *hasbian* (a creative word for "traitor").

praised for being "disloyal to civilization"—a phrase that Adrienne Rich borrowed from Lillian Smith. Rich, writing in 1978, claims, "[W]e have a strong antiracist female tradition, despite all efforts by the patriarchy to polarize its creature-objects, creating dichotomies of privilege and caste, skin-color and age and condition of servitude" (1978, 285). She describes a particular white woman's use of her power as a slave owner as owing to "false loyalty to a system against which she had at first instinctively revolted, and which was destroying her integrity" (1978, 283), invoking the idea of false consciousness in which the woman failed to see that her true allegiance was to women, not to her slave-owning husband.[12] Minnie Bruce Pratt, writing in 1984, extends the theme of white women's betrayal of their white communities, analyzing this betrayal in terms of the fears it brings up for white women involved in antiracist work. She points out: "We don't want to lose the love of the first people who knew us; we don't want to be standing outside the circle of home, with nowhere to go" (1984, 48). She describes the feeling of betraying her mother in whose eyes her antiracist actions were wrong: "She loved me and felt much pain, and shame: I was going the wrong way; I had walked away, and seemed to have turned my back on home" (1984, 48). And yet Pratt speaks of this betrayal proudly, perhaps even self-righteously, emphasizing that racial justice demands such betrayal on her part, whether the betrayal be of her home community or of her subsequent chosen political communities. She asks, "[C]an I maintain my principles against my need for the love and presence of others like me? It is lonely to be separated from others because of injustice, but it is also lonely to break with our own in opposition to that injustice" (1984, 50).

Mab Segrest's 1994 *Memoir of a Race Traitor* has a somewhat different tone. Although she, like Pratt, explores the pain of betraying her white family through her extensive antiracist work, her reference to herself as a race traitor is simply an acknowledgment that this is what she has (accurately) been named; it is the Klan and neo-Nazi groups that use this term as a label for whites like herself. White race traitors are merely one of the many targets of white supremacist groups. For instance, Segrest cites a declaration by a member of the neo-Nazi White Patriot party who writes: "I declare war against Niggers, Jews, Queers, assorted Mongrels, white Race traitors, and despicable informants . . . so fellow Aryan Warriors strike now" (1994, 143). While the term *race traitor* is spoken as an insult, Segrest embraces rather than refuses it, proud of her at times life-threatening work against white supremacists. Meanwhile, however, Segrest recognizes that betraying one's family by crossing racial boundaries may not, for white people, originate in antiracist politics; racial transgression may simply be a convenient way for a white person to rebel against her family. Segrest refers to a black participant in an antiracism workshop who made this

12. I am not interested here in whether or not Rich's analysis is right; in fact, I think her use of the concept of false consciousness and her highlighting of white women's "instinctive" rebellions against racism are quite problematic. My point is simply that she has given a positive valuation to disloyalty.

point: "White people use Black people to draw boundaries in homes where family members' identities are enmeshed, [the participant] explained, in response to a white woman's pleased story of how upset she had made her parents in her adolescence by dating Black men" (1994, 24–25). Thus Segrest attempts to disentangle her family betrayals from her authentic betrayals of white racial unity. Ultimately, she claims that being a race traitor is not a betrayal of her kin; she writes, "[I]t's not my people, it's the *idea* of race I am betraying" (1994, 4).

White race traitors endorse their betrayals as attempts to renounce their own privilege or even to destroy the possibility for privileged membership by anyone in the group by undermining its unity. This is the position of Noel Ignatiev and John Garvey, editors of the journal *Race Traitor*, which they founded "to serve as an intellectual center for those seeking to abolish the white race" (Garvey and Ignatiev 1996, 10). They speak of the white race as a club and advocate acts of dissent that "aim to dissolve the club, to break it apart," claiming that "the weak point of the club is its need for unanimity" (1996, 11). In gender politics, "refusing to be a man" (Stoltenberg 1989) may be a similar form of betrayal.

Sandra Harding argues directly for "traitorous identities" for anyone in unjustly privileged social locations (1991, chap. 11). According to Harding, disloyalty—in the form of acting counter to the expectations for someone in one's social location or of drawing on the insights and the work of marginalized people and using it as a starting point for thinking critically about one's own self—serves to generate liberatory knowledge. Lisa Heldke further develops Harding's position and points out, among other things, that betraying an over-privileged identity as white or as a man (or as a heterosexual, etc.) does *not* involve ceasing to be white or to be a man (etc.). Heldke writes:

> I am more inclined to see the process as one of dismantling an identity I inhabit, in order to rebuild it, rather than attempting to step outside that identity, in order to rebuild it from without, as it were. Traitorousness requires me to insist on my whiteness—to insist that I and others recognize my whiteness as always relevant, always a factor in the way I conceive the world and others; and to work to detect that factor in the places where it is presently most undetectable to me. (1998, 93)

Because in her view the aim is not to exit whiteness itself, there would be room for thinking of this critical process of dismantling and rebuilding identity from within as one that exhibits loyalty, rather than disloyalty—not loyalty to the racist practices currently associated with an identity as white, but rather loyalty to the community of people with whom (and as one of whom) one will be reconstructing the identity. But importantly, the critical act of remaking whiteness—even from within—is presented by Heldke as a traitorous act, revealing an assumption that loyalty and deep criticism are incompatible, or perhaps that given a critique of whiteness as a legitimate basis for exclusive group membership, there is no justifiable reason for loyalty, for loyalty serves to sustain the group itself as an exclusive group.

Thus it seems that whether or not one believes that white race traitors committing acts of betrayal—or males who are disloyal to masculinity, and so on—ought to divest themselves of their identities or ought to critique the identities from within, the point is that betrayal, rather than loyalty, is what has been recommended with respect to the identities built on domination. Within this discourse, loyalty with respect to unjustly privileged groups is taken to constitute acquiescence to others' subordination precisely because profound criticism—which is what is called for—is understood as irreconcilable with loyalty, or because the existence of the potential object of loyalty (for instance, a community built on white identity) is itself thought to be unjust. Because acts of loyalty to whiteness or to masculinity (or to other dominant identities) are assumed to entail supporting others' oppression, those who have membership in these oppressor groups but who are committed to refusing to support others' oppression are advised to opt for disloyalty toward the oppressor group.

IV

So far I have primarily been taking note of the widespread assumption within both feminist communities and the communities of racialized groups involved in liberatory struggles that certain attitudes or acts qualify one as a traitor to one's community and that this is a terrible thing to be if those one is betraying are subordinated people, while at the same time disloyalty to an unjustly privileged group may actually be praised. I am not interested here in whether there is a legitimate critique of the actions or characters of those who are accused of being traitors to oppressed groups (for instance, a critique of "sleeping with the enemy" or of passing); rather, I am interested in the fact that one can condemn another member of an oppositional community by calling her or him a traitor. The implication of this is that loyalty to such a community—or, more vaguely, to others who share an oppressed identity—is considered to be a virtue. Meanwhile, there is some shared understanding that for loyalty to be praiseworthy, one must have correctly identified the proper object of one's loyalty and must reject dominant groups as potential objects of loyalty. While there is much disagreement over what does and what does not count as a treasonous self, one thing seems clear given the discourse on loyalty within the context of resistance: to be called loyal is to be praised, if and only if the loyalty is to those on the side of the right and the good.

One might at this point say that indeed, loyalty is a virtue when it is loyalty to those struggling for liberation, and disloyalty is a virtue when it is disloyalty to the oppressors. Thus, for instance, black racial loyalty is a virtue, and white racial loyalty is morally and politically reprehensible. However, this answer comes too fast, for it is not yet obvious that loyalty is unproblematic when it is loyalty to oppressed communities or communities of resistance; nor is it clear that loyalty cannot function subversively (and consequently be praiseworthy) when it is loyalty to dominant groups. The belief that the value or disvalue of loyalty is determined by the goodness of the object of loyalty (hence, that loyalty is valuable when directed toward oppressed/resistant groups and not valuable when directed toward oppressor groups) may be misguided; perhaps it is better not to ask whether a group *as it is* is worthy of my loyalty, but rather to ask: can and should I offer my loyalty critically toward the groups that are in some way mine, whether or not they are groups whose values *as given* I can endorse?

A key question here will be whether loyalty is compatible with criticism. Within the context of resistance movements, only those who are caught in the conflicted position of trying to be loyal to different groups with sometimes opposing beliefs—such as feminists of color—have been led to insist that the loyal self can meanwhile be a highly critical self. One would hope that all oppositional communities would recognize the need to nurture their members' abilities to continually subject the communities' beliefs and practices to criticism. But the discourses that I cited above reveal that both feminist communities and racialized communities of color have fallen into the mistake of silencing internal dissent, for they have tended to portray departures from the communities' hegemonic beliefs and practices or variations on the defining features of the identity on which the community is based as reprehensible acts of treason. Those who stand at the intersection of competing commitments have had insight into the damage such a curtailing of criticism does; some feminists of color have maintained that they are the ones who are truly loyal to their communities of color and that part of their loyalty is manifested by the work of feminist critique that they carry out with respect to their home cultures. Thus it is necessary to now consider these insights in more detail, asking whether one can salvage loyalty as a virtue by arguing that loyalty is compatible with exercising one's critical faculties—as, for instance, Moraga and Anzaldúa both contend that it is—and then considering: if loyalty and critique can combine, how deeply critical can one be without becoming a traitor?

Contemporary communitarians, having adopted Aristotelian assumptions about the sociality of humans, tend to count loyalty as a virtue because of its role in sustaining community connections; thus they are loath to relinquish the claim that loyalty is a praiseworthy trait. Among communitarians, those who reject the conservatism that threatens to accompany a commitment to community also positively value critique of or resistance to all practices of domination, even when such practices are located in the very communities within which their own selves may be constituted (including self-proclaimed oppositional communities). The challenge—if one is to preserve loyalty as a virtue—is in making room for a critical disposition in a self conceived as socially constituted within a community, especially when the object of critique becomes the community itself.

Marilyn Friedman has tried to meet this challenge—without specifically endorsing loyalty, but at least recognizing the value of community—by distinguishing between different sorts of communities within which a person may have her/his identity constituted or reconstituted. The self that is social and yet critical of traditional communities (for traditional communities, Friedman has in mind "communities of place" such as those based on families, neighborhoods, schools, and so on) can opt for a "community of choice" built on friendships, urban networks, or other voluntary associations (Friedman 1993, chap. 9). By recommending chosen over unchosen connections, Friedman aims to release women from oppressive gender norms typical of traditional communities. But because the choosing self that Friedman describes is one who is inclined to actually leave a community upon becoming highly critical of its values, this sort of self does not model how to be both loyal and critical; the self that aims to relocate in a community of choice demonstrates no loyalty to the community (of place, presumably) from which she/he flees.

Michael Walzer's work on the "connected critic" develops a better model of the coexistence of loyalty and critique; Walzer presents the practice of social critique as best carried out from a position within, rather than outside of and at a distance from, the object of criticism. The "connected critic . . . earns his [*sic*] authority, or fails to do so, by arguing with his fellows. . . . [He], angrily and insistently, sometimes at considerable personal risk . . . objects, protests, and remonstrates. This critic is one of us" (Walzer 1987, 39). Describing and mocking the stereotypical picture of the (unconnected) leftist critic—which Walzer contends does not accurately represent what real, historical leftist critics have been like—Walzer writes:

> The stereotypical leftist critic breaks loose from his local and familial world (bourgeois, petty-bourgeois, conformist, religious, sheltered, provincial, and so on), escapes with much attendant drama, detaches himself from all emotional ties, steps back so as to see the world with absolute clarity, studies what he sees (scientifically, in accordance with the most advanced views), discovers universal values as if for the first time, finds these values embodied in the movement of the oppressed (class, nation, gender, his own or the other—so long as the "finding" is objective, it doesn't matter), decides to support the movement and to criticize its enemies, who are very often people such as he once was. (1988, 225–226)

Walzer finds this story of critique unconvincing in part because he does not think values develop as universals, unbound to the particulars of any location; further, Walzer finds the picture not just implausible but also undesirable: one should not *want* to be disconnected. What is lacking in the stereotypical leftist critic is loyalty, and Walzer both argues for the strong claim that criticism is not possible "as a social practice in the absence of loyalty" (1988, 236) and implies that the alternative to situated criticism, becoming a "critic-at-large surveying the whole world, critical of modernity, popular culture, mass society, bureaucracy, science and technology, the welfare state, and anything else that turns up" (1988, 227), is unappealing.[13]

13. Jonathan Allen (1998) makes the point that Walzer confuses or conflates two meanings of being connected, namely, he moves without argument from the claim that critique requires situatedness (one sense of being connected) to the claim that it requires loyalty (another sense of being connected).

If Walzer is right about the implausibility and undesirability of being a social critic who is unbound to any particular community, and if connection requires loyalty (presumably because without its members' loyalty the community may dissolve), what will be needed is an account of how to engage loyally in critique or how to dissent without losing one's community. Alasdair MacIntyre, in a discussion of patriotism, suggests what may be thought of as guidelines for the loyal critic by identifying the outer limits of loyal critique.[14] For MacIntyre, patriotism, which he takes to be a species of loyalty, does not require completely unconditional and uncritical acceptance of the status quo. He presents a distinction between the varieties of criticism that patriotism permits and those that it does not, and in so doing develops a version of patriotism in which one can be critical and yet still be bounded in one's moral thinking by the ties one has simply because one has been constituted through the particularities of one's own family, community, or nation.

Before offering his distinction, MacIntyre describes patriotism simply as

> one of a class of loyalty-exhibiting virtues (that is, if it *is* a virtue at all) . . . all [of which] exhibit a peculiar action-generating regard for particular persons, institutions or groups, a regard founded upon a particular historical relationship of association between the person exhibiting the regard and the relevant person, institution or group. ([1984] 1994, 308)

MacIntyre emphasizes some of the communitarian bases for considering patriotism to be a virtue. For instance, by noting that the very foundation for all morality resides not in impartial thinking—which he considers to be impossible for humans as social creatures—but rather in what one learns as a being situated in very particular relationships, he points out that if the communities that constitute our selves depend for their existence on their members' loyalty, disloyalty destroys the ground on which morality rests. In destroying one's community, he thinks, one destroys one's moral self.[15]

While this sort of communitarian thinking has resonated with some feminists, feminists cannot fully embrace communitarianism in light of concerns such as those voiced by Friedman about the ways that traditional and often oppressive communities affect women; while constitutive communities are

14. For a debate initiated by MacIntyre's discussion of patriotism, see Nathanson 1989 and 1992, and Gomberg 1990.

15. As Ruth Ginzberg points out, if one has more than one moral community, expulsion from one moral community (or destruction of that community) does not completely destroy one's moral self, since one is not dependent exclusively on that community. She writes:

> I risk genuine "demoralization" when my moral judgments differ enough from those of my moral community for me to be excommunicated, for if I am expelled from my moral community, some piece of my moral agency itself is at stake. I say "some piece of" my moral agency is at stake because most of us are simultaneously members of a number of moral communities. One rarely loses one's membership in all of one's moral communities at once. (1991, 138)

indeed necessary for one's identity, one needs to resist the communities' power to be damaging to one's self.[16] It is in response to this problem that Friedman recommends that one choose one's community/ies critically rather than just accept the community in which one finds oneself. However, this does not adequately solve the problem of how to respond if one's community has values or practices that are objectionable; after all, *any* community—even a chosen one—may present one with a mix of values that one can endorse and those that one cannot, and the exit option will quickly wear thin if one feels compelled to leave any community that is significantly flawed. Fortunately, the situation is not as dichotomous as Friedman imagines: if one can stay planted in a community that one has not (fully) chosen, but work to transform the community itself by engaging in critique from within, one need neither accept the community as given nor leave it entirely.[17] Since staying and engaging in critique will allow one to preserve loyalty as a virtue to be exercised toward a community—and thus will enable the preservation of another good, namely, the community itself—critique will be more satisfactory than exit.

In his discussion of patriotism, MacIntyre also appears concerned about the damage a constitutive community may do to one's self and concerned about the unacceptable values that one's community (or national) membership may implicate one in (though his concerns are clearly not from a feminist perspective). He writes: "Patriotism turns out to be a permanent source of moral danger" ([1984] 1994, 315), thus expressing his worry that patriotism does not allow for thoroughgoing criticism of the object of loyalty—in this case, the nation. He admits:

> [T]he morality of patriotism is one which precisely because it is framed in terms of the membership of some particular social community with some particular social, political and economic structure, must exempt at least some fundamental structures of that community's life from criticism. Because

16. In addition to Friedman 1993, see Weiss 1995 for a feminist consideration of communitarianism.

17. María Lugones rejects Friedman's community of place/community of choice distinction for a similar reason, arguing that while the concept of a community of choice is useful because it introduces the notion of critical distance from a community, Friedman errs in positing the position of critique and resistance as necessarily located outside of a community of place. Instead of accepting Friedman's characterization of communities of place as traditional and internally homogeneous with respect to values and practices, Lugones insists that communities of place are themselves locations of contestation and resistance, where identities are constituted complexly: "Why not think that as contradictory identities are formed within communities of place, these communities are revealed as not univocal, passing on and embodying an undisturbed common sense, but as complex and tense sites of identity formation?" (Lugones 2003, 185–186). If communities of place can sustain internal critique, one does not have to leave them in order to be a political resister. As Lugones contends, "Resistant negotiation of everyday life does not require the formation of associations that lift one from community of place; it rather constitutes life in communities of place" (2003, 186). She suggests bell hooks's "Homeplace: A Site of Resistance" (in hooks 1990) as a text that demonstrates the presence and the value of resistance within a community of place.

> patriotism has to be a loyalty that is in some respects unconditional, so in just those respects rational criticism is ruled out. ([1984] 1994, 313–314)

However, MacIntyre argues, it is not the case that everything about the nation must be unconditionally accepted by the patriot. It is, he thinks, an essential task of those defending patriotism to distinguish between what may and what may not be subjected to criticism and possibly rejected by the patriot (or, analogously, by anyone who exhibits one of the other varieties of loyalty). This motivates MacIntyre's distinction between what may and what may not be loyally (patriotically) critiqued:

> Whatever is exempted from the patriot's criticism the status quo of power and government and the policies pursued by those exercising power and government never need be so exempted. What then is exempted? The answer is: the nation conceived *as a project*, a project somehow or other brought to birth in the past and carried on so that a morally distinctive community was brought into being which embodied a claim to political autonomy in its various organized and institutionalized expressions. ([1984] 1994, 314)

One might have thought that loyalty, functioning like any other Aristotelian virtue, would name the mean, in this case the mean between the deficiency of disloyalty and the excess state of blind loyalty, where blind loyalty would include completely uncritical acceptance of and support for its object. Thus, one response to the claim that loyalty requires that one suspend one's critical faculties could be that only the excess—blind loyalty—requires this, while proper loyalty can include a moderate amount of criticism. But MacIntyre's distinction between different *kinds* of criticism is more helpful. Instead of claiming that loyalty is compatible with moderate criticism, one can claim that loyalty is compatible with even the highest possible level of criticism, as long as the criticism does not aim to destroy or even to call into question the existence of the group, qua group, to which one is loyal.

In MacIntyre's discussion of patriotism, the "group" whose existence one is forbidden to critically undermine is the nation. What about other potential objects of group loyalty? Communities of place will function much like nations (though smaller), as will other "given" rather than "chosen" communities; their members, whose identities have been deeply constituted within these communities, depend on the continued existence of their communities for the maintenance of their own moral (or social) identities. Many racial or ethnic communities (regardless of whether they are located in a particular space or dispersed spatially but held together by social meanings) will function in this way, providing identities for their members such that the members' identities are dependent on the continued existence of the communities. These communities may, when based on racially or ethnically marginalized identities, be generally sites of resistance—for instance, resistance to racial domination—though one might find in connection with racial communities more fully chosen oppositional communities made up of those who take an explicit stance against racism. Even communities of choice—which is how any community built around the project of liberatory politics may be described when its members have consciously committed to a political stance (such as feminism) and on that basis committed to the oppositional community—may be identity-conferring and function similarly: their members lose their own identities if they lose or destroy the communities. Thus in focusing on the question of whether loyalty is a virtue for communities of resistance, I could consider a range of communities (those given, those chosen, those exhibiting a mixture) while requiring only the feature that the community be identity-conferring or constituting with respect to its members. Loyal criticism, within any of these communities, will have a specific limit: one may not aim to undermine through one's critique the existence of the community as a community, and therefore one must exempt from one's criticisms the defining elements of the community.

V

Following MacIntyre, I will proceed now under the assumption that one cannot be said to be loyal to a group if one calls into question or undermines its basis for existence. One might maintain other loyalties—for instance, to individual members of a group—but a group itself cannot be said to be the object of one's loyalty while one acts to deconstruct it. However, this understanding of loyalty (based on MacIntyre's distinction) could set off alarms for the political resister: given precisely this account of loyalty, loyalty may be problematic for feminist communities and for communities of liberatory racial politics, for indeed sometimes the continued existence of that which defines the community as a community is what must be called into question for liberatory purposes. There are several potential motivations for critiquing—and ultimately rejecting—the continued existence of a community as a community. Both gender terms and racial designations have been targets of deconstructive critiques, and to the extent that gender or race defines the identities which ground a liberatory political struggle, such critiques may undermine the very existence of an oppositional community formed around these identities. One could not, for instance, deconstruct the concept of "woman" and remain loyal to women understood as a group or to any specific "women's community" that depended on the concept "woman." Recognition of the intersectional nature of identities also complicates many potential objects of group loyalty under oppression: neither a gender-based group nor a race-based group (etc.) should be protected from the deconstruction that loyalty forbids, because categories of gender and race (etc.) become problematic bases for identity if oppressions are experienced as interlocked. Groups (formerly) based on gender or race only ought to survive *as* groups (and thus be objects of loyalty) if they trade a crude identity-based politics for something more complex.

If one were to agree with any of the motivations for aiming to undermine the basis for particular oppositional communities then, since this is precisely what loyalty rules out (according to MacIntyre), one will have to forfeit loyalty.

Movements that aim to deconstruct or subvert identity, or to complicate identity beyond recognition, could be characterized as a politics that necessarily involves betrayal of the identities—and communities—that are undermined. There may be times when betrayal is exactly what is called for.

It will be useful to look at some examples of the deconstruction of what have been taken to be proper objects of group loyalty for members of oppressed groups. For instance, a term such as *lesbian* or *lesbian-feminist* may function well both to give definition to a political project (such as resisting compulsory heterosexuality) and to delineate the boundaries of a community—and thus may have been thought to name a proper object of group loyalty—but lesbian (identity) politics and lesbian community have been giving way and might best continue to (partially or fully) give way to differently constituted politics and communities. Loyalty to lesbian community may be misplaced, and betrayal—as long as it stems from the right motivation (namely, seeing a need to deconstruct the identity) and not, for instance, from fear or from a desire for individual advantage—may serve liberatory ends. The understanding of "lesbian" is under constant contestation; some critiques aim to subvert the identity "lesbian" or at least to make the enactment of "lesbian" only one among a grand proliferation of possible gender/sexual performances such that it no longer serves as a unifying identity (Butler 1990). Such critiques would count under MacIntyre's distinction as disloyal, because they aim to dissolve a certain collectivity as a collectivity.

The emergence of the term *queer*—where *queerness* "includes the impulse to take apart that identity from within" (Gamson 1996, 397)—perhaps best exemplifies a politics that actually calls for disloyalty (in the name of liberatory aims) because of the way that acts of disloyalty do the work of abandoning or relinquishing the defining terms of a community. As Judith Butler writes:

> If the term "queer" is to be a site of collective contestation, the point of departure for a set of historical reflections and futural imaginings, it will have to remain that which is, in the present, never fully owned, but always and only redeployed, twisted, queered from a prior usage and in the direction of urgent and expanding political purposes. This also means that it will doubtless have to be yielded in favor of terms that do that political work more effectively. Such a yielding may well become necessary in order to accommodate—without domesticating—democratizing contestations that have and will redraw the contours of the movement in ways that can never be fully anticipated in advance. (1993, 228)

The suggested deconstruction of racial designations—primarily based on the points that racial terms do not name natural categories but rather emerged for purposes of racial subordination and that one cannot embrace such terms without reinforcing racism—follows a similar pattern. Those arguing for the deconstruction or abandonment of racial identities would be, according to MacIntyre's distinction, disloyal because they question the actual existence of the racialized collectivity to which they are in one way or another expected to show allegiance. For instance, Naomi Zack (1992) argues for a position of deracination (that is, the refusal of all racial designations), claiming that undermining the foundation of the racialized community designated by the term *black* will help to undermine racism itself.

I do not want to rule out the deconstructive move, and I recognize in it an element of truth about relying on terms that arose and can be utilized for purposes of oppression; the identity terms that deconstructive critiques target can subjectify the self, and there is an ossifying and limiting effect that identity categories have on members of communities captured by the identity terms. Nevertheless, I believe that the postmodern position from within which deconstructive critiques emerge dispenses with identity too easily, and with it sacrifices the possibility of constitutive community (and the loyalties that can be commanded by such communities) and the sources of support, knowledge, and politically resistant energy and motivation that identity-conferring communities can sustain. The value of deconstruction (once it is understood as calling for disloyalty) does not necessarily outweigh the value of maintaining identities, especially if the identities can be understood—reconstructed—as much more complex than the simple categories of, for instance, gender or race. Critical moves to question or reject identities that form the foundations of particular communities come into conflict with arguments for the reassertion of identities, both claiming to be the more truly liberatory move. Thus there is much debate within theories of political resistance over whether to dispense with or conserve—or significantly transform but ultimately hold onto—identities, a debate that I can only touch on here.

For instance, referring to the proposed deconstruction of gay and lesbian identities (along the lines that Butler suggests), Joshua Gamson argues that "the logic and political utility of deconstructing collective categories vies with that of shoring them up; each logic is true, and neither is fully tenable" (1996, 396). Taking gay and lesbian identity-based politics as an example of the strategy of shoring up identities, he points out that the advocates of this strategy "do not do justice to the subversive and liberating aspects of loosened collective boundaries" (1996, 408). On the other side, however, are the failures of a politics focused on subverting identity: "queer theory and politics tend to run past a critique of the particular, concrete forces that make sexual identity, in stabilized and binary form, a basis for discipline, regulation, pleasure, and political empowerment" (1996, 408); deconstructive strategies do not pay attention to "the very concrete and violent institutional forms to which the most logical answer is resistance in and through a particular collective identity" (1996, 408). Thus disloyalty may serve a deconstructive strategy by undermining an identity or a community but may simultaneously be politically dangerous if it risks in concrete ways the welfare of the members of the community.

The value of a deconstructive strategy with respect to race has been similarly contested by those who see racial identities as important sources of solidarity, support, and political action. For instance, Zack's position has been countered by others, such as Lewis Gordon, who would not concede that Zack's disloyalty is to a collectivity that ought to and can dissolve. Rather, she and those who agree with her position of deracination—for instance, other mixed-race people who refuse to accept any racial designations or at least refuse the designation of black—are engaging in the perpetuation of racism by rejecting blackness, while their darker-skinned kin do not have the option of doing so. While those who identify as mixed-race cannot be said to be buying into whiteness, Gordon writes, "to reject the importance of being white in no way addresses the social revulsion with being black" (1995, 392). Because Gordon believes that racist ideology is premised on two principles, namely, "(1) be white, but above all, (2) don't be black" (1995, 389), a disloyalty to blackness through a refusal to accept it as a racial designation is consistent, for him, with the premises of racism. The disloyalty could be further characterized as an abandonment of others to a form of oppression that a select few, through their disloyalty, can escape individually. While Zack, then, intends for her critical position of deracination to serve liberatory aims even if it is disloyal to a racial collectivity that asks for loyalty from her, there is good reason for questioning whether liberatory aims really are served.

This points to a significant danger of the deconstructive strategy: the motivations for dispensing with marginal identities are often suspect, for they arise quite often not from an accurate assessment of the harm the identity category does to all those captured by it, but rather from a desire for individual escape. Those advocating for their release from constraining identity categories—that is, advocating for disloyalty since their aim is to destroy the identity categories that ground "their" communities—may be masking more clearly hurtful forms of treason: divesting themselves individually of an oppressed identity while leaving others behind to suffer the consequences of remaining inevitably marked by an identity that persists regardless of the deconstructive attempt. Anthony Appiah seems guilty of this. He, like Zack, aims not only to expose the fact that racial categorization is scientifically invalid but furthermore to count this fact as significant for racial politics; yet his position goes even further than Zack's in some ways because beyond questioning the legitimacy of race as an organizing category, he asserts an individualist objection to any collectivity whatsoever. Against a position such as Appiah's, Gordon points out that the marks of collective identities do not disappear out of the lives of the oppressed no matter how hard postmodern critics wish the identities away. Gordon argues:

> The anti-race people . . . miss the point. Even if they show that race is a social construction, even if they show that races are no more than cultural or social formations, even if they show that races are pseudo-scientific fictions, they still need to address the ways in which phenomena understood as racial phenomena are lived. (1995, 388)

It is not that Appiah completely disregards the importance of the collective identity of blacks; however, what he expresses most strongly is a simultaneous wish to be able to break with the collectivity for the sake of a more autonomous self. In the following passages he acknowledges the need for the collectivity but also complains of the restraint that membership in a collectivity places on him, describing his desire to break with it:

> An African-American after the Black Power movement takes the old script of self-hatred, the script in which he or she is a nigger, and works, in community

> with others, to construct a series of positive black life scripts. . . . And if one is to be black in a society that is racist then one has constantly to deal with assaults on one's dignity. In this context, insisting on the right to live a dignified life will not be enough. . . . One will end up asking to be respected *as a black*. (1996, 98)

Appiah insists that he is sympathetic to this story and that "it may even be historically, strategically necessary for the story to go this way," but he then says:

> We need to go on to the next necessary step, which is to ask whether the identities constructed in this way are ones we can all be happy with in the longer run. What demanding respect for people *as blacks* or *as gays* requires is that there be some scripts that go with being an African-American or having same-sex desires. . . . It is at this point that someone who takes autonomy seriously will want to ask whether we have not replaced one kind of tyranny with another. If I had to choose between Uncle Tom and Black Power, I would, of course, choose the latter. But I would like not to have to choose. (1996, 98–99)

For Appiah, given the conflict he describes, loyalty would be misguided since he finds the racial collectivity that presses a claim upon his loyalty to be itself based on a concept that he rejects and even at times characterizes as the very source of his oppression.

Those who advocate the dissolution of races need to consider the possibility that at the present moment the preservation of racialized identities may still be necessary for liberatory purposes. Furthermore, they must consider whether their questioning the basis for the racial collectivity—which one could think of as an act of betrayal—*could* even serve to dissolve a racial category. I think that in many cases—including cases involving the current racial categories—the collectivity that one betrays does not dissolve as a result; though some people may escape the category to one degree or another by disassociating from it, others are left behind in it. Naomi Scheman makes this point:

> Though I never chose to be a Jew . . . I can embrace that identity, make it mine, struggle with it, make it fit; or I can ignore it, reject its relevance to what I think matters about me, find myself elsewhere. So it is with being a woman—Jews are the people the Nazis round up; women are the people misogynists target for rape: in either case I can claim an identity informed but not determined by those who define it by their hate, or I can disown the identity and find other ground on which to stand. If social ontology were up to me, I don't think there'd be either Jews or women: I don't think I'd have constructed religion or gender. But the supposition doesn't make sense: social ontology couldn't be up to me, or even us; it's a matter of history. And, in the light of history, it is a matter of honor not to walk away from the people with whom history has given me "a shared fate." (1992, 191)[18]

18. Scheman cites Evelyn Torton Beck (1989, 175) for the phrase "a shared fate."

While the deconstruction of the racial categories that name oppressed or marginalized groups may be counter to liberatory aims—and disloyalty in the name of deconstruction may cover up suspicious motivations such as individual gain premised on the abandonment of others—this does not mean that *no* collective identities should be eradicated through disloyalty. As Marilyn Frye points out, while racialized communities of people of color may pursue liberatory aims by strengthening racial identification, white people may help to undermine racism through disloyalty to white racialized communities precisely because such disloyalty can deconstruct the racial category of whiteness, a category that functions to unjustly lend privilege and authority to those included in it. There is an asymmetry between oppressed racialized groups and privileged racialized groups with respect to the value of their abolishing their respective racial categories. While white women, Frye claims, should contribute to the "demolition" of the white race, this does not imply that "women of other races should take the same approach to their racial categorization and their races" (1992, 165). She argues:

> [T]he social-constructedness of race and races in the racist state has very different meanings for groups differently placed with respect to these categories. The ontological freedom of categorical reconstruction may be generic, but what is politically possible differs for those differently positioned, and not all the political possibilities for every group are desirable. (1992, 164)

Because the aim is actually to destroy a racial category in the case of whiteness, being loyally critical of a community based on that category would not go far enough; if maintenance of the category of whiteness requires its members' allegiance, the disposition most consistent with eradicating the category of whiteness is one of disloyalty toward it.

While I have argued that the deconstructive move with respect to categories of racially oppressed groups seems dangerous—and thus disloyalty cannot necessarily be recommended—this does not mean that the identity categories must be left untouched. Loyalty, after all, leaves lots of room for critique, even if it sets a limit. Racially marginalized identities and the communities formed around them may still be the targets of critique, as long as the critique aims at transformation rather than destruction. Without such critical remaking of identity-related communities, there will be many within these communities for whom loyalty would become a burden, perhaps so large a burden that being loyal would be utterly self-sacrificial: for instance, as suggested by both Moraga and Anzaldúa's writings, the Chicana lesbian loyally committed to (unreconstructed) Chicano culture agrees to a life of erasure.

If one is to be loyal, then, one is advised to be loyally critical; because objects of group loyalty—at least under conditions of oppression—are far from perfect, loyalty seems most promising as a virtue precisely when it is exercised critically. However, even when a loyal member of a community such as a racially marginalized community is highly critical, the virtue of loyalty exercised in this context may still be burdensome. There is a heavy toll on the loyal critic, the political resister who remains situated; in many cases such a resister becomes a sort of outcast even among her/his own people, never fully supported or accepted. Furthermore, communities may be relatively impervious to change even when subjected to internal critique, and to the extent that the objections and protestations delivered by the loyal critic fail to result in significant change, the one who is loyal may still have to endure a community whose practices are oppressive to her/himself. Loyalty, under these conditions, becomes another burdened virtue. Notwithstanding and even in recognition of this, political resisters may accept the burden of remaining (loyally) within a community that serves, in some ways badly, as a "home" but that nevertheless is better than the alternative of floating unmoored, being what Walzer dubbed the "critic-at-large."

The better possibility, of course, is a community that can avoid being too traditional (and marked with internal dynamics of domination and subordination) but also avoid becoming precarious in the way that some oppositional communities—always subject to deconstructive moves—are. For such communities to exist, identity must be rethought, and there are some promising and creative attempts at resuscitating identity under way. One such attempt comes out of the post-positivist realist position that aims at "reclaiming identity."[19] This position navigates between essentialist understandings of identity and the postmodernist repudiation of identity, rejecting both by noting that neither of these two polar stances discriminate adequately between different identities; postmodernist critiques of identity describe a violent subjectifying force as the primary feature of all identities, as if different marginalized identities did not carry distinctive experiences and thus distinctive possibilities for knowledge and political activation. As Linda Alcoff puts it, one needs "to make distinctions between kinds of processes in which identities are formed, all of which may not be coercive impositions" (Alcoff 2000, 323). Paula Moya further explains:

> Prevailing theories of identity lack the intellectual resources to distinguish between different kinds of identities. We contend that a theory of identity is inadequate unless it allows a social theorist to analyze the epistemic status and political salience of any given identity and provides her with the resources to ascertain and evaluate the possibilities and limits of different identities. Neither "essentialist" nor "postmodernist" theories of identity can do this. (Moya 2000a, 7)

Another recent critical attempt to remake identity-based politics is found in Lani Guinier and Gerald Torres's concept of "political race" (Guinier and Torres 2002), a concept designed specifically to surpass identity politics. Rather than deconstructing race, Guinier and Torres propose that one think of the racially marginalized as like the miner's canary: their lack of well-being, like the

19. See the essays collected under the title *Reclaiming Identity: Realist Theory and the Predicament of Postmodernism* (Moya and Hames-García, eds., 2000), especially Moya, "Introduction: Reclaiming Identity" and "Postmodernism, 'Realism,' and the Politics of Identity," and Alcoff, "Who's Afraid of Identity Politics?"

canary's, signals the presence of a toxic atmosphere (namely, failed democracy) that will ultimately poison not just themselves but others as well. Thus, organizing around race, instead of stagnating with the celebration of a racial category as identity politics does, leads to a much wider systemic critique. "Unlike identity politics," they insist, "political race is not about being but instead is about doing" (Guinier and Torres 2002, 16); the community based on political race is an activist community, overlapping but not coextensive with a community designated by an ordinary racial term such as "black."

Thus, there is the possibility of unpacking complex understandings of identity and of building communities that—more adequately than the communities formed around simple categories of identity—resist internally duplicating the larger society's dynamics of domination and subordination. This produces some hope for there being objects of group loyalty for political resisters, where the exercise of loyalty would not be too heavily burdened by either the damaging aspects of the community or by the need for constant internal critique. It is, however, a fragile hope, for even the communities that understand identity complexly are unstable, experimental, and liable to becoming obsolete at some future moment. Given the persistent susceptibility of these communities to a critique that will undermine the basis of the community itself—which is exactly what loyalty forbids—it seems that a proper object of group loyalty, especially a loyalty that would not meanwhile be burdensome, may be hard to hold onto.

VI

Given the sorts of identities and communities that are available under conditions of oppression, group loyalty can be a virtue only when it is exercised highly critically and when the object of loyalty is not the sort of group that would best be deconstructed rather than transformed. Political resisters thus may face two stumbling blocks regarding loyalty. First, when they are loyal to a group that calls for critique but not deconstruction, they are burdened with a commitment to a community that may still do significant damage to their selves (because the community has not yet been critically transformed in ways that would reduce its internal dynamics of domination and subordination) and with the hardships of always being a critic, never fully belonging as a comfortably accepted member. Second, when political resisters consider loyalty to communities that—as their own critical judgments may lead them to believe—would better be deconstructed, they find not that they are saddled with loyalty as a burdened virtue, but rather that loyalty becomes altogether unavailable as a virtue. In these cases disloyalty is morally prescribed.

To claim that there are instances in which one should engage in disloyalty, however, is not to say that disloyalty becomes the virtue; one can maintain, rather, that loyalty is the virtue but one that cannot be either developed or exercised (or both) in certain contexts. Because proper loyalty requires, like any Aristotelian virtue, that one determine when and how much and toward what object one should be loyal, then even if loyalty is appropriate under some circumstance, conditions of oppression may not always create the right opportunities for it. This is simply to apply something that Aristotle recognized: one cannot have perfect virtue—the virtue of what he calls a good man—in a corrupt *polis*, though one may still be a good *citizen* (see *Pol.* 1276b28–35). Certain virtues may at times simply be unavailable to a person. For instance, for Aristotle, when a citizen is not ruling, that citizen cannot express or develop the virtues associated with ruling and therefore cannot have complete or perfect virtue. Along similar lines, in the case of loyalty it may be that certain situations make the virtue of loyalty unavailable because of the absence of a good object of loyalty, namely, a group or community that ought not to be subject to deconstruction.

Aristotle makes a point about friendship that is also relevant to this consideration of loyalty. True or perfect friendship is, for him, indicative of virtue; it can only take place between good men who are similar in their goodness (*NE* 1156b8–24). Friendship of this sort both requires virtue of the friends, and it also enhances their virtuous characters. But there are times, Aristotle says, when one may have to leave a friendship—that is, engage in something quite like a betrayal of one's friend. This occurs in the case that one's friend—whom one had taken to be good—turns out to be irremediably bad (*NE* 1165b13–23).[20] In recognizing that one must leave the friendship, one acknowledges the loss of that hoped-for opportunity for the exercise and development of virtue, as that opportunity turned out not to be actualizable. And so it is with one's loyalties to any community. If one's critique reaches the limit and reveals that the community is based on an identity that ought not to be, one may be compelled to betray the community in an attempt to deconstruct it and to thus forgo the possibility of having those virtues such as loyalty that only a good (enough) community—like a good friendship—could foster.

Thus, loyalty can be a virtue, but a virtue that like any other virtue requires that it be exercised in the right way. In particular, proper loyalty—at least the sort of group loyalty I have been exploring—presupposes that the community toward which one is to be loyal is one that may need to be critiqued, but not eliminated. Oppression creates communities that are precarious as good objects of loyalty and thereby tends to make loyalty either burdened—if one accepts the position of loyal critic—or unavailable, if the critique reaches its limit and turns into a deconstructive project. While feminist communities and the communities of liberatory racial politics may at times be the sort of communities that proper loyalty requires, maintaining a disposition of loyalty even in these communities does create a "permanent source of moral danger" (MacIntyre [1984] 1994, 315), for there is always the possibility of the collectivity's "going bad," whether in the mild sense of becoming socially or politically obsolete or ineffective under changed conditions, or whether in a more severe sense of becoming thoroughly corrupt.

20. Aristotle also notes that if one friend remained the same but the other "became better and far outstripped him in excellence [virtue]" (*NE* 1165b23–24), the more virtuous friend would have grounds for terminating the friendship.

Conclusion

Eudaimonistic Virtue Ethics under Adversity

Throughout this book I have both made use of and critically proposed revisions to eudaimonistic virtue ethics in the Aristotelian tradition. In this conclusion I would like to take stock of what a eudaimonistic virtue ethics might look like after my revisions.

While I have obviously seen some liberatory value in eudaimonistic virtue ethics, here I will highlight the presence of a fundamental problem with applying a eudaimonistic virtue ethics such as Aristotle's. The problem arises because of an assumption of his that I believe to be correct: that virtue is necessary but not sufficient for *eudaimonia* or flourishing. This fact creates a tension whenever those conditions that, in addition to virtue, are necessary for flourishing, are actually absent. This typically happens under the adverse circumstances created by oppression, where the external or background conditions necessary for flourishing will tend to be lacking or diminished. Furthermore, under these conditions it may frequently be the case that a trait (say, courage) necessary for flourishing will require a sacrifice of something else (say, one's physical or psychological health) that is also necessary for flourishing. Under these conditions, the project of identifying and developing the virtues and the venture of aiming at a flourishing life may not coincide, as they usually do in, say, Aristotle's ethics. Aristotle's discussions of virtue usually take for granted that the background conditions for virtue are being met: luck has been sufficiently good, material needs have been fulfilled, enough leisure time has been available, no great adversity is presenting itself. He does consider how things change under adversity or tragedy, but (aside from some attention to war) he does not focus on systemic sources of adversity that would cause some people's lives to be predictably fraught with terrible conditions. Under conditions that are difficult but not terrible, one can talk about the virtues that "shine through" (*NE* 1100b30) adversity. But when conditions are truly disastrous, talk of the virtues becomes irrelevant for *eudaimonia*, since *eudaimonia* is simply out of reach; according to Aristotle, one is "talking nonsense" if one describes the "victim on the rack" as happy, no matter how virtuous he may be (*NE* 1153b19–21).

As Martha Nussbaum (1986) has argued, there is a fragility to the good life, and disastrous luck, among other things, can destroy its possibility. For victims of oppression, life conditions are quite likely to present the sorts of "bad luck"—such as the systemically based bad luck stemming from what Claudia Card (1996) has called the "unnatural lottery"—that tell against the possibility of flourishing. Thus a context of oppression pushes to the foreground the insufficiency—rather than (just) the necessity—of virtue for flourishing. Utilizing a eudaimonistic virtue ethics to analyze phenomena of oppression has led me to emphasize—rather than simply acknowledge, as Aristotle does—that the relationship between virtue and flourishing is a contingent one, and that the insufficiency of virtue for flourishing is often more salient than its necessity. Now it is time to examine how the insufficiency of virtue significantly changes the way a eudaimonistic virtue ethics can be utilized.

I have argued in this book for the existence of the burdened virtues, virtues that have the unusual feature of being regularly disjoined from their bearer's own flourishing. I have suggested that the concept of burdened virtues implies that eudaimonism must be rethought in certain ways, because contrary to the usual pattern of connection between a virtue and its bearer's flourishing, here is a set of virtues that could only actualize their potential to be partly constitutive of a flourishing life if the background conditions were different. To wrap up and see where my revisions of eudaimonism have left me, I will address the following central question: how, under conditions of oppression, does one determine what the virtues are?

Aristotle cannot provide much guidance in answering this question, not only because he does not think about oppression or other systemically based and relentlessly adverse conditions, but also because his methodology for arriving at a table of the virtues is notoriously suspect. He does not even derive his understanding of virtue from his conception of *eudaimonia*; rather, it goes the other way around: the definition of *eudaimonia* is dependent on knowing what the virtues are. Thus, for Aristotle, *eudaimonia* is an "activity of soul in conformity with excellence [virtue]" (*NE* 1098a16–17). Much contemporary work in virtue ethics assumes that one can work toward identifying the virtues by beginning with the concept of flourishing and then asking which traits are conducive to or constitutive of flourishing.[1] This would work well if virtue were both necessary and sufficient for flourishing. It also works in a rough sort of a way even if virtue is insufficient for flourishing, as long as it is also the case most of the time that everything else that is necessary for flourishing—such as the right material conditions—obtains. But, under conditions of great adversity, the necessary background conditions for flourishing tend *not* to obtain. Oftentimes, then, there will be traits that should be counted as virtues but whose bearers will nevertheless be unable to flourish. In

1. See Simpson 1997, both for comments on Aristotle's methodology and for the claim that contemporary virtue ethicists, unlike Aristotle, try to work from a conception of flourishing to an account of the virtues.

those cases, beginning with a conception of flourishing and trying to move from there toward a table of the virtues will not work; it will not uncover the virtues that are disconnected from flourishing. Without a consistent connection between virtue and flourishing, how, even given a working conception of flourishing, is one to determine what the virtues are?

I am going to begin my answer to this question in a roundabout way, by referring to Rosalind Hursthouse's (1999) claim that examining cases of dilemmas whose resolution leaves a moral remainder reveals an important distinction between "action guidance" and "action assessment." I will then try out a parallel distinction between what I will call "trait guidance" and "trait assessment," where one provides *trait guidance* when one identifies or decides which traits to cultivate, and one engages in *trait assessment* when one evaluates a trait's goodness, that is, when one determines whether a trait is to count as a virtue.

To illustrate the relevance of the distinction between action guidance and action assessment within a virtue ethics framework, Hursthouse asks one to consider an agent who is faced with a difficult but resolvable moral dilemma, a dilemma in which either action that the agent could take would be morally problematic; another way to put this is to say that the dilemma is resolvable but only with a remainder. Since the dilemma is resolvable, there will be a clear-enough answer to the questions, "what shall I do?" or "what is the right decision to make regarding which action to take?" and other variations on these questions. The answers to these questions provide action guidance. However, it would be a mistake to conflate these questions with questions like "which action is the right one?" or "which action is good?" since, given that both available actions will leave a troubling moral remainder, the answer is "neither." These latter questions are ways of soliciting action assessment (Hursthouse 1999, 49–51). When one faces a choice between two bad or wrong actions in a dilemma, although one action may clearly be the better one, that does not make it good or right; these are cases where, in Hursthouse's words, action guidance and action assessment may "come apart" (1999, 50). Hursthouse argues that a virtuous agent, given (because she/he is virtuous) that she/he has done nothing blameworthy to create the dilemma in the first place, may still be said to act well when faced with such a dilemma, as long as she/he acts with the appropriate painful or regretful feelings about what she/he must do. But a nonvirtuous agent who creates a dilemma through wrongdoing (such as making a promise that should not have been made because it cannot be kept without committing some other moral wrong) now cannot be said to be acting well, even if she/he chooses correctly given the options the dilemma presents. A truly tragic dilemma complicates things further, regardless of whether the agent did anything blameworthy to create the dilemma. Here, Hursthouse argues, action guidance and action assessment come apart even for a virtuous agent, for despite the agent's having chosen correctly which action to take, either action is so terrible that "even a virtuous agent cannot emerge with her life unmarred" (1999, 74). Thus while correct action guidance could lead the agent to choose the action correctly (if one action is better than the other), an assessment cannot mark that action as good; this is so because

> although [good action] is conceptually linked to morally correct (right) decision and to "action of the virtuous agent," it is *also* conceptually linked to "good life" and *eudaimonia*... [and] the actions a virtuous agent is forced to in tragic dilemmas fail to be good actions because the doing of them, no matter how unwillingly or involuntarily, mars or ruins a good life. (1999, 74)

Turn now to what appears to be a parallel distinction between trait guidance and trait assessment and to considering whether and when these two may also come apart from each other. Tragic dilemmas can cause *action* guidance and *action* assessment to come apart because although one can decide which action to take, none of the available actions, given such a dilemma, can be linked to a good life, and an action must be linked to a good life to be assessed as good. *Trait* guidance and *trait* assessment will come apart similarly just in case a trait that it is best to cultivate turns out to be assessed as not a good trait, that is, not a virtue. However, failing to connect (straightforwardly) to a good life need not disqualify a trait from being a virtue, precisely because virtue is insufficient for flourishing; under adverse conditions, traits that still can be assessed as virtues may fail to manifest any connection to a good life. These are the burdened virtues. It is still possible for trait guidance and trait assessment to come apart, for in certain bad conditions, the best traits for one to have may not be virtues at all, in which case the right decision (when asked for trait guidance) will be to develop the least bad of the traits among those that are possible. But in other cases, there will be virtues that one can maintain but that will nevertheless not be identifiable as virtues through their connection to a good life. One will need some other way of identifying these virtues.

When the background conditions are conducive to living well, and there are traits that are both the right ones to choose when asked for trait guidance and the ones to label as good when asked for trait assessment, one will be able to say the following about a hypothetical trait v_1:

Trait v_1 tends to enable its bearer to make the right decisions and to perform good actions (given the assumption that these are available); and, having trait v_1 is conducive to or partly constitutes living a good life.

Trait v_1 is a virtue that is not burdened. For instance, given background conditions of a just polity, satisfaction of material needs, fulfilling and nurturing connections with others, and good-enough luck, one can list many traits that would be virtues in this clean sense: generosity, compassion, friendliness, trustworthiness, honesty, (and, straying far from Aristotle) creativity, (or, returning to something much more Aristotelian) temperance, and so on. One might disagree about the particular traits that belong or do not belong on this list, but in general the assessment of traits is easy given such fantastically favorable external conditions. One can, in order to identify instances of trait v_1, use that loose methodology of beginning with a conception of flourishing and working backward from there to see which traits are conducive to or partly constitutive of such flourishing.

However, when things are not simple, as they are not in real life, many traits that one would point to when asked for trait guidance will nevertheless not fit the description of trait v_1. For instance, consider the trait discussed in chapter 4: sensitivity and attention to others' suffering. A properly moderate level of this trait may be the best choice when faced with an overwhelming level of others' suffering, suffering that has been caused by great injustice; it is clearly better than indifference and probably better than such a high level of compassion that one drowns in others' pain. But is it "good" in the way that trait v_1 is? It does not connect straightforwardly to the good life, since in a really good life, there would not be the sorts of injustices that caused such enormous suffering, and one would consequently not experience the constant anguish of attending to such suffering and guilt at being unable to attend to more. Under better conditions, sensitivity and attention to others' suffering would be a virtue, but it would not make the kinds of demands on an agent that it makes under terrible conditions. Under circumstances of great injustice and its resultant high levels of suffering, this trait becomes burdensome and, as such, does not connect well to the concept of flourishing.

Despite the lack of a direct tie to a good life, however, I am unwilling to forfeit this trait and others like it as potential virtues. While they are not connected to flourishing in the traditional way and thus will not be found on a list of traits that meet this criteria, it may be possible to identify traits like this as virtues by seeing how they *would* connect to a good life if only—counterfactually—conditions were better. Consider the following description of a hypothetical trait v_2:

> When good actions are unavailable, trait v_2 tends to enable its bearer to choose as well as possible, with the appropriate feelings, such as regret or anguish, toward what cannot be done. Furthermore, trait v_2 is a trait that *would* be good—in the straightforward sense of conducive to or constitutive of flourishing—if conditions were better and presented a truly good option, for in such a case trait v_2 would operate without the encumbrance of a moral remainder, and thus without the negative feelings that attach to it.

Trait v_2 is a burdened virtue. This term acknowledges about a trait that it is not a straightforward virtue in the way that trait v_1 is (it is a *burdened* virtue), and the term meanwhile names the trait as belonging to a category of traits that count as virtues (it is a burdened *virtue*) and that can be identified as such because their connection to flourishing can still be shown in some way—in this case, through an imagined counterfactual. Employing this counterfactual allows one to still make use of a variation on the methodology of working from a conception of flourishing to a list of the virtues, but instead of asking which traits succeed in connecting to a good life, one searches for traits that have the potential to be partly constitutive of a good life despite their failure (given adverse conditions) to actually function compatibly with a good life.

The trait of sensitivity and attention to others' suffering could instantiate trait v_2. Under conditions of enormous and widespread injustice and the suffering that it causes, the trait is terribly demanding, to the point where its bearer cannot be said to be living well: attending to even a tiny fraction of those who suffer requires taking on great pain, and meanwhile one is disturbed by the overwhelming level of need to which one necessarily will fail to attend. Both of these feelings burden the bearer of this trait, and no moderate state can be found in which this does not happen. Nevertheless, such sensitivity and attention to others' suffering is still a sort of virtue in the way that trait v_2 is described to be: it enables its bearer to choose and act as well as possible under the circumstances (even though this may involve taking on great pain), with accompanying regret or sorrow at what cannot be done; and, it is a trait that would be clearly—or at least less problematically—good if only conditions were remarkably better and there were not such vast and unjust suffering to attend to, but only the regular sorts of sufferings that may be a part of any human life.

In the case of trait v_2 the adverse external conditions interfere with flourishing in such a way that if only the bad conditions were to be improved, trait v_2 would reveal itself as connected to flourishing. But not all traits that seem to be burdened virtues fit this pattern, because adverse conditions may alter the relationship between virtue and flourishing in deeper ways. For instance, when there are injustices or relations of domination that can only be changed through struggle, there may be a conflict between on the one hand living as if flourishing were currently possible, and on the other hand working to bring about better conditions (and more possibilities for flourishing) in the future. Perhaps a sympathetic attitude toward another person—even if that person is dominating others—would reflect a virtue one would do well to have if, counterfactually, no relation of domination were present. But under the actual conditions, an opposite trait—the refusal to extend any sympathy toward those whom one must politically oppose—might be better recommended for overcoming structures of domination. This latter trait may be the one that should count as a (burdened) virtue, but it will not be identifiable through the methodology used to uncover traits like trait v_2. It may seem that this methodology ought to work for *any* trait that is to count as a virtue, because the methodology takes account of the insufficiency of virtue for flourishing (through the device of the counterfactual) that otherwise rules out finding the virtues by working backward from a conception of flourishing.

Thus the question arises: should this sort of trait—which would not be partly constitutive of flourishing even under good external conditions—be permitted to count as a (burdened) virtue? Answering negatively reflects a commitment to an utterly perfectionist virtue ethics that, I would contend, renders virtue ethics not very useful for theorizing about oppression and resistance, or even about life under any but the most ideal conditions. While bad luck—including luck of the systemic variety—can certainly destroy or damage the virtues, I want to leave room for a range of assessments of traits even under persistent adversity. A trait's goodness could be found in its potential to help its bearer engage in noble pursuits, such as struggling to end oppression, or simply in its tendency to enable its bearer to live as well as possible even under poor conditions.

I have called traits that are good in these ways burdened virtues, despite their not fitting the description of trait v_2. Consider those traits discussed in chapters 5 and 6, traits that one might choose (though perhaps mistakenly) when asked for trait guidance for purposes of political resistance: unrelenting anger or rage at injustice and a withholding of sympathy for the oppressors; courage to struggle even when the costs are great, along with a willingness to take on those costs and make sacrifices; loyalty to one's comrades and those with whom one casts one's lot in the context of struggle. It is possible (though far from clear) that these traits would be the best ones to cultivate, given the constraints of oppression—if, for instance, they are the traits needed for engaging in committed resistance and not giving in to injustice or subordination. While they may be directly detrimental to their bearers' (and others') well-being, their alternatives may be worse (for instance, self-hatred or depression in place of anger; a resigned acceptance of unjust hierarchies in place of a willingness to take great risks in struggling for justice). They are clearly not virtues in the way that trait v_1 is, and they will not be identifiable as virtues simply by working backward from a conception of flourishing, for they do not connect easily to flourishing; each carries a cost to its bearer (and probably to others). They also will tend not to qualify as instances of trait v_2, because unlike a trait such as sensitivity and attention to others' suffering, the traits required for political resistance might not be virtues at all under better conditions; indeed, it is the very conditions of oppression that create the need for resisters with these character traits. Thus, these burdened virtues—if they are virtues at all—will not even be discoverable by posing the sort of counterfactual that worked in the case of trait v_2.

Failing to fit the criteria for trait v_2, these traits of the politically resistant self could better be characterized as instances of the following hypothetical trait v_3:

Trait v_3 is chosen because it is judged to be the best trait to cultivate in the circumstances, even though it is not conducive to or constitutive of anyone's flourishing at present; it does, however, tend to enable its bearer to perform actions with the aim of eventually making flourishing lives more possible overall (for the bearer of trait v_3 and/or for others).

There is an inconsistency between means and ends in the case of these traits, with the result that while these traits might contribute to eventual flourishing, they could not be described as partly *constitutive* of a good life. Their claim to being connected to flourishing at all lies in the fact that they are chosen and pursued with eventual flourishing in mind, since the goal of resistance is to end the conditions of oppression that interfere with the good life. However, this connection to a flourishing or good life is extremely unreliable, because the room for error is great, and the costs of judging wrongly may be enormous: how can one know which oppositional strategies, if any, could succeed in bringing about better conditions? What can and cannot be justified in the name of liberation, especially given the impossibility of predicting the results of one's actions? (Can the willing sacrifice of one's own life be justified? Perhaps. How about the kidnapping or torture of the "enemy"? Very doubtful.) There is a danger here of glorifying traits that, while purportedly aimed at liberation, facilitate morally horrifying actions.

Is trait v_3 a burdened virtue, namely, should it still count as any sort of a virtue at all? I believe that some instances of trait v_3 will qualify as burdened virtues, and others will not. The idea of a burden attached to a trait is that there is some level of cost that is to be weighed against what is otherwise excellent about the trait. But somewhere on this continuum, a burden becomes so great that it no longer makes sense to assess the trait as good (though it is possible that the trait would still be chosen as the best among terrible options); this can happen when the means/ends split becomes too profound. Furthermore, since trait v_3 is chosen because *it is judged to be* the best trait to cultivate in the circumstances, it is possible that some instances of trait v_3 will have been wrongly judged to be choiceworthy. If one gets things wrong at the level of trait guidance—as I am suggesting some oppositional political movements will inevitably do given the difficulty of the decisions to be made and the unpredictability of results—one cannot expect the (erroneously) chosen trait to be, even beyond that, actually good.

While the description of trait v_3 covers those traits that enable resistance to oppression, some traits simply help one to survive and live as well as possible under oppression, without particularly empowering one to engage in political resistance. These traits, also, may at times be the best ones to develop even though they cannot be assessed in any unqualified way as excellences of character. They can be counted as examples of trait v_4:

> Trait v_4 tends to enable its bearer to make the best possible decisions and to perform the best possible actions; and, having trait v_4 is conducive to or partly constitutes living as well as possible, though because trait v_4 carries a cost to its bearer (and perhaps to others), it is only choiceworthy when bad conditions are present and a good life is unattainable.

The cost associated with the traits that instantiate trait v_4 lies in the way a self with these traits is diminished or compromised. For instance, being adept at lying to or manipulating people in positions of power may help one to survive subordination but would not be a good trait under egalitarian conditions. Keeping oneself in a state of psychological denial or numbness may be necessary for getting through otherwise devastating loss or for tolerating a form of victimization—such as battering—from which one cannot escape. Disassociation or splitting can be coping mechanisms for child victims of sexual abuse. None of these traits connects to a life that could be described as good in a straightforward way, though each trait saves its bearer from enduring something worse. Nor would any of these traits be virtues under counterfactually good conditions, for these are not traits that one would need for flourishing. Unlike instances of trait v_3, these traits do not even have the noble aim of bringing about eventual liberation, though one may want to characterize them as manifesting a praiseworthy will to go on, to not let oppression stamp out one's very life. Thus one might want to call them burdened virtues—with an enormously high burden—or, in order to draw attention to the enormity of the suffering that each of these traits indicates the presence of, one might simply want to call them cases of moral damage and not refer to them as virtues at all. While I am advocating a version of virtue ethics that has a non-perfectionist slant, there is a limit to how awful something can be while still qualifying as a virtue, even a burdened virtue.

With the introduction of the category of burdened virtues, trait assessment can now be seen as more nuanced than just marking a trait as a virtue, a vice, or a trait toward which one could be morally indifferent. If one is willing to accept a trait as a virtue even though it typically fails to be connected to a good life, then trait guidance and trait assessment need not always come apart under bad conditions: traits that one chooses as the best possible options when asked for trait guidance *may* also count among those that one assesses to be virtues; they will be burdened virtues, but still virtues.

In response to the question about how one is to identify the virtues under oppression, one can now point to the ways that traits v_2, v_3, and v_4 (and I will leave open the possibility that there are some additional ways of counting as a burdened virtue, because these may not exhaust the ways that a trait that carries a cost can still be praiseworthy) can be identified as virtues. Their marks of excellence are earned either by being a trait that would be good under better conditions (trait v_2), or by being a trait whose goodness or nobility comes from its potential to help bring about a world in which flourishing will be more possible (trait v_3), or by being a trait that can improve a life even if that life cannot be truly good (trait v_4). In any of these cases, the trait can (though will not necessarily) fall into the category of a burdened virtue, a category that captures those traits that would be missed if one were to simply work backward from a conception of full flourishing to a discovery of what is conducive to or constitutive of that sort of flourishing. Of course, oppression is not all-encompassing and many clear-cut virtues may survive fine even (or perhaps especially) in abject conditions and be discoverable by investigating which traits are conducive to or partly constitutive of flourishing. But a methodology for constructing a table of the virtues that looks only for these sorts of traits—and not also for burdened virtues—will not be particularly helpful in a context in which burdening is endemic.

The insufficiency of virtue for flourishing together with the adverse conditions that make this insufficiency of constant relevance have suggested these revised guidelines for identifying virtues, guidelines that recognize that a trait may be a virtue even if it is burdened by a lack of a direct and uncompromised connection to flourishing. This raises another question, about the value of eudaimonistic virtue ethics under oppression: if (burdened) virtues are not directly linked to flourishing, is it still useful to continue to center the concept of flourishing at all under conditions of oppression? Specifically, will a theory with an unattainable sort of flourishing at the center of it make moral life, under oppression, always appear to be a matter of compromise and failure?

My first response to this question is to remember that oppression takes many forms and that while some experiences of oppression are of misery and failure to flourish, not all are. Thus flourishing may not always be out of reach under oppression. Though I would not want to romanticize oppression by pointing to any special joys to be found in, for instance, poverty or slavery, it would also be an exaggeration to describe all experiences of oppression as relentless wretchedness. I say this not to lend legitimacy to oppressive practices; after all, some of what is wrong with oppression may be found not in its tendency to interfere with flourishing but rather in its ability to deny its victims their freedom.[2]

Nevertheless, when the eudaimonistic claim that flourishing is central to moral life is combined with a recognition that one faces unjust barriers to flourishing and that the virtues one is able to develop are largely burdened with their lack of a simple connection to a good life, one may end up with quite a pessimistic outlook. Indeed, a loss of hope and a turn to nihilism is, as Cornel West has pointed out in the case of black Americans, a serious danger for oppressed people.[3]

I acknowledge this dangerous possibility of hopelessness, and if eudaimonism in the context of adverse conditions necessarily led into this abyss I would want to reject it. However, I see the spirit of eudaimonism preserved in a phenomenon that is the opposite of hopelessness and that, perhaps amazingly, survives even the worst sorts of oppression: the affirmation and embrace of life.[4] The choice to go on living, to insist upon life—with its sufferings and its joys—is an existential choice of great significance under oppression, and this choice captures something crucial about eudaimonism.[5] In fact, this phenomenon of affirming life may offer insights into how one is to conceive of *any* human flourishing, for in choosing life one chooses what is at the core of a *good* life.

2. Thanks to Bat-Ami Bar On (who, in turn, may owe the point to her reading of Arendt) for emphasizing this point to me.

3. See "Nihilism in Black America" in West 1993.

4. Thanks to Andrés Molina Ochoa, whose unpublished story "Erika's Case" led me to see this.

5. Lewis Gordon has identified Camus's (1955 [1942]) question "Why go on?" as having special relevance for blacks in the face of antiblack racism and sees black existential philosophy as in part addressing the choice to go on living as a significant existential choice under oppression. See Gordon 1997 and "Africana Philosophy of Existence" in Gordon 2000.

Works Cited

Alarcón, Norma. 1981. "Chicana's Feminist Literature: A Re-vision through Malintzin/ or Malintzin: Putting Flesh Back on the Object." In *This Bridge Called My Back: Writings by Radical Women of Color*, ed. Cherríe Moraga and Gloria Anzaldúa, 182–190. New York: Kitchen Table: Women of Color Press.

———. 1994. "Traddutora, Traditora: A Paradigmatic Figure of Chicana Feminism." In *Scattered Hegemonies: Postmodernity and Transnational Feminist Practices*, ed. Inderpal Grewal and Caren Kaplan, 110–136. Minneapolis: University of Minnesota Press.

Alcoff, Linda Martín. 2000. "Who's Afraid of Identity Politics?" In *Reclaiming Identity: Realist Theory and the Predicament of Postmodernism*, ed. Paula Moya and Michael Hames-García, 312–344. Berkeley: University of California Press.

Allen, Jonathan. 1998. "The Situated Critic or the Loyal Critic? Rorty and Walzer on Social Criticism." *Philosophy and Social Criticism* 24 (6): 25–46.

Annas, Julia. 1992. "The Good Life and the Good Lives of Others." *Social Philosophy and Policy* 9 (2): 133–148.

———. 1993. *The Morality of Happiness*. Oxford: Oxford University Press.

———. 1998. "Virtue and Eudaimonism." In *Virtue and Vice*, ed. Ellen Frankel Paul, Fred Miller, Jr., and Jeffrey Paul, 37–55. Cambridge: Cambridge University Press.

Anzaldúa, Gloria. 1987. *Borderlands/La Frontera*. San Francisco: Spinsters/Aunt Lute.

Appiah, K. Anthony. 1996. "Race, Culture, Identity: Misunderstood Connections." In *Color Conscious: The Political Morality of Race* by K. Anthony Appiah and Amy Gutmann, 30–105. Princeton, NJ: Princeton University Press.

Arendt, Hannah. 1958. *The Human Condition*. Chicago: University of Chicago Press.

———. 1963. *On Revolution*. New York: Penguin.

Aristotle. 1984. *The Complete Works of Aristotle: The Revised Oxford Translation*, ed. Jonathan Barnes. Princeton, NJ: Princeton University Press.

Armstrong, Elizabeth. 1995. "Traitors to the Cause? Understanding the Lesbian/Gay 'Bisexuality Debates.'" In *Bisexual Politics*, ed. Naomi Tucker, 199–218. New York: Harrington Park.

Ault, Amber. 1996. "The Dilemma of Identity: Bi Women's Negotiations." In *Queer Theory/Sociology*, ed. Steven Seidman, 311–330. Cambridge: Blackwell.

Bar On, Bat-Ami. 1993. "Marginality and Epistemic Privilege." In *Feminist Epistemologies*, ed. Linda Alcoff and Elizabeth Potter, 83–100. New York: Routledge.

——. 2001. "Violent Bodies." In *Feminists Doing Ethics*, ed. Peggy DesAutels and Joanne Waugh, 63–75. Lanham, MD: Rowman and Littlefield.

Bartky, Sandra Lee. 1990. *Femininity and Domination*. New York: Routledge.

——. 1997. "Sympathy and Solidarity: On a Tightrope with Scheler." In *Feminists Rethink the Self*, ed. Diana Tietjens Meyers, 177–196. Boulder, CO: Westview.

——. 1999. "In Defense of Guilt." In *On Feminist Ethics and Politics*, ed. Claudia Card, 29–51. Lawrence: University Press of Kansas.

Bauman, Zygmunt. 1989. *Modernity and the Holocaust*. Cambridge: Polity.

Beck, Evelyn Torton. 1989. "Naming Is Not a Simple Act." In *Twice Blessed: On Being Lesbian, Gay, and Jewish*, ed. Christie Balka and Andy Rose, 171–181. Boston: Beacon.

Bell, Derrick. 1992. *Faces at the Bottom of the Well: The Permanence of Racism*. New York: Basic.

Berkman, Alexander. 1970. *Prison Memoirs of an Anarchist*. Pittsburgh, PA: Frontier.

Bishop, Sharon. 1987. "Connections and Guilt." *Hypatia* 2 (1): 7–23.

Blum, Lawrence. 1980. "Compassion." In *Explaining Emotions*, ed. Amélie Oksenberg Rorty, 507–518. Berkeley: University of California Press.

Blum, Lawrence, Marcia Homiak, Judy Housman, and Naomi Scheman. 1973–1974. "Altruism and Women's Oppression." *Philosophical Forum* 5 (1–2): 222–247.

Bolte, Angela. 1998. "The Outcast Outlaw: Incorporating Rage into an Account of the Emotions." *American Philosophical Association Newsletters: Newsletter on Feminism and Philosophy* 98 (1): 46–48.

Brink, David. 1990. "Rational Egoism, Self, and Others." In *Identity, Character, and Morality*, ed. Owen Flanagan and Amélie Oksenberg Rorty, 339–378. Cambridge, MA: MIT Press.

——. 1997. "Self-Love and Altruism." *Social Philosophy and Policy* 14 (1): 122–157.

Broadie, Sarah. 1991. *Ethics with Aristotle*. Oxford: Oxford University Press.

Brown, Wendy. 1995. *States of Injury*. Princeton, NJ: Princeton University Press.

Butler, Judith. 1990. *Gender Trouble: Feminism and the Subversion of Identity*. New York: Routledge.

——. 1993. *Bodies That Matter: On the Discursive Limits of "Sex."* New York: Routledge.

Calhoun, Cheshire. 1995. "Standing for Something." *Journal of Philosophy* 92 (5): 235–260.

Camus, Albert. [1942] 1955. *The Myth of Sisyphus and Other Essays*. Translated by Justin O'Brien. New York: Knopf.

Card, Claudia. 1985. *Virtues and Moral Luck*. Series 1, Institute for Legal Studies, Working Papers. University of Wisconsin-Madison, Law School, November.

——. 1996. *The Unnatural Lottery: Character and Moral Luck*. Philadelphia, PA: Temple University Press.

Carmichael, Stokely, and Charles Hamilton. 1967. *Black Power: The Politics of Liberation*. New York: Random House.

Carr, Brian. 1999. "Pity and Compassion as Social Virtues." *Philosophy: The Journal of the Royal Institute of Philosophy* 74 (289): 411–429.

Clark, Kenneth. 1955. *Prejudice and Your Child*. Boston: Beacon.

——. 1965. *Dark Ghetto: Dilemmas of Social Power*. New York: Harper and Row.

Cleaver, Eldridge. 1968. *Soul on Ice*. New York: Dell.

Combahee River Collective. 1981. "A Black Feminist Statement." In *This Bridge Called My Back: Writings by Radical Women of Color*, ed. Cherríe Moraga and Gloria Anzaldúa, 210–218. New York: Kitchen Table: Women of Color Press.
Conly, Sarah. 2001. "Why Feminists Should Oppose Feminist Virtue Ethics." *Philosophy Now* 33: 12–14.
Coyne [Walker], Margaret Urban. 1985. "Moral Luck?" *Journal of Value Inquiry* 19: 319–325.
Cuomo, Chris. 1999. "Feminist Sex at Century's End: On Justice and Joy." In *On Feminist Ethics and Politics*, ed. Claudia Card, 269–287. Lawrence: University Press of Kansas.
Davion, Victoria M. 1991. "Integrity and Radical Change." In *Feminist Ethics*, ed. Claudia Card, 180–192. Lawrence: University Press of Kansas.
Davis, Angela. 1997. "Race and Criminalization: Black Americans and the Punishment Industry." In *The House That Race Built*, ed. Wahneema Lubiano, 264–279. New York: Random House.
Dayan, Yaël. 1960. *Envy the Frightened*. New York: Dell.
Donner, Wendy. 2002. "Feminist Ethics and Anger: A Feminist Buddhist Reflection." *American Philosophical Association Newsletters: Newsletter on Feminism and Philosophy* 1 (2): 67–70.
Driver, Julia. 1996. "The Virtues and Human Nature." In *How Should One Live?*, ed. Roger Crisp, 111–129. Oxford: Clarendon.
Du Bois, W. E. B. [1903] 1969. *The Souls of Black Folk*. New York: Signet Classic.
Epstein, Helen. 1979. *Children of the Holocaust: Conversations with Sons and Daughters of Survivors*. New York: Penguin.
Fanon, Frantz. 1967. *Black Skins, White Masks*. New York: Grove.
Feinberg, Joel. 1984. *Harm to Others*. Oxford: Oxford University Press.
Ferguson, Ann. 1995. "Feminist Communities and Moral Revolution." In *Feminism and Community*, ed. Marilyn Friedman and Penny Weiss, 367–397. Philadelphia, PA: Temple University Press.
Fletcher, George P. 1993. *Loyalty: An Essay on the Morality of Relationships*. New York: Oxford University Press.
Foot, Philippa. 1978. *Virtues and Vices*. Berkeley: University of California Press.
Friedman, Marilyn. 1993. *What Are Friends For?* Ithaca, NY: Cornell University Press.
Frye, Marilyn. 1983. *The Politics of Reality*. Trumansburg, NY: Crossing Press.
——. 1992. "White Woman Feminist." In *Willful Virgin*, 147–169. Freedom, CA: Crossing Press.
Funderburg, Lise. 1994. *Black, White, Other*. New York: Morrow.
Gamson, Joshua. 1996. "Must Identity Movements Self-Destruct? A Queer Dilemma." In *Queer Theory/Sociology*, ed. Steven Seidman, 395–420. Cambridge: Blackwell.
Garvey, John, and Noel Ignatiev, eds. 1996. *Race Traitor*. New York: Routledge.
Geras, Norman. 1998. *The Contract of Mutual Indifference: Political Philosophy after the Holocaust*. New York: Verso.
Gibian, Ruth. 1992. "Refusing Certainty: Toward a Bisexuality of Wholeness." In *Closer to Home: Bisexuality and Feminism*, ed. Elizabeth Reba Weise, 3–16. Seattle, WA: Seal.
Ginzberg, Ruth. 1991. "Philosophy Is Not a Luxury." In *Feminist Ethics*, ed. Claudia Card, 126–145. Lawrence: University Press of Kansas.
Glasgow, Douglas. 1980. *The Black Underclass*. New York: Vintage.
Gomberg, Paul. 1990. "Patriotism Is Like Racism." *Ethics* 101: 144–150.
Gordon, Lewis. 1995. "Critical 'Mixed Race'?" *Social Identities* 1 (2): 381–395.

——. 1997. "Introduction: Black Existential Philosophy." In *Existence in Black: An Anthology of Black Existential Philosophy*, ed. Lewis Gordon, 1–9. New York: Routledge.
——. 1999. "A Short History of the 'Critical' in Critical Race Theory." *American Philosophical Association Newsletters: Newsletter on Philosophy and the Black Experience* 98 (2): 23–26.
——. 2000. *Existentia Africana: Understanding Africana Existential Thought*. New York: Routledge.
Grier, William, and Price Cobbs. 1968. *Black Rage*. New York: Basic.
Guinier, Lani, and Gerald Torres. 2002. *The Miner's Canary: Enlisting Race, Resisting Power, Transforming Democracy*. Cambridge, MA: Harvard University Press.
Halwani, Raja. 2003. *Virtuous Liasions*. Chicago, IL: Open Court.
Hamilton, Charles V. 1992. "Afterword." In *Black Power: The Politics of Liberation* [1967] by Kwame Ture [Stokely Carmichael] and Charles Hamilton, 201–218. New York: Random House.
Hampton, Jean. 1997. "The Wisdom of the Egoist: The Moral and Political Implications of Valuing the Self." *Social Philosophy and Policy* 14 (1): 21–51.
Harding, Sandra. 1991. *Whose Science? Whose Knowledge?* Ithaca, NY: Cornell University Press.
Hartfield, Bernadette W. 1995. "A Response to María Lugones's 'Hard-to-Handle Anger.'" In *Overcoming Sexism and Racism*, ed. Linda Bell and David Blumenfeld, 219–226. Lanham, MD: Rowman and Littlefield.
Heldke, Lisa. 1998. "On Being a Responsible Traitor." In *Daring to Be Good: Essays in Feminist Ethico-Politics*, ed. Bat-Ami Bar On and Ann Ferguson, 87–99. New York: Routledge.
Hill, Thomas. 1973. "Servility and Self Respect." *Monist* 57 (1): 87–104.
Hoagland, Sarah Lucia. 1988. *Lesbian Ethics*. Palo Alto, CA: Institute of Lesbian Studies.
Hoagland, Sarah Lucia, and Julia Penelope, eds. 1988. *For Lesbians Only: A Separatist Anthology*. London: Onlywomen.
Homiak, Marcia. 1999. "On the Malleability of Character." In *On Feminist Ethics and Politics*, ed. Claudia Card, 52–80. Lawrence: University Press of Kansas.
Hooker, Brad. 1996. "Does Moral Virtue Constitute a Benefit to the Agent?" In *How Should One Live?*, ed. Roger Crisp, 141–155. Oxford: Clarendon.
hooks, bell. 1990. "Homeplace: A Site of Resistance." In *Yearning: Race, Gender and Cultural Politics*, 41–49. Boston: South End.
——. 1993. *Sisters of the Yam: Black Women and Self-Recovery*. Boston: South End.
——. 1995. *Killing Rage: Ending Racism*. New York: Holt.
Hursthouse, Rosalind. 1995. "Applying Virtue Ethics." In *Virtues and Reasons*, ed. Rosalind Hursthouse, Gavin Lawrence, and Warren Quinn, 57–75. Oxford: Clarendon.
——. 1999. *On Virtue Ethics*. Oxford: Oxford University Press.
Jaggar, Alison. 1989a. "Feminist Ethics: Some Issues for the Nineties." *Journal of Social Philosophy* 20: 91–107.
——. 1989b. "Love and Knowledge: Emotion in Feminist Epistemology." In *Gender/Body/Knowledge*, ed. Alison Jaggar and Susan Bordo, 145–171. New Brunswick, NJ: Rutgers University Press.
——. 1991. "Feminist Ethics: Projects, Problems, Prospects." In *Feminist Ethics*, ed. Claudia Card, 78–104. Lawrence: University Press of Kansas.
Jaspers, Karl. [1947] 1961. *The Question of German Guilt*. Translated by E. B. Ashton. New York: Capricorn.

Kekes, John. 1998. "The Reflexivity of Evil." In *Virtue and Vice*, ed. Ellen Frankel Paul, Fred Miller, Jr., and Jeffrey Paul, 216–232. Cambridge: Cambridge University Press.
King, Martin Luther, Jr. 1963. *Why We Can't Wait*. New York: Harper and Row.
———. 1986. *I Have a Dream: Writings and Speeches That Changed the World*, ed. James Melvin Washington. New York: HarperCollins.
———. 2003. "A Long, Long Way to Go" [1965]. In *Ripples of Hope: Great American Civil Rights Speeches*, ed. Josh Gottheimer, 258–265. New York: Basic Civitas.
La Caze, Marguerite. 2001. "Envy and Resentment." *Philosophical Explorations* 4 (1): 31–45.
Leighton, Stephen. 1988. "Aristotle's Courageous Passions." *Phronesis: A Journal for Ancient Philosophy* 33 (1): 76–99.
Lewis, Oscar. 1961. *The Children of Sanchez*. New York: Random House.
Lorde, Audre. 1984. "The Uses of Anger: Women Responding to Racism" and "Eye to Eye: Black Women, Hatred, and Anger." In Lorde, *Sister Outsider*, 124–133, 145–175. Trumansburg, NY: Crossing Press.
Loury, Glenn. 1995. *One by One from the Inside Out: Essays and Reviews on Race and Responsibility in America*. New York: Simon and Schuster.
Lugones, María. 1991. "On the Logic of Pluralist Feminism." In *Feminist Ethics*, ed. Claudia Card, 35–44. Lawrence: University Press of Kansas.
———. 1995. "Hard-to-Handle Anger." In *Overcoming Sexism and Racism*, ed. Linda Bell and David Blumenfeld, 203–217. Lanham, MD: Rowman and Littlefield.
———. 2003. "Enticements and Dangers of Community and Home for a Radical Politics." In *Pilgrimages/Peregrinajes: Theorizing Coalition against Multiple Oppressions*, 183–205. Lanham, MD: Rowman and Littlefield.
MacIntyre, Alasdair. 1981. *After Virtue*. Notre Dame, IN: University of Notre Dame Press.
———. [1984] 1994. "Is Patriotism a Virtue?" In *Communitarianism: A New Public Ethics*, ed. Markate Daly, 307–318. Belmont, CA: Wadsworth.
Mayer, Arno. 1988. *Why Did the Heavens Not Darken?* New York: Pantheon.
McFall, Lynne. 1991. "What's Wrong with Bitterness." In *Feminist Ethics*, ed. Claudia Card, 146–160. Lawrence: University Press of Kansas.
McLaren, Margaret. 2001. "Feminist Ethics: Care as a Virtue." In *Feminists Doing Ethics*, ed. Peggy DesAutels and Joanne Waugh, 101–118. Lanham, MD: Rowman and Littlefield.
Meyers, Diana T. 1997. "Emotion and Heterodox Moral Perception: An Essay in Moral Social Psychology." In *Feminists Rethink the Self*, ed. Diana T. Meyers, 197–218. Boulder, CO: Westview.
Mills, Charles. 1997. *The Racial Contract*. Ithaca, NY: Cornell University Press.
Moraga, Cherríe. 1983. "A Long Line of Vendidas." In Moraga, *Loving In the War Years*, 90–144. Boston: South End.
———. 1993. *The Last Generation*. Boston: South End.
Morgan, Robin, ed. 1970. *Sisterhood Is Powerful*. New York: Random House.
Moya, Paula. 2000a. "Introduction: Reclaiming Identity." In *Reclaiming Identity: Realist Theory and the Predicament of Postmodernism*, ed. Paula Moya and Michael Hames-García, 1–26. Berkeley: University of California Press.
———. 2000b. "Postmodernism, 'Realism,' and the Politics of Identity." In *Reclaiming Identity: Realist Theory and the Predicament of Postmodernism*, ed. Paula Moya and Michael Hames-García, 67–101. Berkeley: University of California Press.
Moya, Paula, and Michael Hames-García, eds. 2000. *Reclaiming Identity: Realist Theory and the Predicament of Postmodernism*. Berkeley: University of California Press.

Moynihan, Daniel P. 1965. *The Negro Family: The Case for National Action*. Washington, DC: Office of Policy Planning and Research, U.S. Department of Labor.
Myrdal, Gunnar. 1944. *An American Dilemma*. New York: Harper.
Nagel, Thomas. 1979. "Moral Luck." In *Mortal Questions*, 24–38. Cambridge: Cambridge University Press.
Nathanson, Stephen. 1989. "In Defense of 'Moderate Patriotism.'" *Ethics* 99: 535–552.
———. 1992. "Is Patriotism Like Racism?" *American Philosophical Association Newsletters: Newsletter on Philosophy and the Black Experience* 91 (2): 9–12.
Nelson, William. 1996. "Eudaimonism and Justice." *Southwest Philosophy Review* 12 (1): 247–256.
Noddings, Nel. 1984. *Caring: A Feminine Approach to Ethics and Moral Education*. Berkeley: University of California Press.
Nussbaum, Martha. 1986. *The Fragility of Goodness*. Cambridge: Cambridge University Press.
———. 1996. "Compassion: The Basic Social Emotion." *Social Philosophy and Policy* 13 (1): 27–58.
———. 1999. *Women and Human Development: The Capabilities Approach*. Cambridge: Cambridge University Press.
———. 2001. *Upheavals of Thought: The Intelligence of Emotions*. Cambridge: Cambridge University Press.
Okin, Susan Moller. 1996. "Feminism, Moral Development, and the Virtues." In *How Should One Live?*, ed. Roger Crisp, 211–229. Oxford: Clarendon.
Pakula, Alan, writer/director. 1982. *Sophie's Choice*. Based on a novel by William Styron. Universal.
Pateman, Carole. 1988. *The Sexual Contract*. Stanford, CA: Stanford University Press.
Pears, David. 1980. "Courage as a Mean." In *Essays on Aristotle's Ethics*, ed. Amélie Oksenberg Rorty, 171–187. Berkeley: University of California Press.
Pettit, Philip. 1988. "The Paradox of Loyalty." *American Philosophical Quarterly* 25 (2): 163–171.
Phillips, D. Z. 1964–1965. "Does It Pay to Be Good?" *Proceedings of the Aristotelian Society* 65: 45–60.
Plato. 1961. *The Republic*. Translated by Paul Shorey. In *Plato: The Collected Dialogues*, ed. Edith Hamilton and Huntington Cairns. Princeton, NJ: Princeton University Press.
Potter, Nancy. 2001. "Is Refusing to Forgive a Vice?" In *Feminists Doing Ethics*, ed. Peggy DesAutels and Joanne Waugh, 135–150. Lanham, MD: Rowman and Littlefield.
———. 2002. *How Can I Be Trusted? A Virtue Theory of Trustworthiness*. Lanham, MD: Rowman and Littlefield.
Pratt, Minnie Bruce. 1984. "Identity: Skin Blood Heart." In *Yours in Struggle* by Elly Bulkin, Minnie Bruce Pratt, and Barbara Smith, 9–63. Ithaca, NY: Firebrand.
Prior, William. 2001. "*Eudaimonism* and Virtue." *Journal of Value Inquiry* 35: 325–342.
Putnam, Daniel. 1997. "Psychological Courage." *Philosophy, Psychiatry, and Psychology* 4 (1): 1–11.
———. 2001. "The Emotions of Courage." *Journal of Social Philosophy* 32 (4): 463–470.
Rawls, John. 1971. *A Theory of Justice*. Cambridge, MA: Harvard University Press.
———. 1993/1996. *Political Liberalism*. New York: Columbia University Press.
———. 1999. *The Law of Peoples*. Cambridge, MA: Harvard University Press.
———. 2001. *Justice as Fairness: A Restatement*, ed. Erin Kelly. Cambridge, MA: Belknap Press of Harvard University Press.

Rich, Adrienne. 1978. "Disloyal to Civilization: Feminism, Racism, Gynephobia." In Rich, *On Lies, Secrets, and Silence*, 275–310. New York: Norton.

Rogers, Kelly. 1994. "Aristotle on the Motive of Courage." *Southern Journal of Philosophy* 32: 303–313.

——. 1997. "Beyond Self and Other." *Social Philosophy and Policy* 14 (1): 1–20.

Rorty, Amélie Oksenberg. 1986. "The Two Faces of Courage." *Philosophy: The Journal of the Royal Institute of Philosophy* 61: 151–171.

Rousseau, Jean-Jacques. 1979. *Emile*. Translated by Allan Bloom. New York: Basic.

Royce, Josiah. 1908. *The Philosophy of Loyalty*. New York: Macmillan.

Ruddick, Sara. 1989. *Maternal Thinking: Toward a Politics of Peace*. Boston: Beacon.

Rust, Paula C. 1995. *Bisexuality and the Challenge to Lesbian Politics: Sex, Loyalty, and Revolution*. New York: New York University Press.

Sartre, Jean-Paul. 1949 [French, 1948]. *Dirty Hands*. In Sartre, *No Exit and Three Other Plays*, 129–248. Translated by L. Abel. New York: Knopf.

Scheman, Naomi. 1992. "Jewish Lesbian Writing: A Review Essay." *Hypatia* 7 (4): 186–194.

——. [1980] 1993. "Anger and the Politics of Naming." In *Engenderings: Constructions of Knowledge, Authority, and Privilege*, 22–35. New York: Routledge.

Scott, Daryl Michael. 1997. *Contempt and Pity: Social Policy and the Image of the Damaged Black Psyche, 1880–1996*. Chapel Hill: University of North Carolina Press.

Segrest, Mab. 1994. *Memoir of a Race Traitor*. Boston: South End.

Sherman, Nancy. 1993. "The Virtues of Common Pursuit." *Philosophy and Phenomenological Research* 53 (2): 277–299.

Shklar, Judith. 1984. *Ordinary Vices*. Cambridge, MA: Harvard University Press.

Simpson, Peter. 1997. "Contemporary Virtue Ethics and Aristotle." In *Virtue Ethics: A Critical Reader*, ed. Daniel Statman, 245–259. Washington, DC: Georgetown University Press.

Snow, Nancy. 1994. "Self-Blame and Blame of Rape Victims." *Public Affairs Quarterly* 8 (4): 377–392.

——. 2002. "Virtue and the Oppression of Women." *Canadian Journal of Philosophy* Supplementary Volume 28 on Feminist Moral Philosophy: 33–62.

Sparks, Holloway. 1997. "Dissident Citizenship: Democratic Theory, Political Courage, and Activist Women." *Hypatia* 12 (4): 74–110.

Spelman, Elizabeth V. 1988. *Inessential Woman*. Boston: Beacon.

——. 1989. "Anger and Insubordination." In *Women, Knowledge, and Reality*, ed. Ann Garry and Marilyn Pearsall, 263–273. Boston: Unwin Hyman.

——. 1991. "The Virtue of Feeling and the Feeling of Virtue." In *Feminist Ethics*, ed. Claudia Card, 213–232. Lawrence: University Press of Kansas.

——. 1997. *Fruits of Sorrow*. Boston: Beacon.

——. 1999. "Anger." In *Wicked Pleasures*, ed. Robert Solomon, 117–132. Lanham, MD: Rowman and Littlefield.

Steele, Shelby. 1990. *The Content of Our Character: A New Vision of Race in America*. New York: St. Martin's.

Steinberg, Stephen. 1981. *The Ethnic Myth: Race, Ethnicity, and Class in America*. Boston: Beacon.

——. 1995. *Turning Back: The Retreat from Racial Justice in American Thought and Policy*. Boston: Beacon.

Stocker, Michael. 1990. *Plural and Conflicting Values*. Oxford: Oxford University Press.

Stoltenberg, John. 1989. *Refusing to Be a Man*. Portland, OR: Breitenbush.

Sumner, L. Wayne. 1998. "Is Virtue Its Own Reward?" In *Virtue and Vice*, ed. Ellen Frankel Paul, Fred Miller, Jr., and Jeffrey Paul, 18–36. Cambridge: Cambridge University Press.

Szwajgier, Adina Blady. 1990. *I Remember Nothing More*. New York: Pantheon.

Taylor, Gabriele. 1996. "Deadly Vices." In *How Should One Live?*, ed. Roger Crisp, 157–172. Oxford: Clarendon.

Taylor, Gabriele, and Sybil Wolfram. 1968. "The Self-Regarding and Other-Regarding Virtues." *Philosophical Quarterly* 18 (72): 238–248.

Tessman, Lisa. 1998. "Dangerous Loyalties and Liberatory Politics." *Hypatia* 13 (4): 18–39.

———. 2000. "Moral Luck in the Politics of Personal Transformation." *Social Theory and Practice* 26 (3): 375–395.

———. 2001. "Critical Virtue Ethics: Understanding Oppression as Morally Damaging." In *Feminists Doing Ethics*, ed. Peggy DesAutels and Joanne Waugh, 79–99. Lanham, MD: Rowman and Littlefield.

———. 2002a. "Do the Wicked Flourish? Virtue Ethics and Unjust Social Privilege." *American Philosophical Association Newsletters: Newsletter on Feminism and Philosophy* 1–2: 59–63.

———. 2002b. "On (Not) Living the Good Life: Reflections on Oppression, Virtue and Flourishing." *Canadian Journal of Philosophy* Supplementary Volume 28 on Feminist Moral Philosophy: 3–32.

Tolman, Deborah, and Tracy Higgins. 1996. "How Being a Good Girl Can Be Bad for Girls." In *"Bad Girls"/"Good Girls": Women, Sex, and Power in the Nineties*, ed. Nan Bauer Maglin and Donna Perry, 205–225. New Brunswick, NJ: Rutgers University Press.

Tormey, Judith Farr. 1973–1974. "Exploitation, Oppression and Self-Sacrifice." *Philosophical Forum* 5 (1–2): 206–221.

Von Wright, Georg Henrik. 1963. *The Varieties of Goodness*. London: Routledge and Kegan Paul.

Walker, Margaret Urban. 1993. "Moral Luck and the Virtues of Impure Agency." In *Moral Luck*, ed. Daniel Statman, 235–250. Albany: State University of New York Press.

———. 1998. *Moral Understandings: A Feminist Study in Ethics*. New York: Routledge.

Walzer, Michael. 1973. "Political Action: The Problem of Dirty Hands." *Philosophy and Public Affairs* 2 (2): 160–180.

———. 1987. *Interpretation and Social Criticism*. Cambridge, MA: Harvard University Press.

———. 1988. *The Company of Critics*. New York: Basic.

Weiss, Penny. 1995. "Feminism and Communitarianism: Comparing Critiques of Liberalism." In *Feminism and Community*, ed. Marilyn Friedman and Penny Weiss, 161–186. Philadelphia, PA: Temple University Press.

West, Cornel. 1993. *Race Matters*. Boston: Beacon.

Wilkes, Kathleen. 1980. "The Good Man and the Good for Man in Aristotle's Ethics." In *Essays on Aristotle's Ethics*, ed. Amélie Oksenberg Rorty, 341–357. Berkeley: University of California Press.

Williams, Bernard. 1973. "Ethical Consistency." In *Problems of the Self*, 166–186. New York: Cambridge University Press.

———. 1981a. "Conflicts of Values." In *Moral Luck*, 71–82. New York: Cambridge University Press.

———. 1981b. "Moral Luck." In *Moral Luck*, 20–39. New York: Cambridge University Press.

——. 1985. *Ethics and the Limits of Philosophy*. Cambridge, MA: Harvard University Press.

Williams, Bernard, and Thomas Nagel. 1976. "Moral Luck." *Proceedings of the Aristotelian Society* 50: 115–151.

Williams, Patricia. 1995. *The Rooster's Egg: On the Persistence of Prejudice*. Cambridge, MA: Harvard University Press.

Wilson, James. 1991. *On Character*. Washington, DC: American Enterprise Institute for Public Policy Research.

Witmer, Helen Leland, and Ruth Kotinsky, eds. 1951. *Personality in the Making: The Fact-Finding Report of the Mid-Century White House Conference on Children and Youth*. New York: Harper.

Wolff, Robert Paul. 1968. *The Poverty of Liberalism*. Boston: Beacon.

Woolfrey, Joan. 2002. "Feminist Awareness as Virtue: A Path of Moderation." *American Philosophical Association Newsletters: Newsletter on Feminism and Philosophy* 1–2: 64–67.

Yoshizaki, Amanda. 1992. "Breaking the Rules: Constructing a Bisexual Feminist Marriage." In *Closer to Home: Bisexuality and Feminism*, ed. Elizabeth Reba Weise, 155–162. Seattle, WA: Seal.

Young, Iris Marion. 1990. *Justice and the Politics of Difference*. Princeton, NJ: Princeton University Press.

——. 2000. *Inclusion and Democracy*. Oxford: Oxford University Press.

Young, Stacey. 1992. Breaking Silence about the "B-word": Bisexual Identity and Lesbian-Feminist Discourse." In *Closer to Home: Bisexuality and Feminism*, ed. Elizabeth Reba Weise, 75–90. Seattle, WA: Seal.

Zack, Naomi. 1992. "An Autobiographical View of Mixed Race and Deracination." *American Philosophical Association Newsletters: Newsletter on Philosophy and the Black Experience* 91 (1): 6–10.

Index

action-centered ethics, 20–23
action guidance and action assessment, 130n32, 161–162
activism. *See* resistance, political
African-Americans, 15, 26n14, 34n1, 47, 64–65, 116, 121–122, 124n20, 136n5, 138–139, 150–153, 168
  and anger. *See* anger, in African-Americans
  and damage imagery, 6, 36, 39–45, 48
  stereotypes of, 35, 43–44, 103, 129–130
  See also racism
agency, 17–18, 25–26, 29, 38
Alarcón, Norma, 137n6, 137n7, 138
Alcoff, Linda Martín, 155
Allen, Jonathan, 145n13
Amnesty International, 82, 83n2, 98
anger, 37, 57, 106
  in African-Americans, 116–117, 121–122, 124n20, 129–130
  in African-American women/women of color, 116–117, 121–123
  Aristotle's account of. *See* Aristotle, and anger
  feminist analysis of, 8, 116–123
  as harmful, 9, 30, 96, 121, 124–127, 129–130, 165
  at oppression/oppressors, 6, 8, 13, 30–31, 96, 113–127, 165
  in women, 116–123
anguish, 5
  at others' suffering, 8, 80–90, 98, 104–106, 163
Annas, Julia, 58n5, 70n31, 75n36
Anzaldúa, Gloria, 138, 144, 154
Appiah, K. Anthony, 152–153
Arendt, Hannah, 90n15, 168n2
Aristotle, 54n2, 65, 74n34, 84–86, 91–95, 156–157
  and anger, 8, 69n29, 84, 118–120, 121n16, 122–123, 125
  and character, 21, 29, 89, 111
  and continence/incontinence, 21, 92
  and courage, 87n7, 92–94, 96, 104, 125–128
  and the distinction between self-regarding and other-regarding virtues, 62–63, 70–76
  and the doctrine of the mean, 83–85, 120, 122–126, 148
  and *eudaimonia*, 35, 51, 53, 58–59, 71–76, 94, 110, 159–160
  and external goods/conditions, 35, 49, 57, 87n7, 94, 108–111, 159
  and friendship, 59, 70n31, 74, 87n7, 157
  and interdependence, 58–59, 62, 72–76, 86, 144
  and justice/injustice, 36, 66n21, 71–72, 74n34, 75, 126, 133
  and luck, 5, 27, 29, 35, 73, 89, 94, 109–111, 159

Aristotle (*continued*)
  and mixed actions, 8, 108–111, 113–114, 124
  and pity, 8, 84n4, 91–93, 101–102, 104
  and the relationship of virtue to flourishing, 4, 7, 11, 35, 49, 51, 57–59, 62–63, 70–76, 94, 107–108, 159–160
  sexism of, 21n11, 74–75
Armstrong, Elizabeth, 140n10
Ault, Amber, 140n10

Bar On, Bat-Ami, 50n13, 78n40, 168n2
Bartky, Sandra Lee, 4, 24–26, 29, 36n3, 37, 65n20, 90n14, 90n15, 97n21, 128n30
Bauman, Zygmunt, 105n34
Bell, Derrick, 10
Berkman, Alexander, 116–117
betrayal, 135–144, 150–154
bisexuals, 139–140
Bishop, Sharon, 88n9, 111n3
Black Power movement, 46n10, 64–65, 117, 152–153
blacks, black Americans. *See* African-Americans
blaming the victim, 33–35, 37–39, 42, 46–47, 56
Blum, Lawrence, 66n22, 105n31
Bolte, Angela, 122n19
Brink, David, 62n15, 76n38
Broadie, Sarah, 92–93
Brown, Wendy, 68–69
Brown v. Board of Education, 39, 65
Butler, Judith, 150–151

Calhoun, Cheshire, 18n7
Camus, Albert, 168n5
Card, Claudia, 6, 12–13, 15, 17–21, 23–24, 26, 36, 49, 50n11, 54n2, 69, 112n5, 160
care ethics, 66–68, 81–82
Carmichael, Stokely, 46n10, 65
Carr, Brian, 91n17
character, 20–23, 115
  Aristotle's account of. *See* Aristotle, and character
  and conservatism, 42–43, 45–46, 49
  development of, 12, 14–15, 29, 36, 42–43
  evaluation of, 52, 128
  influences on, 42–43, 108, 111, 131
  possibilities for transforming, 6, 15–16, 18–19, 23–25, 45, 50, 55, 89, 128–129 (*see also* politics of personal transformation)
  and relationship to flourishing, 23, 49, 107, 111
Chicano/as and Latino/as, 115n7, 137–138, 154
Civil Rights movement, 113, 117
Clark, Kenneth, 64–65
Cleaver, Eldridge, 122n18
Cobbs, Price, 116, 124n20
Combahee River Collective, 136n5
communitarianism, 61n12, 134n3, 144–149
community, 144–149, 151, 154–157
  as community of resistance. *See* oppositional community
  feminist, 9, 128–129, 135–151, 157
  lesbian, 139–141, 150–151
  as an object of loyalty. *See* loyalty, to an oppressed group or oppositional community
  racial, 9, 135–139, 144, 148–157
compassion, 50n12, 55, 63, 68, 77, 82, 84n4, 90n13, 90n15, 101–104, 105n31, 113, 116, 162–163
  See also suffering, unjust, sensitivity and attention to others'
Conly, Sarah, 11n1
consciousness-raising, 19, 24, 119
conservatives and neo-conservatives, 39–48
continence/incontinence, 21–22, 24–25, 67n25, 135
  Aristotle's account of. *See* Aristotle, and continence/incontinence
courage, 57, 68, 122, 135n4, 159
  Aristotle's account of. *See* Aristotle, and courage
  as harmful, 96, 125–128
  as painful, 96, 127
  of political resisters, 8, 96, 115–116, 125–128, 165
  in women, 50, 67–68n25, 127n27
Coyne [Walker], Margaret Urban. *See* Walker, Margaret Urban
criticism and self-criticism, 8, 116, 128–129

culture of poverty thesis, 40, 43–44
Cuomo, Chris, 97

Davion, Victoria, 18n7
Davis, Angela, 44
Dayan, Yaël, 125n23
dilemmas, moral, 8, 28, 31, 108, 111–112, 124–125, 130, 161–162
  dirty hands, 8, 88n9, 89–90n12, 108, 110–112
  tragic, 28, 31, 87–89, 110, 161–162
Doctors without Borders, 83
domination, 54–57, 74–79
  vices of. *See* vice(s), of domination
Donner, Wendy, 117n10
Driver, Julia, 60n10
Du Bois, W. E. B., 34

economic inequality, 13–14, 35, 40, 54–55, 64, 74, 77, 84, 103
epistemic privilege, 78–79, 155
epistemology of ignorance, 79
Epstein, Helen, 98n22
eudaimonia, 57–59, 110–112, 162
  Aristotle's account of. *See* Aristotle, and *eudaimonia*
  defined, 35, 51, 53, 160
  See also flourishing
eudaimonism, 3, 23, 33, 85–86, 107, 167–168
  critical revisions of, 7, 73–76, 86–87, 97, 108, 159–160

Fanon, Frantz, 36n3, 65n20
fear, 44, 55, 91, 93, 103–105, 125–127
Feinberg, Joel, 53n1
feminism, 22
  and evaluation of character traits, 15–16
  as a liberatory movement. *See* liberatory movements, feminist
feminist ethics, 5, 20–23, 66–67, 97, 135
  in relation to virtue ethics, 11n1, 23
Ferguson, Ann, 16n6
Fletcher, George P., 134n3
flourishing, 23, 86, 101–102, 162–168
  ancient Greek conception of, 7, 57–60, 62, 70, 74–75, 78
  barriers to, 4, 6, 13, 23, 35, 49, 56, 89, 96, 127, 159, 163, 166, 168
  distinguished from happiness, 7, 57–62, 78
  external conditions necessary for, 26, 35, 51, 57, 94–96, 109, 159–168
  giving an account of, 13n2, 51–52
  and the goals of liberatory movements, 51–52, 57, 70, 75–76, 78, 107–108, 114, 135
  intersubjective agreement about, 77–79
  and relationship to virtue. *See* virtue, and relationship to flourishing
  subjective accounts of, 51n15, 60–62, 78
Foot, Philippa, 60n10, 62n14
Friedman, Marilyn, 15n4, 61n12, 144–147
Frye, Marilyn, 26n15, 117n9, 118, 120, 123, 140, 154
Funderburg, Lise, 138

Gamson, Joshua, 140n10, 150–151
Garvey, John, 142
Geras, Norman, 82, 85, 98–101, 105
Gibian, Ruth, 140
Ginzberg, Ruth, 127n27, 135n4, 146n15
Glasgow, Douglas, 34n1
Gomberg, Paul, 146n14
good life, the. *See* flourishing
Gordon, Lewis, 34, 151–152, 168n5
Grier, William, 116, 124n20
guilt, 8, 37, 82, 88n9, 89, 96–97, 111–112, 117, 163
Guinier, Lani, 155–156

Halwani, Raja, 11n1
Hamilton, Charles V., 46n10, 65
Hampton, Jean, 63n16
happiness. *See* flourishing; flourishing, distinguished from happiness
Harding, Sandra, 142
Hartfield, Bernadette W., 122n19
health, psychological, 26n14, 39, 42, 65, 108, 114, 124n20, 129–130, 159, 166
Heldke, Lisa, 142
heterosexism, 15, 115, 137–138, 150
Higgins, Tracy, 38n5
Hill, Thomas, 65–66
Hoagland, Sarah Lucia, 67n24, 69, 139n8
Holocaust, the, 82, 89, 96n20, 99, 105
  survivors of, 97–98

Homiak, Marcia, 11n1, 25n13, 66n22
homophobia. *See* heterosexism
Hooker, Brad, 56n4, 60n10, 63
hooks, bell, 26n14, 122, 129–130, 139, 147n17
hopelessness, 37, 47, 49, 57, 106, 168
Hursthouse, Rosalind, 28–29, 31, 55–56, 60n10, 87–89, 111n3, 130n32, 161–162

identity, 9, 69, 142–156
identity politics, 136, 149–156
Ignatiev, Noel, 142
inclusion, 7, 74–77
  as unattainable, 86–87
indifference, 54, 74n35, 113
  contract of mutual, 82, 98–101
  as a meta-vice, 77–80, 100
  to others' suffering, 8, 77–80, 82–90, 98–100, 104–106, 163
integrity, 18, 20, 24, 26, 29, 50, 79, 113, 115, 127n27
interdependence, 7, 58–59, 62, 73–76, 86, 117
  Aristotle's account of. *See* Aristotle, and interdependence

Jaggar, Alison, 20–21, 23, 119, 128n30
Jaspers, Karl, 96
Johnson, President Lyndon, 40
joy, 85, 97–98, 168
justice/injustice, 36, 54–55, 58, 62n14, 62n15, 63, 69, 76–77, 84–85, 90, 97, 100–106, 126–127, 130–131, 164–165
  Aristotle's account of. *See* Aristotle, and justice/injustice

Kant, Immanuel, 13, 36, 66, 107
Kekes, John, 56n4
King, Jr., Martin Luther, 113

La Caze, Marguerite, 69n27
Latino/as. *See* Chicano/as and Latino/as
Leighton, Stephen, 128n29
lesbians and lesbian politics, 24, 42, 115n7, 117n9, 118, 137–141, 150–151, 154
Lewis, Oscar, 40
liberalism, 51n15, 61n13, 99–101
liberals, 39–41, 46–48
liberatory movements, 51–52, 106–109, 113–117, 129, 166
  African-American, 8, 46n10, 64, 113, 117, 129–130, 136n5, 152–153 (*see also* Black Power movement; Civil Rights movement)
  Chicano/a, 115n7, 137–138
  feminist, 8, 22, 36, 50, 65, 115n7, 117–123, 136–142
  as objects of loyalty. *See* loyalty, to an oppressed group or oppositional community
  radical, 27, 46n10, 113–116, 136n5
Lorde, Audre, 116–117, 119, 121–122
Loury, Glenn, 42
loyalty, 116, 133–134
  as burdensome, 9, 128–129, 134, 154–157
  as contrary to liberatory ends, 9, 133–136, 149–157
  to an oppressed group or oppositional community, 9, 128–129, 133–140, 143, 148–157, 165
  to an oppressor group, 140–143, 154
  as portrayed within liberatory movements, 134–143
  and relationship to criticism, 8–9, 128–129, 135–140, 142–157
Lugones, María, 79, 122–123, 147n17
lying, 37, 55, 69, 166

MacIntyre, Alasdair, 11n1, 60n11, 146–150, 157
Mayer, Arno, 105n32
McFall, Lynne, 69n27
McLaren, Margaret, 11n1
Meyers, Diana T., 119
Mills, Charles, 79, 98–99n23
mixed-race identity, 138–139, 151–152
Moraga, Cherríe, 137–138, 144, 154
moral damage, 4–5, 12, 17–18, 23–27, 29–30, 33–34, 36–38, 46–50, 63, 94, 108, 167
  denial of, 34, 47–48
  recovery from, 20, 46–48, 115
  and relationship to psychic damage, 36–39, 65
  and victim-blaming, 6, 33–34, 37–46

moral luck, 5–6, 12, 16–18, 20, 23, 25–31, 36–38, 54n2, 89, 94, 109–112, 164
  defined, 13
  and relationship to flourishing, 23, 27, 110–112
  types of, 12–15, 27, 29
moral remainder, 3, 5, 8, 88, 124, 130n32, 161, 163
Moya, Paula, 155
Moynihan, Daniel P., 40–42
Myrdal, Gunnar, 40

Nagel, Thomas, 14, 17
Nathanson, Stephen, 146n14
Nelson, William, 76n38
Nietzsche, Friedrich, 68–69
Noddings, Nel, 66–67, 81–82
Nussbaum, Martha, 50n12, 51n15, 86n5, 89, 90n13, 91n17, 101–103, 111–112, 133n1, 160

Okin, Susan Moller, 11n1, 67
oppositional community, 16n6, 19n8, 27, 31, 46–47, 49, 52, 115, 128–130, 133–136, 144, 148–150, 155–156
oppression, 19n8, 49–50, 54–57, 66, 114–131, 157
  internalization of, 36–37, 49, 65–68, 121–122, 128–129
  living as well as possible under, 23, 52, 164–167
  moral damage under, 4, 18–20, 24, 27, 29–30, 33–34, 45, 56, 69, 108–109, 167 (*see also* moral damage)
  as multiple, interlocking systems, 13–14, 122, 136n5, 144, 149
  as pervasive, 55–56, 61, 109
  psychological, 36–37, 65
  and relationship to flourishing, 3–4, 7, 10, 23, 25–27, 34–36, 49, 57, 95, 107–109, 159–161, 163–168
  structural sources of, 27, 35, 40, 46–48, 55, 109
  struggles against. *See* liberatory movements
  theories of, 56

pain, 21–22, 25, 28–29, 65, 85, 88–98, 104–106, 120, 126, 161, 164
  as interfering in flourishing, 85, 89, 94
Pateman, Carole, 98–99n23
Pears, David, 128n29
pessimism, 4, 9–10, 168
Pettit, Philip, 134n3
Phillips, D. Z., 60n10
Plato, 58–59, 62n15, 70n30
politics of personal transformation, 6, 12, 15–17, 22–26, 50, 55
Potter, Nancy, 11n1, 69n27
Pratt, Minnie Bruce, 141
Prior, William, 74n34
privilege, unjust, 7, 19, 33, 53–58, 68, 75–79, 100, 102–104
  and associated character traits, 54–58, 61–62, 68–69, 75–80
  rejection of, 55, 140–143, 154
psychic damage, 36–42, 65. *See also* moral damage
Putnam, Daniel, 127n27

queers/queer politics, 138, 150–151

racism, 15, 35, 39–45, 47, 54–55, 64, 66, 74, 77–79, 103, 115, 117, 121–123, 129–130, 135, 138, 140–142, 148–156
  blamed on blacks, 40–45
  denial of, 45
  and self-hate. *See* self-hate
rape, 31, 38, 54, 83, 137
Rawls, John, 28n16, 61n13, 98–100, 103, 126
regret, 8, 29, 89, 111, 124, 130–131, 161, 163–164
  as agent-regret, 5–6, 12–13, 27–28, 30–31, 38n6, 88n9, 119
  as a mark of virtue, 28, 31, 88, 112–113
  at the self one is, 12, 30
resentment, 44, 57, 68–69
resistance, political, 3, 98, 151–156, 165–166
  as burdensome, 95, 108, 128, 165
  and the politically resistant self, 8, 31, 107–109, 112–131, 165
  as praiseworthy, 95, 107–109, 113–114, 130, 164, 166–167
  radical, 113–123

responsibility, 22, 26, 31, 37, 49
in relation to control, 12–13, 17–18, 20, 23, 28, 30, 38
types of, 17
Rich, Adrienne, 141
Rogers, Kelly, 63n16, 87n7, 127n28
Rorty, Amélie Oksenberg, 125n22
Rousseau, Jean-Jacques, 101n26, 102n28
Royce, Josiah, 134n3
Ruddick, Sara, 81–82
Rust, Paula C., 139–140

Sartre, Jean-Paul, 112
Scheman, Naomi, 66n22, 119n13, 153
Scott, Daryl Michael, 39–42
Segrest, Mab, 141–142
self-defense, women's, 31, 38, 50, 119
self-hate, 19, 64–65, 67, 121, 165
self-interest, 67, 70, 79, 86, 99–104
self-respect, 64–66
self-sacrifice, 5, 16, 66–67, 86–87, 96, 107, 115, 126–128, 154, 159, 165
separatist politics, 46n10, 113, 115n7, 117–118, 122–123, 139–140
servility, 65–67
sexism, 35, 55, 64, 66, 74, 77, 84, 118, 122, 135, 137–138
Aristotle's. *See* Aristotle, sexism of
Sherman, Nancy, 71n32, 72n33
Shklar, Judith, 56n4
Simpson, Peter, 160n1
Snow, Nancy, 11n1, 38n6
Socrates, 35n2, 53, 58
Sophie's Choice, 89
Sparks, Holloway, 127n27
Spelman, Elizabeth V., 68, 90n15, 91n16, 93n18, 118–120, 123
Steele, Shelby, 45
Steinberg, Stephen, 40, 47
Stocker, Michael, 88n9, 89–90n12, 110–111
Stoics, the, 35n2
Stoltenberg, John, 142
structural change, 27, 45–50
suffering, unjust, 166–167
indifference to. *See* indifference, to others' suffering
as pervasive, 80, 84–89, 95
sensitivity and attention to others', 8, 80–96, 98–106, 108, 163–165
Sumner, L. Wayne, 60n10, 61–62, 77–78
Szwajgier, Adina Blady, 105n33

Taylor, Gabriele, 60n10, 67–68n25
Tolman, Deborah, 38n5
Tormey, Judith Farr, 66n22
Torres, Gerald, 155–156
Ture, Kwame. *See* Carmichael, Stokely

vice(s), 61
of domination, 33, 54–58, 61–63, 67–68, 75–80
of oppressed people, 18–19, 34, 57, 67–69
virtue(s)
barriers to the development of, 36, 54n2, 56–57, 73, 89
as benefiting their possessor, 55, 60, 62n14, 67n25, 70, 73
burdened, 4, 7, 9, 34n1, 95–98, 106–109, 111–114, 116, 121, 124–131, 134, 154–157, 160, 162–168
feminine, 16, 66, 69
how to identify a, 9, 19n8, 20, 49–52, 159–167
for living with bad luck, 27–31, 94, 159
as a mean, 83–87, 90, 120–126, 148
multiple and conflicting, 60
painful, 28, 90–98, 108
and pleasure, 83–84, 91–94
of political resistance, 50, 96, 107–109, 114–131, 165
that reflect dominant values, 48
and relationship to flourishing, 7, 19n8, 28, 35, 37, 49–53, 56–63, 73–80, 94–98, 107–112, 114–117
self-regarding and other-regarding, 61–75, 86–87, 90
virtue ethics, 21–23, 37, 48–49, 53, 56, 87, 167
ancient Greek, 53, 59
critical revisions of, 34, 73–74
contemporary, 55–56, 60–64, 70, 78, 160
neo-Aristotelian, 11n1, 34, 73
in relation to feminist ethics. *See* feminist ethics, in relation to virtue ethics

for theorizing about oppression, 11, 73, 164, 167
voluntarism, 12, 23–26, 45–46
Von Wright, Georg Henrik, 62n14, 67n25
vulnerability, 29, 86n5, 101–104, 111–113, 129

Walker, Margaret Urban, 13, 18n7, 20, 28–29, 39n7
Walzer, Michael, 88n9, 111n3, 112, 145–146, 155
Warren, Chief Justice Earl, 39, 65
weakness of the will. *See* continence/incontinence
Weiss, Penny, 147n16
West, Cornel, 47, 168
whites/whiteness, 39–40, 55, 77–79, 140–143, 154
Wilkes, Kathleen, 70n30
Williams, Bernard, 5–6, 12–15, 17–18, 25, 27–30, 37, 87n8, 88, 111n3, 124
Williams, Patricia, 44n9
Wilson, James, 42–43
Wolff, Robert Paul, 133–134
Wolfram, Sybil, 67–68n25
Woolfrey, Joan, 11n1

Yoshizaki, Amanda, 140
Young, Iris Marion, 35, 76n37, 77–78
Young, Stacey, 140n11

Zack, Naomi, 139, 150–152